Developmental Psychology

Penney Upton
University of Worcester

Series editor:
Dominic Upton
University of Worcester

 Pearson

Harlow, England • London • New York • Boston • San Francisco • Toronto • Sydney
Dubai • Singapore • Hong Kong • Tokyo • Seoul • Taipei • New Delhi
Cape Town • São Paulo • Mexico City • Madrid • Amsterdam • Munich • Paris • Milan

C000000508

Pearson Education Limited
Edinburgh Gate
Harlow
Essex CM20 2JE
England

and Associated Companies throughout the world

Visit us on the World Wide Web at:
www.pearson.com/uk

First published 2012

ISBN 978-0-273-73516-8

British Library Cataloguing-in-Publication Data
A catalog record for this book is available from the British Library

Library of Congress Cataloging-in-Publication Data
Upton, Penney.
  Psychology express : developmental psychology / Penney Upton, Dominic Upton. -- 1st ed.
     p. cm.
  Includes bibliographical references and index.
  ISBN 978-0-273-73516-8 (pbk.)
  1. Developmental psychology. I. Upton, Dominic. II. Title.
  BF713.U68 2011
  155--dc23

                                                  2011019203

Typeset in 9.5/12.5pt Avenir Book by 30

Contents

The PsychologyExpress series

→ **UNDERSTAND QUICKLY**
→ **REVISE EFFECTIVELY**
→ **TAKE EXAMS WITH CONFIDENCE**

'All of the revision material I need in one place – a must for psychology undergrads.'
Andrea Franklin, Psychology student at Anglia Ruskin University

'Very useful, straight to the point and provides guidance to the student, while helping them to develop independent learning.'
Lindsay Pitcher, Psychology student at Anglia Ruskin University

'Engaging, interesting, comprehensive . . . it helps to guide understanding and boosts confidence.'
Megan Munro, Forensic Psychology student at Leeds Trinity University College

'Very useful . . . bridges the gap between Statistics textbooks and Statistics workbooks.'
Chris Lynch, Psychology student at the University of Chester

'The answer guidelines are brilliant, I wish I had had it last year.'
Tony Whalley, Psychology student at the University of Chester

'I definitely would (buy a revision guide) as I like the structure, the assessment advice and practice questions and would feel more confident knowing exactly what to revise and having something to refer to.'
Steff Copestake, Psychology student at the University of Chester

'The clarity is absolutely first rate . . . These chapters will be an excellent revision guide for students as well as providing a good opportunity for novel forms of assessment in and out of class.'
Dr Deaglan Page, Queen's University, Belfast

'Do you think they will help students when revising/working towards assessment? Unreservedly, yes.'
Dr Mike Cox, Newcastle University

'The revision guide should be very helpful to students preparing for their exams.'
Dr Kun Guo, University of Lincoln

'A brilliant revision guide, very helpful for students of all levels'.
Svetoslav Georgiev, Psychology student at Anglia Ruskin University

Introduction

Not only is psychology one of the fastest-growing subjects studied at university worldwide, it is also one of the most exciting and relevant subjects. Over the past decade the scope, breadth and importance of psychology have developed considerably. Important research work from as far afield as the UK, Europe, USA and Australia has demonstrated the exacting research base of the topic and how this can be applied to all manner of everyday issues and concerns. Being a student of psychology is an exciting experience – the study of mind and behaviour is a fascinating journey of discovery. Studying psychology at degree level brings with it new experiences, new skills and knowledge. As the Quality Assurance Agency (QAA) has stressed:

> psychology is distinctive in the rich and diverse range of attributes it develops – skills which are associated with the humanities (e.g. critical thinking and essay writing) and the sciences (hypotheses-testing and numeracy).   (QAA, 2010, p. 5)

Recent evidence suggests that employers appreciate the skills and knowledge of psychology graduates, but in order to reach this position you need to develop your skills, further your knowledge and, most of all, successfully complete your degree to your maximum ability. The skills, knowledge and opportunities that you gain during your psychology degree will give you an edge in the employment field. The QAA stresses the high level of employment skills developed during a psychology degree:

> due to the wide range of generic skills, and the rigour with which they are taught, training in psychology is widely accepted as providing an excellent preparation for many careers. In addition to subject skills and knowledge, graduates also develop skills in communication, numeracy, teamwork, critical thinking, computing, independent learning and many others, all of which are highly valued by employers.   (QAA, 2010, p. 2)

This book is part of a comprehensive new series, Psychology Express, that helps you achieve these aspirations. It is not a replacement for every single text, journal article, presentation and abstract you will read and review during the course of your degree programme. It is in no way a replacement for your lectures, seminars or additional reading. A top-rated assessment answer is likely to include considerable additional information and wider reading – and you are directed to some of these readings in this text. This revision guide is a conductor: directing you through the maze of your degree by providing an overview of your course, helping you to formulate your ideas and directing your reading.

Each book within Psychology Express presents a summary coverage of the key concepts, theories and research in the field, within an explicit framework of revision. The focus throughout all of the books in the series will be on how you should approach and consider your topics in relation to assessment and exams. Various features have been included to help you build up your skills and knowledge ready for your assessments. More details about these can be found in the guided tour for this book on p. viii.

By reading and engaging with this book, you will develop your skills and knowledge base and in this way you should excel in your studies and your associated assessments.

Psychology Express: Developmental Psychology is divided into 11 chapters and your course has probably been divided up into similar sections. However, we the series authors and editor, must stress a key point: do not let the purchase, reading and engagement with the material in this text restrict your reading or your thinking. In psychology, you need to be aware of the wider literature and how it interrelates and how authors and thinkers have criticised and developed the arguments of others. So even if an essay asks you about one particular topic, you need to draw on similar issues raised in other areas of psychology. There are, of course, some similar themes that run throughout the material covered in this text, but you can learn from other areas of psychology covered in the other texts in this series, as well as from material presented elsewhere.

We hope you enjoy this text and the others in the Psychology Express series, which cover the complete knowledge base of psychology.

- *Biological Psychology* (Emma Preece): covering the biological basis of behaviour, hormones and behaviour, sleeping and dreaming, and psychological abnormalities.

- *Cognitive Psychology* (Jonathan Ling and Jonathan Catling): including key material on perception, learning, memory, thinking and language.

- *Developmental Psychology* (Penney Upton): from pre-natal development through to old age, the development of individuals is considered. Childhood, adolescence and lifespan development are all covered.

- *Personality and Individual Differences* (Terry Butler): normal and abnormal personality, psychological testing, intelligence, emotion and motivation are all covered in this book.

- *Social Psychology* (Jenny Mercer and Debbie Clayton): covering all the key topics in Social Psychology including attributions, attitudes, group relations, close relationships and critical social psychology.

- *Statistics in Psychology* (Catherine Steele, Holly Andrews and Dominic Upton): an overview of data analysis related to psychology is presented, along with why we need statistics in psychology. Descriptive and inferential statistics and both parametric and non-parametric analysis are also included.

- *Research Methods in Psychology* (Steve Jones and Mark Forshaw): research design, experimental methods, discussion of qualitative and quantitative methods and ethics are all presented in this text.

- *Conceptual and Historical Issues in Psychology* (Brian M. Hughes): the foundations of psychology and its development from a mere interest into a scientific discipline. The key conceptual issues of current-day psychology are also presented.

This book, and the companion volumes in this series, should cover all your study needs (there will also be further guidance on the website.) It will, obviously, need to be supplemented with further reading and this text directs you towards suitable sources. Hopefully, quite a bit of what you read here you will already have come across and the text will act as a jolt to set your mind at rest – you do know the material in depth. Overall, we hope that you find this book useful and informative as a guide for both your study now and in your future as a successful psychology graduate.

Revision note

- *Use evidence based on your reading, not on anecdotes or your 'common sense'.*
- *Show the examiner you know your material in depth – use your additional reading wisely.*
- *Remember to draw on a number of different sources: there is rarely one 'correct' answer to any psychological problem.*
- *Base your conclusions on research-based evidence.*

Explore the accompanying website at www.pearsoned.co.uk/psychologyexpress

→ Prepare more effectively for exams and assignments using the answer guidelines for questions from this chapter.

→ Test your knowledge using multiple choice questions and flashcards.

→ Improve your essay skills by exploring the You be the marker exercises.

Guided tour

→ Understand key concepts quickly

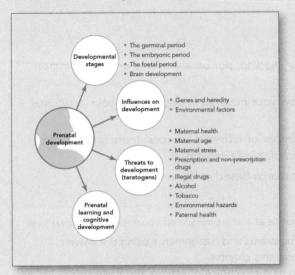

Start to plan your revision using the **Topic maps**.

Grasp **Key terms** quickly using the handy definitions. Use the flashcards online to test yourself.

Key terms

Nativism: the belief that skills and abilities have a genetic basis – they are therefore innate. For example, according to this view our level of cognitive ability is predetermined by inheritance.

Empiricism: the theory that all knowledge and skills are acquired through experience. This forms the basis of Locke's philosophy that the child is born a blank slate, knowing nothing, and the behaviourist approach that development is based on learning.

→ Revise effectively

KEY STUDY

Elias and Berk (2006). Self regulation in young children: Is there a role for sociodramatic play?

This study tested the idea that socio-dramatic play can contribute to the development of self-regulation. A longitudinal design was used in which 51 three- and four-year-olds were observed playing in their preschool classrooms. Children were observed at the start of the school year (Time 1) then again, four–five months later (Time 2). Standardised measures were used to record the children's involvement in socio-dramatic play and self-regulatory skills. Child temperament and verbal abilities were also assessed. Children who were involved in more episodes of socio-dramatic play at Time 1 showed better self-regulation by Time 2. In contrast, those engaged in more solitary pretend play were less likely to show self-regulation at Time 2. The longitudinal nature of this study strengthens its predictive validity and strongly suggests that socio-dramatic play influences the development of self-regulation. Furthermore, because the researchers also measured each child's verbal ability, they were able to show that more interaction with others and self-regulation were not simply a function of better communication skills. This is important because there is evidence that verbal ability can influence both socio-dramatic play and self-regulation. Finally, it was found that the benefits of socio-dramatic play for increasing self-regulation were greatest for children rated as having an impulsive temperament. This suggests a potential interventional role

Quickly remind yourself of the **Key studies** using the special boxes in the text.

Test your knowledge

3.1 What are gross motor skills?

3.2 How are fine motor skills useful for psychological functioning in later life?

3.3 Briefly describe the main principles of Dynamic Systems Theory.

Answers to these questions can be found on the companion website at:
www.pearsoned.co.uk/psychologyexpress

Prepare for upcoming exams and tests using the **Test your knowledge** and **Sample question** features.

Compare your responses with the **Answer guidelines** in the text and on the website.

Answer guidelines

✱ *Sample question*   Essay

Play is essential to a child's development. Discuss.

Approaching the question

Your answer should aim to provide an analysis of the main functions of play that have been described in the literature. A discussion of the possible threats to play that have been suggested in recent times will help illustrate the importance often placed on play in contemporary Western society.

Important points to include

● Begin by defining play and discussing the difference between immediate and delayed purpose for activities such as play.

● Discuss the theoretical approaches to play, comparing classic views, which considered the origins of play, to more current approaches, looking at the

Chapter 2: Test your Knowledge questions

The following are a copy of the Test your Knowledge questions found in this chapter of your book.

Have a go at answering the question, referring to the 'Answer Guidelines' for extra help in how to frame

The Biology of the visual system

1. Name the image-forming structures of the eye.
Q1: Answer Guidelines
2. What are the three types of retinal cells and what are their functions?
Q2: Answer Guidelines
3. What does retinotopic mapping mean?
Q2: Answer Guidelines
4. Describe the main types of cells in the V1 area.
Q2: Answer Guidelines

Gestalt Theory

5. How did the Gestaltists suggest form is extracted?
Q1: Answer Guidelines
6. Describe the law of Prägnanz.
Q2: Answer Guidelines
7. What is figure-ground segregation?
Q2: Answer Guidelines
8. List four shortcomings of Gestalt theory.
Q2: Answer Guidelines

→ **Make your answers stand out**

Use the **Critical focus** boxes to impress your examiner with your deep and critical understanding.

CRITICAL FOCUS

Multi-causal explanations of the A-not-B error

In revisiting the A-not-B error, Smith et al. (1999) take a new approach, attempting to explain what infants do in the A-not-B task rather than what they cannot do. Their explanation focuses on performance and ultimately raises profound questions about what it means to know. The idea of knowledge as an enduring mental structure that exists independently of behaviour dominates in the study of cognitive development. Indeed, this idea of mental structures that gradually develop over time underlies Piaget's seminal theory of cognitive development. Thus achieving the AB task has always been taken to represent a qualitative change in infant thinking; the task can only be successfully completed once the infant has developed a new schema: the

Make your answer stand out

It is important to remember to take a critical approach to this question. While there is a lot of theory surrounding the purpose of play for development, the empirical evidence is more limited. This does not, however, mean that the ideas cannot be critiqued and a good student will approach this question with an inquiring eye. Can we be sure, for example, that play enhances cognitive skills or does it simply reflect a child's current abilities? Does play help relationships flourish or do other factors (such as a child's motor skills or verbal abilities) mediate both play behaviours and acceptance by peers? The importance of linking your answer to other areas you have studied cannot be highlighted enough. Introducing some of the current debates happening across

Go into the exam with confidence using the handy tips to **make your answer stand out**.

Guided tour of the companion website

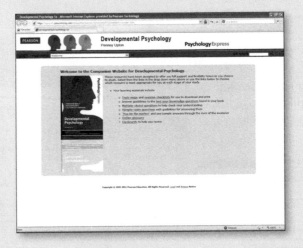

→ Understand key concepts quickly

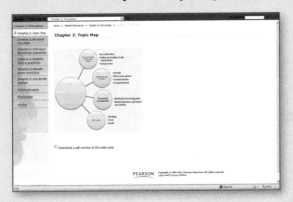

Printable versions of the **Topic maps** give an overview of the subject and help you plan your revision.

Test yourself on key definitions with the online **Flashcards**.

→ **Revise effectively**

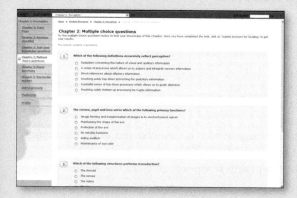

Check your understanding and practise for exams with the **Multiple choice questions**.

→ **Make your answers stand out**

Evaluate sample exam answers in the **You be the marker** exercises and understand how and why an examiner awards marks.

Put your skills into practice with the **Sample exam questions**, then check your answers with the guidelines.

All this and more can be found at
www.pearsoned.co.uk/psychologyexpress

Acknowledgements

Author's acknowledgements

Many thanks to Lee Badham, Tracey Price and Emma Jackson for their technical assistance.

A big thank you must also go to my husband for his advice and encouragement whilst writing this textbook and to my children – Francesca, Rosie and Gabriel – who have taught me a lot about the practical aspects of child development.

Series editor's acknowledgements

I am grateful to Janey Webb and Jane Lawes at Pearson Education for their assistance with this series. I would also like to thank Penney, Francesca, Rosie and Gabriel for their dedication to psychology.

Dominic Upton

Publisher's acknowledgements

Our thanks go to all reviewers who contributed to the development of this text, including students who participated in research and focus groups, which helped to shape the series format:

Dr Andy Cochrane, National University of Ireland, Maynooth

Dr Kate Eames, Coventry University

Dr Julian Lloyd, University of Chester

Dr Debbie Riby, Newcastle University

Student reviewer:

Steff Copestake, student at the University of Chester

We are grateful to the following for permission to reproduce copyright material:

Figures 11.1, 11.2 and 11.3 adapted from data from the Office for National Statistics licensed under the Open Government Licence v.1.0.

Themes, theories and key figures in developmental psychology

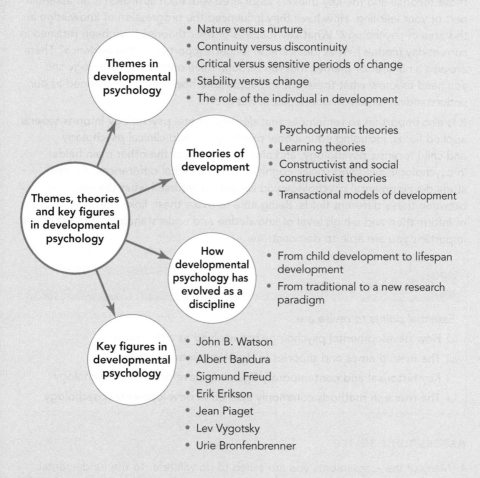

Themes in developmental psychology
- Nature versus nurture
- Continuity versus discontinuity
- Critical versus sensitive periods of change
- Stability versus change
- The role of the indivdual in development

Theories of development
- Psychodynamic theories
- Learning theories
- Constructivist and social constructivist theories
- Transactional models of development

Themes, theories and key figures in developmental psychology

How developmental psychology has evolved as a discipline
- From child development to lifespan development
- From traditional to a new research paradigm

Key figures in developmental psychology
- John B. Watson
- Albert Bandura
- Sigmund Freud
- Erik Erikson
- Jean Piaget
- Lev Vygotsky
- Urie Bronfenbrenner

A printable version of this topic map is available from
www.pearsoned.co.uk/psychologyexpress

Introduction

Developmental psychology is the scientific study of age-related changes in mind and behaviour. Originally it was believed that the development of all our skills and abilities was completed in childhood. We now understand that development is a lifelong process; change does not stop because we have reached adulthood. The chapter therefore provides an overview of the lifespan approach to the study of development and shows you the value of examining changes that occur in adulthood, as well as those that occur in childhood.

There are a number of other prominent theories that underpin much of the contemporary thinking in developmental psychology. A critical understanding of these theories and the key thinkers associated with each approach is an essential part of your learning. How have they influenced the progression of knowledge in this area of psychology? What key features of their theories have been retained in current-day models? What ideas are no longer supported by the evidence? There are also a number of themes that run through developmental psychology and you need to know what these are and appreciate how they have changed as our understanding of human development has grown.

It is also important to remember that developmental psychology informs several applied fields, including educational psychology, child clinical psychology and child forensic psychology, and also complements the other main fields in psychology, including social, cognitive and individual differences. As you study developmental psychology you should ask yourself what the links are between these different fields. Being able to make these links shows synthesis of information and a high level of knowledge and understanding – skills that it is important you are able to demonstrate.

> → *Revision checklist*
>
> *Essential points to revise are:*
> - ❑ How developmental psychology has evolved as a discipline
> - ❑ The main themes and theories in developmental psychology
> - ❑ Key historical and contemporary figures in developmental psychology
> - ❑ The research methods commonly applied in developmental psychology

Assessment advice

- Many of the assessments you are asked to do will refer to the fundamental issues in developmental psychology that are covered in this chapter.
- Issues such as whether development is influenced by genes or environment is one of the most far-reaching debates in this area of psychology. The

relevant issues may be stated clearly, as in the example assessment question presented below, or they may be implicit. For example, a common question in cognitive development concerns the merits and problems of Piaget's theory of cognitive development. You might also be asked to compare and contrast this theory with another theory such as that of Vygotsky. In both cases the question has not mentioned discontinuous v. continuous development; however a good student will recognise that this is an important consideration in Piaget's theory and will talk about this explicitly.

● Recognising the main themes and theories in developmental psychology is essential, both for questions that tackle these issues directly and also for answering other topic-based questions. This chapter outlines the main issues, but they will be cross-referenced to other chapters where more details are provided.

Sample question

Could you answer this question? Below is a typical essay question that could arise on this topic.

 Sample question   **Essay**

To what extent do theoretical models of development reflect the idea that psychological development involves both biological and environmental influences?

Guidelines on answering this question are included at the end of this chapter, whilst further guidance on tackling other exam questions can be found on the companion website at: **www.pearsoned.co.uk/psychologyexpress**

Themes in developmental psychology

There are a number of themes that run right through developmental psychology. These are:

● the influence of nature verses nurture
● continuity versus discontinuity in change
● critical verses sensitive periods of development
● stability verses change
● the role of the individual in development.

Nature versus nurture

- This debate concerns the relative contributions of inheritance and the environment in determining our knowledge and behaviour.
- The argument that development is rooted in nature developed from the teachings of philosophers such as Plato and Descartes, who supported the idea that we are born with knowledge and *innate* skills.
- The opposing view, that environmental influences cause developmental progression, stems from the ideas of thinkers such as John Locke, who argued for the concept of *tabula rasa* – the idea that the mind is a blank slate at birth, with experience determining what we know.
- In developmental psychology this debate centres around two main questions.
  - Are children born with innate knowledge or skills or is this acquired from interaction with the environment?
  - Is development driven by external factors or by something inside each individual?
- Nature refers to:
  - traits, abilities and capacities that are inherited
  - it includes anything produced by the predetermined unfolding of genetic information
  - development that relies on nature alone is known as *maturation*.
- In contrast, nurture refers to:
  - environmental influences that shape development
  - it usually implies social and cultural factors that shape our environment and the way in which the behaviours of those around us influence our development
  - this includes the way we are raised as children, the attitudes and behaviours of our peer group, our experiences and even the choices we make as we get older; societal factors such as the socio-economic circumstances in which we find ourselves may also be important.
- This debate predominates in some areas more than others. For example, it is an important question in language acquisition, which will be considered in Chapter 5.
- In contemporary psychology the consensus view is that development results from an interaction between genes and environment and the debate now concerns the relative role of nature and nurture for different aspects of development.

Continuity versus discontinuity

- This issue concerns whether development follows a smooth, continuous path or it is a discontinuous stage-based process.

- In continuous change:
  - development is gradual and cumulative
  - changes are quantitative in nature
  - the underlying processes that drive change are the same over the course of the lifespan
  - each behaviour or skill builds upon a previous one and later development can be predicted from experiences in early life
  - physical growth and changes in height are examples of continuous change in childhood.
- In discontinuous change:
  - development occurs in distinct, usually abrupt, stages
  - each stage is qualitatively different from the last
  - examples from nature include the caterpillar that turns into butterfly or the tadpole which becomes a frog.
- The question for developmental psychology is whether psychological skills and abilities in childhood are qualitatively different from those of adults or are children merely mini adults who simply lack the knowledge that comes with experience?
- One area in which this debate has been of primary concern is cognitive development, which will be reviewed in Chapter 7.
- Psychologists generally agree that neither approach is complete and it is likely that some processes may be better described as continuous and others as occurring through stages.
- There is also some suggestion that continuous and discontinuous processes may interact.

Critical versus sensitive periods of change

- A critical period is a specific time during development when a particular event has its greatest impact.
- In developmental psychology, a critical period for development usually implies that certain environmental stimuli are needed if typical development is to occur.
- Attachment theory, which will be considered in Chapter 4, suggests that there may be a critical period for emotional development.
- Better understanding of the plasticity and resilience of human nature have led to a reassessment of this idea.
- Most development psychologists now agree that, rather than suffering permanent damage from a lack of stimuli during early periods of development, it is more likely that people can use later experiences to help them overcome deficits.

- It is now more common to talk about sensitive rather than critical periods.
- In a sensitive period we may be more susceptible to particular stimuli. However, the absence of that stimuli does not always result in irreversible damage.

Stability versus change

- This issue concerns the extent to which early traits and characteristics persist throughout life or are able to change. Does the shy child become a shy adult? Can a shy child become a gregarious adult?
- The stability–change issue involves the degree to which we merely become older versions of our younger selves.
- Theorists who believe in stability in development often argue from a *nativist* stance, emphasising the role of heredity for the development of psychological characteristics. We inherit aspects of our personality, for example, in much the same way that we inherit eye colour.
- From this perspective, we cannot change our psychological self, only learn to control it. Thus the shy child remains shy as an adult even if they learn to act in an outgoing manner in social situations.
- From an empiricist viewpoint, stability in psychological characteristics stems from the impact of early experiences that cannot be overcome.
- An individual is shy not because of a genetic predisposition, but because during early experiences interacting with others they encountered considerable stress, leading them to avoid social interaction.
- This has much in common with the idea described in the preceding section, that there are critical periods of development during which specific experiences permanently influence later behaviour.
- The majority of contemporary theorists believe that there is potential for change throughout the lifespan.
- Later experiences are believed to be able to influence development just as early ones can.
- However, there is still some debate as to how much change is possible. Baltes (2003) argues that while adults are able to change, their capacity to do so is less than that of a child and diminishes over time.
- On the other hand, Kagan (2003) argues that personality traits such as shyness have a genetic basis, yet he also provides evidence that even these inherited traits can be subject to change over time.

The role of the individual in development

- This concerns the extent to which development is driven by external factors or by something inside each individual. Is the child an active agent who influences their own development or a passive agent who merely responds to forces in the developmental progression?

- Traditional views of development see the individual as passive in their development.

- Empiricists see the child as a passive recipient of stimuli, while nativists see the child as passively following a biological programme.

- Most contemporary theories of development recognise an active role for children in their own development.

- This thinking has its roots in the philosophy of Kant, who argued for a synthesis of nativism and empiricism. He proposed that:

  - we are born with certain mental structures that help us to interpret input from our senses in particular ways

  - however, it is only through interaction with the environment that these structures order and organise experience

  - individuals play an active role in this development as organisers of this experience.

- Modern theories of development recognise the child as central to their own development.

- The individual is able to influence development directly through the choices they make and, increasingly as they get older, by selecting their environment.

- They are also able to affect development indirectly through their behaviour, which can affect how others respond to them and to some extent the experiences they encounter.

Key terms

Nativism: the belief that skills and abilities have a genetic basis – they are therefore innate. For example, according to this view our level of cognitive ability is predetermined by inheritance.

Empiricism: the theory that all knowledge and skills are acquired through experience. This forms the basis of Locke's philosophy that the child is born a blank slate, knowing nothing, and the behaviourist approach that development is based on learning.

? Sample question — Problem-based learning

Your local school wants to start a new after-school history club for children it is thought will benefit from extended learning opportunities and it would like your advice from a developmental perspective. Initially the focus will be on life in the 1950s. The club will have a varied programme, including library and Internet research, trips to local museums and visits from experts, including local people who grew up in the post-war years. It will culminate in a weekend spent at a local historic house, where the children will experience a 1950s lifestyle. The club will be expensive to run and only a limited number of places are available. None of the children have studied

▶

history before, so the school wants to select club members based on their parents' educational level. Only children whose parents are educated to A level or above will be invited to join.

What do you think the school believes about the role of the individual in learning and development? Does it see the child as having an active or passive role, for example?

Do you think it sees cognitive development as based in nature or nurture?

Based on your knowledge of developmental theory, what advice would you give the school about its approach to teaching history and its methods of selecting pupils to participate in the history club?

Test your knowledge

1.1 What is the contemporary view of the nature–nurture debate?

1.2 What are the four main features of continuous change in development?

1.3 Why are critical periods no longer commonly referred to in developmental psychology?

1.4 What is the stability–change issue?

1.5 What is the traditional view of the role of the individual in development?

Answers to these questions can be found on the companion website at: www.pearsoned.co.uk/psychologyexpress

Theories of development

Psychodynamic theories

Proponents of the psychodynamic perspective believe that behaviour is motivated by inner forces, memories and conflicts, of which a person has little awareness or control. These inner forces usually result from childhood experiences and continue to influence behaviour across a person's lifespan. The best-known theorists of this perspective are Sigmund Freud and Erik Erikson.

Learning theories

This perspective suggests that the key to understanding development lies in observable behaviour and an individual's response to environmental stimuli. The assumption here is that behaviour is a learnt response to *reinforcement* provided by the environment. The learning and conditioning principles described in the behavioural theories of B. F. Skinner and John B. Watson account for human development.

One area that behaviourist theories do not explain is the type of learning that takes place when someone learns by observing a model. Called *social learning* by Albert Bandura, this is the process in which someone imitates the behaviour observed in another person when it appears to have reinforcing consequences and inhibits such behaviour when the observed consequence is punishment.

Constructivist and social constructivist theories

Constructivism argues that learning and development occur when an individual interacts with the environment around them. Individuals are seen as active learners who construct their own understanding and knowledge of the world as a result of their actions within the environment. Development is suggested to take place in sequential stages and children's thinking is proposed to be different from that of adults. The best known theorist of this perspective is Jean Piaget, who developed an important theory of cognitive development.

Social constructivist theories are a variant of this perspective that emphasise the influence of the social and cultural environment on development. The social context of development and an individual's interactions with other people are seen to play an important role in development. The most significant theorists to take account of social and cultural factors in development are Lev Vygotsky and Urie Bronfenbrenner.

Transactional models of development

Transactional models of development also represent a valuable way of describing the interplay of nature and nurture in development. Most often applied to explaining the development of positive and negative outcomes for children and in particular the development of atypical behaviours, this approach was first described in the mid-1970s. One of the most significant theorists in this field is Sameroff (1991; Sameroff & Chandler, 1975), who describes a transactional model of development as one in which the mutual effects that children and adults have on modifying each other's behaviour is emphasised. A transactional process is one in which one person's behaviour in a dyad affects the other person's behaviour, which in turn influences the first person's behaviour and so on. In this way, expectations for behaviour and another person's responses to that behaviour, are established. Interactions are therefore dynamic, reciprocal and circular. This model represents an important move away from issues of cause and effect in adult/child relationships; the emphasis is on the dynamics of the meshing of the bidirectional influences – each partner's behaviour is contingent upon the other's and both partners become changed as the cycle of interactions proceed.

CRITICAL FOCUS

Where does knowledge come from?

In her paper 'Nativism, empiricism and the origins of knowledge', Spelke (1998) argues that the age-old nature–nurture debate remains an essential research topic in cognitive development. She also notes that intuition is a poor guide to human cognitive development – 'common sense' explanations of human cognition have rarely been validated.

While reading this paper, think very carefully about the idea often cited in popular culture that psychology is 'just common sense'. Why are the findings of psychologists often deemed to be 'obvious'? Is this simply a good example of hindsight bias?

An important issue highlighted by this paper is the idea that 'the preconceptions of scientists can never be eliminated from science'. To what extent are we objective observers of human behaviour? Can we ever be truly objective and, if not, how should the researcher deal with their own 'intuition' or preconceptions about how we develop? What sort of things might influence such preconceptions?

Test your knowledge

1.6 What do psychodynamic theorists believe motivates behaviour?

1.7 What type of learning is not explained by behaviourism?

1.8 What is the difference between constructivist and social constructivist theories?

Answers to these questions can be found on the companion website at:
www.pearsoned.co.uk/psychologyexpress

Further reading Key developmental theories

Key reading

Spelke, E. S. (1998). Nativism, empiricism and the origins of knowledge. *Infant Behaviour and Development, 21*(2), 181–200

Bronfenbrenner, U. (1999). Environments in developmental perspective: Theoretical and operational models. In S. L. Friedman & T. D. Wachs (Eds.), *Measuring environment across the lifespan: Emerging methods and concepts*, (pp. 3–28). Washington DC: APA Press. Available online at: http://readtogether.uncg.edu/hdf/facultystaff/Tudge/Bronfenbrenner%201999.pdf

How developmental psychology has evolved as a discipline

There are two key issues to remember with regard to the progress of developmental psychology as a discipline:

- a change in the focus of interest from development in childhood to development across the lifespan
- a gradual shift in the way that this developmental change has been studied.

From child development to lifespan development

- Early studies of children began in the second half of the nineteenth century with baby biographies, which were some of the first studies in human development.
- The most famous baby biography is one kept by Darwin of his infant son's development, which he later reported in an article that appeared in the journal *Mind* in 1877. While not scientifically sound, these single *case studies* made human development a legitimate topic for study.
- Darwin also focused attention on the significance of the immaturity of human's infants in his book *On the Origin of Species* (1859).
- Darwin's theory of recapitulation, which proposed that individual development replicates the evolution of the species ('*Ontogeny* recapitulates *phylogeny*'), was also popular at this time.
- For example, in the very early stages of development the human embryo looks like a fish, even having gill slits. This fits well with the evolutionary idea that humans evolved from other vertebrates.
- In 1891, G. Stanley Hall tried to make the study of children more scientific than the baby biographies had previously been by using questionnaires in an attempt to collect more objective data and to explore 'the contents of children's minds'.
- At around the same time in England, James Sully (1842–1923) established a new subject at London University called 'Child Psychology'.
- In the early twentieth century, adolescence also began to be studied as a distinct life stage.
- One of the first psychologists to study and write about adolescence was G. Stanley Hall (1904), who suggested that this was an important period of change, typified by intense emotional turmoil, which he called 'storm and stress'.
- The continuation of psychological development throughout adulthood as well as childhood and adolescence was recognised in the second half of the twentieth century.
- Erik Erikson (1950) developed one of the most important theories, which suggested that psychological development continues across the lifespan.

- However, traditional theory continued to dominate thinking in developmental psychology for much of the twentieth century.
- According to the traditional view:
  - the study of human development is divided into separate, self-contained age-related specialities: infancy, childhood, adolescence, adulthood and gerontology (old age)
  - most developmental change is believed to occur in childhood and adolescence
  - adulthood is a period of relative stability
  - old age is believed to be characterised by decline.
- The lifespan perspective began to emerge as a distinct discipline in the 1960s and 1970s and continues to gain in popularity.
- According to the lifespan perspective:
  - developmental change occurs throughout the lifespan
  - adulthood is seen as an important time of growth and change, not the end point of development as it is in the traditional view
  - no age period dominates development; changes in adulthood are as important as those in childhood
  - adulthood and aging are not portrayed as a period of decline; the changes that occur as we age may also be positive
  - development is therefore *multidirectional,* meaning that as some capacities or behaviours decrease, others expand
  - development includes both gain and loss throughout the lifespan and these may even occur together
  - development is *multidimensional,* that is, it consists of biological, social, emotional and cognitive changes, each of which are interrelated
  - the study of development should be seen as *multidisciplinary*; neuroscientists, psychologists, sociologists and medical researchers have different but complimentary perspectives on age-related change
  - thus the social and cultural context of development is seen as highly relevant to developmental change
  - the plasticity of human development – the idea that we retain capacity for change in response to environmental factors right across the lifespan – is emphasised.

From traditional to a new research paradigm

- Traditionally, developmental psychology has used a systematic approach to investigating age-related changes.
- The methods used were based in those used in the natural sciences and followed a *hypothetico-deductive* approach.

- Methods were therefore mainly *experimental*, the aim being to collect objective data and carry out a quantitative analysis to provide accurate descriptions and explanations of how and why change occurs.
- Data collection was usually carried out under controlled conditions in a laboratory.
- An underlying assumption in this traditional scientific *positivist* approach is that there is an objective reality in the world that can be observed, measured and categorised. This method has produced much of the theoretical work and research described in this book.
- However, during the last 20 to 30 years, there has been increasing debate about whether this approach is appropriate for the study of human development.
- Objections to this traditional lab-based research include the following:
  - development is being studied outside of a meaningful social context and the findings may therefore lack *ecological* validity – thus they may no longer hold true when the person is behaving naturally in their everyday setting
  - people's behaviour during a research study may also be changed because of other factors, such as the uneven power relationship between the researcher and the participant – this has been suggested to be a particular issue when working with children
  - the researcher may impose their own ideas of what it is they are measuring on the participant by the research tools that they use and the way they design the study, meaning that the participant's behaviour during the study may be an artefact of participating in the research.
- These objections to the positivist approach have resulted in different emphases in the way that many developmental psychologists conduct their research.
  - Some researchers continue to follow the core principles of the traditional scientific approach, but take the influence of context on people's behaviour into account. A good example of this is the work of Margaret Donaldson (1978), which looked at how children's cognitive performance changed according to the language used and the meaningfulness of the situation.
  - Others have moved to using less traditional methods, such as *observations* and *quasi-experimental* methods, to study people's behaviour in everyday situations.
  - The collection of more *qualitative* data, using open-ended questions in questionnaires and interviews that allow participants to raise ideas that the researcher had not included, has also become more common.
- Other psychologists have had a more radical reaction to the debate about the traditional scientific approach and reject the idea that human thought and behaviour can ever be studied objectively.

- They argue that there is no single objective reality; rather, each of us constructs our own understandings and interpretations of 'reality', which are embedded in the context of our interactions with others. 'Reality' is therefore highly individualised and subjective.

- These psychologists therefore focus their studies on the interactions between people, with the aim of describing the subjective experience of participants and understanding individuality in order to build 'local theories' that apply to the specific social context of an event.

- Unlike 'scientific' theories, these theories are not concerned with generating predictions so much as making sense of phenomena. These are some of the key features of what is referred to as a *qualitative* approach and sometimes called *new paradigm* research.

- The difference between the new paradigm and the traditional approach is illustrated by Greig and Taylor's (1999) suggestion that in the positivist approach children are 'determined, knowable, objective and measurable', whereas in the qualitative approach they are 'subjective, contextual, self-determining and dynamic'.

- It is important to recognise that there is some overlap between these differing approaches, with many researchers using a variety of methods and seeking to gain both quantitative and qualitative data.

Key terms

Hypothetico-deductive: a method of scientific inquiry that begins by formulating a hypothesis or prediction, which is then tested experimentally. The hypothesis is then either confirmed or rejected, depending on the experimental findings.

Experiment: a method of investigating causal relationships between variables or to test a hypothesis. This involves the manipulation of one or more variables (the independent variables), while holding other variables (dependent variables) constant. The effect of changes in the independent variables on the dependent variables is measured, recorded and analysed to determine the relationship between the variables.

Positivist approach: suggests that all human experiences and social behaviours can be reduced to observable, measurable facts.

Ecological validity: the degree to which the behaviours observed during a research study reflect the behaviours that occur in natural settings. In a very controlled study such as a lab-based experiment, ecological validity is low because the setting is artificial and so people may not respond in the way they would in everyday life to a given set of stimuli. It is therefore argued that we are less able to generalise from the behaviours seen in experimental research to real-life behaviours.

Qualitative approach: emphasises the importance of the meaning of experiences to groups or individuals when trying to explain human behaviour and development. It uses non-experimental methods such as in-depth interviews, focus groups and case studies.

Test your knowledge

1.9 How does the traditional model of human psychological development differ from the lifespan approach?

1.10 How might a researcher investigate cognitive development using a positivist research model?

1.11 What are the advantages and disadvantages of the new paradigm approach to studying psychological development?

Answers to these questions can be found on the companion website at: **www.pearsoned.co.uk/psychologyexpress**

 Sample question   *Information provider*

Design an information sheet that shows the different ways in which we can investigate human psychological development. For each one describe the pros and cons and give examples of how these techniques have been used successfully in research studies.

Further reading Evolution of developmental psychology

Topic	Key reading
Research and ethics	Balen, R., Blyth, E., Calabretto, H., Fraser, C., Horrocks, C., & Manby, M. (2006). Involving children in health and social research: 'Human becomings' or 'Active beings'? *Childhood*, *13*(1), 29–48.
Research methods	Greig, A. & Taylor, J. (1999). *Doing research with children*. London: Sage.
Models in developmental psychology	Nesselroade, J. R., & Schmidt McCollen, K. M. (2000). Putting the process into developmental processes. *International Journal of Behavioral Development, 24*(3), 295–300. Available online at: http://nesselroade.cdhrm.org/pdf/Nesselroade,%20Schmidt%20%282000%29.pdf

Key figures in developmental psychology

There are a number of key figures in developmental psychology. These are the theorists whose ideas and research have changed the way we think about human development. G. Stanley Hall, for example, is often called the 'father' of developmental psychology as he carried out some of the first systematic studies of children. He also taught one of the first courses in child development and established scientific journals for the publication of child development research. His beliefs, based on Darwin's theory that children's development recapitulates the evolution of the species, have long since been discredited. However, he retains importance as an historical figure as he inspired a great deal of the work on human development upon which this book is based. The theories of those who followed in Hall's footsteps have also not always stood up to close scrutiny. However, there are some theorists whose work remains critical to our understanding of human development:

John B. Watson (1878–1958)

- Created the behaviourist approach to psychology at the beginning of the twentieth century.
- Believed that human behaviour can be understood in terms of experiences and learning, rejecting the introspective approach of late nineteenth-century theorists, which attempted to understand internal mental experiences based on self-reports.
- Promoted the objective study of observable, measurable behaviours.
- Believed that all behaviour is the product of environment and experience and biological factors had no role in development.
- Believed that all learning takes place through *operant conditioning*, a process of association between a behaviour and the consequence of that behaviour.
- Consequences either reinforce a behaviour, making it more likely to reoccur, or are aversive, thereby decreasing the likelihood of the behaviour reoccurring.
- A reinforcer is any event that strengthens or increases the behaviour that it follows:
  - positive reinforcers are favourable outcomes presented after the behaviour, so, in positive reinforcement, a response or behaviour is strengthened by the addition of something such as praise or a direct reward
  - negative reinforcers involve the removal of an unfavourable outcome after the display of a behaviour, so, in negative reinforcement, a response is strengthened by the removal of something considered unpleasant.
- Punishment occurs when an adverse outcome causes a decrease in the behaviour it follows:
  - positive punishment involves the presentation of an unfavourable outcome in order to weaken the response it follows
  - negative punishment occurs when a favourable outcome is removed after a behaviour occurs.
- Development is believed to be far more complex than behaviourism allows, although modern application of these ideas can still be found in *applied behavioural analysis (ABA)* an intervention programme often used with children with behavioural or learning difficulties.

Example of application of theory: behaviourism

Applied behaviour analysis, or ABA, is often discussed in relation to interventions for children with autism. Probably the most well-known proponent of ABA methods is Ole Ivas Lovaas, an American psychologist whose approach is based on over 30 years of clinical work with institutionalised, non-verbal children diagnosed with autism. He found that these children were able to develop verbal skills through an intense one-to-one behavioural programme. Research carried out by Lovaas suggests that the best results are seen when children enter a programme before the age of 4 years and undergo intensive therapy for 40 hours a week over at least 2 years. Most progress is made when the intervention is followed both at home and school.

An ABA programme begins by recording all aspects of the child's current behaviours and skills. This involves a therapist or behaviour analyst observing the child working and playing with others in a variety of settings, consulting with family, teachers and other professionals working with the child, as well as working directly with the child. In this way a record is produced, which will include medical history, family history, and behavioural history. From this detailed snapshot of the child, the behaviour analyst or therapist begins to make assessments about where there are skill deficits in order to develop a programme that will teach these skills.

Usually the skills that the child needs to learn will be broken down into tasks, and when these tasks are achieved the child is rewarded. Examples of rewards (*reinforcers*) include playing with a favourite toy, verbal praise or even favourite foods. These artificial reinforcers that encourage the child are gradually replaced by more social and everyday reinforcers.

There is a lot of evidence to support the effectiveness of the Lovaas approach. However, there are also criticisms of this approach and the evidence surrounding it. For example, most of the research has been carried out by the Lovaas Institute and other advocates of the method, suggesting a possible conflict of interest. Lovaas himself has also demonstrated that while a large number of children do seem to benefit from the ABA approach, a significant minority do not. Unfortunately, there is as yet no way of assessing who will and won't benefit prior to treatment.

Albert Bandura (1925–)

- Bandura believed behavioural learning theories were inadequate as a framework for understanding human development.
- He suggested that many human behaviours were learnt from observing others' behaviour and attitudes, using this as a model for our own behaviour (*social learning theory*).
- We choose who to imitate – learning is not an automatic response but depends on internal and environmental processes.
- We only imitate the model's behaviour if the model possesses characteristics we find attractive or desirable.
- Other conditions that are necessary if modelling is to be effective include:
  - *attention*: the observer must see the modelled behaviour

- *retention:* the observer must be able to remember the modelled behaviour
- *reproduction:* the observer must have the skills to reproduce the action
- *motivation:* the observer must be motivated to carry out the action they have observed and remembered and must have the opportunity to do so (motivations may include seeing the model's behaviour reinforced, while punishment may discourage repetition of the behaviour).
- Social learning theory has been called a bridge between behaviourist and cognitive learning theories, because it encompasses attention, memory and motivation.

Sigmund Freud (1856–1939)

- Best known in developmental psychology for his controversial model of psychosexual development.
- Personality develops through a series of stages, during which the psychosexual energies of the *id* become focused on different areas of the body as the child grows to adulthood.
- This psychosexual energy, or *libido*, is described as the driving force behind behaviour.
- Freud's model is interactionist: the sequence and timing of the stages is biologically determined. However, successful personality development depends on the environmental experiences of the child at each stage.
- Five stages of development are proposed (see Table 1.1).
- If each psychosexual stage is completed successfully, the result is a healthy personality.
- Unresolved conflicts at any stage lead to fixation and the individual remains stuck in this stage. For example, a person fixated at the oral stage may be overly dependent on others and seek oral stimulation through smoking, drinking or eating.
- Few psychologists today accept this theory of development as accurate:
  - one problem is that concepts such as the libido are impossible to measure and therefore cannot be tested scientifically
  - Freud's theory is based upon retrospective case studies and not empirical research; it is based on the recollections of adult patients, not on actual observation and study of children.

Table 1.1 **Freud's five stages of psychosexual development**

Stage	Age	Characteristics
Oral stage	Birth to 1 year	An infant's primary interaction with the world is through the mouth. The mouth is vital for eating and the infant derives pleasure from oral stimulation through gratifying activities such as tasting and sucking. If this need is not met, the child may develop an oral fixation later in life, examples of which include thumb-sucking, smoking, fingernail-biting and overeating.
Anal stage	1 to 3 years	Freud believed that the primary focus of the libido was on controlling bladder and bowel movements. Toilet training is a primary issue with children and parents. Too much pressure can result in an excessive need for order or cleanliness later in life, while too little pressure from parents can lead to messy or destructive behaviour later in life.
Phallic stage	3 to 6 years	Freud suggested that the primary focus of the id's energy is on the genitals. According to Freud, boys experience an *Oedipal complex* and girls experience an *Electra complex*, or an attraction to the opposite-sex parent. To cope with this conflict, children adopt the values and characteristics of the same-sex parent, thus forming the *superego*.
Latent stage	6 to 11 years	During this stage, the superego continues to develop while the id's energies are suppressed. Children develop social skills, values and relationships with peers and adults outside of the family.
Genital stage	11 to 18 years	The onset of puberty causes the libido to become active once again. During this stage, people develop a strong interest in the opposite sex. If development has been successful to this point, the individual will continue to develop into a well-balanced person.

Erik Erikson (1902–1994)

- Erikson was a psychoanalyst and accepted a lot of Freud's ideas.
- However, he put much more emphasis on the social and cultural aspects of development.
- He also believed that development continued across the lifespan, rather than simply childhood experiences determining adult psychological health.
- There are eight stages of development, from infancy to late adulthood, called 'the eight ages of man' (see Table 1.2).
- In each stage the person confronts, and it is hoped masters, new challenges.
- Each stage builds on the successful completion of earlier stages and the challenges of stages not successfully completed are likely to reappear as problems in the future (see Chapter 10 for more information about this theory).

Table 1.2 Erikson's eight stages of psychosocial development

Stage	Basic conflict	Important events	Outcome
Infancy (birth to 18 months)	Trust v. mistrust	Feeding	Children develop a sense of trust when caregivers provide reliabilty, care and affection. A lack of this will lead to mistrust.
Early childhood (2 to 3 years)	Autonomy v. shame and doubt	Toilet training	Children need to develop a sense of personal control over physical skills and a sense of independence. Success leads to feelings of autonomy; failure results in feelings of shame and doubt.
Preschool (3 to 5 years)	Initiative v. guilt	Exploration	Children need to begin asserting control and power over the environment. Success in this stage leads to a sense of purpose. Children who try to exert too much power experience disapproval, resulting in a sense of guilt.
School age (6 to 11 years)	Industry v. inferiority	School	Children need to cope with new social and academic demands. Success leads to a sense of competence, while failure results in feelings of inferiority.
Adolescence (12 to 18 years)	Identity v. role confusion	Social relationships	Teens need to develop a sense of self and personal identity. Success leads to an ability to stay true to yourself, while failure leads to role confusion and a weak sense of self.
Young adulthood (19 to 40 years)	Intimacy v. isolation	Relationships	Young adults need to form intimate, loving relationships with other people. Success leads to strong relationships, while failure results in loneliness and isolation.
Middle adulthood (40 to 65 years)	Generativity v. stagnation	Work and parenthood	Adults need to create or nurture things that will outlast them, often by having children or creating a positive change that benefits other people. Success leads to feelings of usefulness and accomplishment, while failure results in shallow involvement in the world.
Maturity (65 to death)	Ego integrity v. despair	Reflection on life	Older adults need to look back on life and feel a sense of fulfilment. Success at this stage leads to feelings of wisdom, while failure results in regret, bitterness and despair.

Jean Piaget (1896–1980)

- Piaget was one of the most influential developmental psychologists of the twentieth century. His stage theory of cognitive development revolutionised our view of children's thinking and learning and inspired more research than any other developmental psychologist.

- Piaget was initially interested in the nature of knowledge and how it could be seen as a form of adaptation to the environment, which he called *genetic epistemology*.

- Piaget argued that:

  - the child takes an active role in their own development

  - there are four stages of cognitive development and thinking is qualitatively different at each stage (see Table 1.3)

  - children develop progressively more elaborate and sophisticated mental representations of the world called schemas, based on their own actions on the environment and the consequences of these actions

  - knowledge is constructed through two processes:

    - *assimilation* in which the child evaluates and tries to understand new information, based on existing knowledge of the world

    - *accommodation*, in which the child expands and modifies their mental representations of the world based on new experiences.

- Some of the detail of these stage theories has been criticised and the evidence now suggests that Piaget underestimated children's abilities.

- However, many of his concepts are still accepted and his ideas continue to influence educators across the world. (We will explore Piaget's ideas in greater detail in Chapter 7.)

Table 1.3 **Piaget's stages of cognitive development**

Stage	Approximate age	Characteristics
Sensorimotor	0–2 years	Begins to make use of imitation, memory and thought. Begins to recognise that objects do not cease to exist when they are not in view. Moves from reflex actions to goal-directed activity.
Pre-operational	2–7 years	Gradually develops use of symbols, including language. Able to think operations through logically in one direction. Has difficulties seeing another person's point of view.
Concrete operational	7–11 years	Able to solve concrete problems. Understands some mathematical operations such as classification and seriation.
Formal operational	11 years–adult	Able to solve abstract problems in logical fashion. Becomes more scientific in thinking. Develops concerns about social issues, identity.

Lev Vygotsky (1896–1934)

- Developed his theory at the same time as Piaget but, because he was working in Marxist Russia, while he was aware of Piaget's theories, his work was not known in the West until the 1970s, long after his death.
- Like Piaget, Vygotsky believed that the child actively constructed their knowledge of the world.
- However, he attributed a much greater role to the social and cultural environment of the child than Piaget.
  - Human history is created through the construction and use of cultural tools and it is this inventive use of tools that makes humans unique.
  - Cultural tools include ways of thinking as well as ways of doing and one of the most important cultural tools people use is language.
  - Information about how to use cultural tools is transmitted from one generation to the next through social interaction, although each generation may adapt these cultural tools for its own needs or use it in new ways, a process known as *appropriation.*
- Our knowledge and understanding of the world is constructed in a social context, not, as Piaget thought, by children acting on the environment alone.
- The child follows the adult's example at first, gradually developing the ability to do tasks without help.
- The difference between what a child can do with help and what he or she can do alone is called the *zone of proximal development (ZPD)* and we will explore this further in Chapter 7.
- To be effective, learning must take place within this ZPD. New tasks should neither be too difficult to master with help nor so easy that they can be completed alone.

Urie Bronfenbrenner (1917–2005)

- Developed the *bioecological systems theory*, a model that provides a framework for looking at the different factors which influence human development.
- This model acknowledges the importance of biological factors for development, but also points to the fact that, more than any other species, humans create environments to help shape their own development.
- Development always occurs in a particular social context and this context can change development; it should therefore be possible to develop environments to optimise our genetic potential.
- There are five different aspects of the environment that influence development (see Figure 1.1).
  - *Microsystem* includes the immediate environment we live in and any immediate relationships or organisations we interact with, such as the

family, school, workplace, peer group and neighbourhood. How an individual acts or reacts to other people in the microsystem will affect how they are treated in return. Each individual's unique genetic and biological traits will also affect how others treat them.

- *Mesosystem* describes the connections between immediate environments as the way in which different groups or organisations in the microsystem work together and it is suggested it has an effect on how we develop as individuals. For example, if parents take an active role in the child's schooling and school and home agree on what is best for the child, then development will be well supported and optimal. If, however, the school and home have different goals and attitudes, the child will be given conflicting information from the two environments, which may impact development.

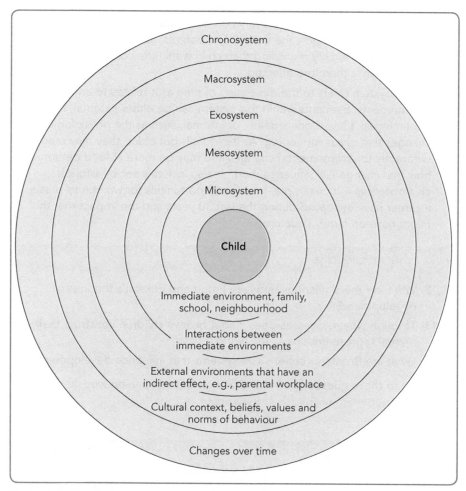

Figure 1.1 Bronfenbrenner's ecological model of development

- *Exosystem* refers to the external environmental settings that only indirectly affect development, such as a parent's workplace. For example, workplace structure can influence the choices a parent makes regarding childcare. Changes in these settings can have both positive and negative effects on microsystem relationships. For instance, a promotion at work may mean more money for treats and activities, but may also mean less time at home for the parent.

- *Macrosystem* is the larger cultural context and includes cultural and social norms and attitudes, national economy, political culture, etc. Although this layer is the most remote from the individual it still influences development – for instance, by shaping how the micro- and exosystems are organised. For example, if it is the belief of the culture that parents alone should be responsible for raising their children, that culture is less likely to provide financial or other resources to help parents. This will then affect the structures in which the parents function. For instances will both parents need to work to support the family? The parents' ability or inability to carry out that responsibility regarding their child within the context of the child's microsystem is therefore affected.

- *Chronosystem* refers to the dimension of time as it relates to an individual's environments. Elements within this system can be either external, such as the timing of a loved one's death, or internal, such as the physiological changes that occur with aging. As individuals get older, they may react differently to environmental changes and may be more able to determine how that change will influence them. It also includes socio-historical circumstances – for example, how the opportunities for women to pursue a career have increased during the last 30 years and the impact that this might have on family structures.

Test your knowledge

1.12 What are the similarities between Freud and Erikson's theories of development?

1.13 Through what processes does Piaget believe children construct their mental representations of the world?

1.14 What are Bronfenbrenner's five systems that influence development?

Answers to these questions can be found on the companion website at:
www.pearsoned.co.uk/psychologyexpress

 Sample question   Essay

Critically evaluate Piaget's model of cognitive development. In particular, what does this approach suggest about the nature of the child and the course of human development?

CRITICAL FOCUS

Cultural tools

According to Vygotsky, cultural tools are essential to our development as human beings, both in evolutionary and individual terms. For example, a hammer is a physical example of a cultural tool. It is a means of knocking sharp objects such as nails into surfaces to create new structures. The form and function of the hammer are the result of generations of cultural evolution and adaptation. The meaning and use of a hammer is not immediately obvious to someone who has never come across one before or who has never needed to knock nails into surfaces. The information about how to use tools is also culturally transmitted. However, each generation may adapt the hammer for its own needs or use it in new ways. Vygotsky calls this *appropriation*. Thus the hammer that we buy from the DIY store in the twenty-first century is very different from the one first constructed by our ancestors. Language is also a cultural tool. Like the hammer, the language we use today is the result of long-term cultural development, adaptation, transmission and appropriation. How do you think the form and function of language has evolved over time? Does language in the twenty-first century differ from that of the nineteenth or twentieth centuries? What examples can you think of from modern society that reflect the ways in which language has been appropriated? What are the advantages and disadvantages of such appropriation?

Further reading Key theorists

Topic	Key reading
Behaviourism	Watson, J. B. (1913). Psychology as the behaviorist views it. *Psychological Review*, *20*, 158–177. Available online at: http://psychclassics.yorku.ca/Watson/views.htm
Genetic epistemology	Piaget, J. (1968). *Genetic epistemology* (1st of series of lectures at Columbia University). Available online at: www.marxists.org/reference/subject/philosophy/works/fr/piaget.htm
Others	Search for writings by Watson, Darwin, Hall, Freud and other key figures at: http://psychclassics.yorku.ca/index.htm
	An electronic resource developed by Christopher D. Green at York University, Toronto, Canada.

Chapter summary – pulling it all together

→ Can you tick all the points from the revision checklist at the beginning of this chapter?

→ Attempt the sample question from the beginning of this chapter using the answer guidelines below.

→ Go to the companion website at www.pearsoned.co.uk/psychologyexpress to access more revision support online, including interactive quizzes, flashcards, You be the marker exercises as well as answer guidance for the Test your knowledge and Sample questions from this chapter.

Answer guidelines

 Sample question   **Essay**

To what extent do theoretical models of development reflect the idea that psychological development involves both biological and environmental influences?

Approaching the question

Your answer should aim to provide an analysis of how human knowledge and skills develop. You will need to consider the role given to biology and environment in the main theoretical approaches to development, including behaviourist, psychodynamic and constructivist approaches.

Important points to include

- Outline the key issues, establishing the historical importance of the nature–nurture argument. Highlight the change in focus over time, such as that the debate is no longer about which matters but, rather, how much each matters.
- Discuss some of the different theoretical approaches, including:
  - behaviourist approaches to development
  - psychodynamic theories
  - social learning theory
  - constructivist approaches.
- For each you will need to:
  - highlight the relative importance given to biology or environment
  - give examples of relevant theorists and show how they have applied their theory to different aspects of development.
  - evaluate the ability of each theory to explain development and identify any gaps in the theories by comparing and contrasting approaches.

Make your answer stand out

It is really easy to fall into the trap of simply describing a number of theories and theorists. A good answer will take a critical stance, evaluating the ability of the theory to explain development and will focus on a range of examples of psychological development, including cognitive, social and emotional skills. Linking your evaluation to other issues in developmental psychology, such as the role of the individual and stability and change, will demonstrate your ability to synthesise the information you have learnt. Evaluating the methodological approaches of any research studies cited will also make your answer stand out.

Explore the accompanying website at www.pearsoned.co.uk/psychologyexpress
- → Prepare more effectively for exams and assignments using the answer guidelines for questions from this chapter.
- → Test your knowledge using multiple choice questions and flashcards.
- → Improve your essay skills by exploring the You be the marker exercises.

2

Prenatal development

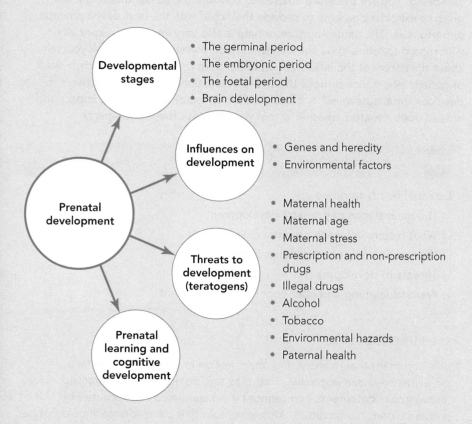

Developmental stages
- The germinal period
- The embryonic period
- The foetal period
- Brain development

Influences on development
- Genes and heredity
- Environmental factors

Prenatal development

Threats to development (teratogens)
- Maternal health
- Maternal age
- Maternal stress
- Prescription and non-prescription drugs
- Illegal drugs
- Alcohol
- Tobacco
- Environmental hazards
- Paternal health

Prenatal learning and cognitive development

A printable version of this topic map is available from
www.pearsoned.co.uk/psychologyexpress

Introduction

It is important to understand the stages of prenatal development so you can see the psychological effects that can occur if this development goes wrong. However, while you need to know what happens during the main stages of prenatal development you must also remember that you are studying psychology, not physiology. It is therefore important to think about the long-term impact of prenatal experiences on later social, emotional and psychological development. For this reason the focus of prenatal development in psychology tends to be on how development may be negatively affected by *teratogens* and the short- and long-term consequences on child development. Of course the flip side of this is the way in which avoidance of teratogens can be beneficial for future infant well-being. You are therefore advised to consider the advice that might be given to expectant parents to provide their child with the best developmental opportunities. The nature–nurture debate is also very important, especially with regard to future skills and behaviour. You therefore need to ask yourself about the nature of the influences on the unborn child: are they clearly a result of genetic inheritance or does the environment alone provide the answers to developmental outcomes? Is it less clear which factor has the most impact and indeed does it matter whether or not we can tease these two apart?

> → **Revision checklist**
>
> *Essential points to revise are:*
> ❏ The main stages of prenatal development
> ❏ What factors influence prenatal development
> ❏ How environment and genetics interact
> ❏ Threats to development
> ❏ Prenatal learning and later cognitive development

Assessment advice

● It is important that in answering any question in psychology you take an *evidence-based* approach. That is to say, do not make generalised or sweeping statements that cannot be substantiated or supported by evidence from the literature. Also remember that the evidence should not be anecdotal. After all, you are not writing an opinion piece; you are crafting an argument that is based on current scientific knowledge and understanding.

● Furthermore, whatever type of assessment you have to undertake, it is important to take an *evaluative* approach to the evidence. Whether you are writing an essay, sitting an exam or designing a webpage, the key advice is to avoid simply describing how development takes place or the impact of teratogens on developmental outcomes. Rather, it is necessary to think about the strength of the evidence in each field you are covering. One of the key skills for psychology students is critical thinking and for this reason the tasks featured in this chapter focus on developing this way of thinking. Thus you are not simply expected to learn a set of facts and figures, but to think about the implications of what we know and how this might be applied in everyday life. Better assessment answers are the ones that take this critical approach.

- Evidence is not static – it was once believed that certain drugs (DES) could help prevent miscarriage, however we now know that they also increase the risk of fertility problems for the sons and daughters of those women who took this hormone during a 30-year period from the 1950s through to the 1970s. Our knowledge of human development is continually evolving and awareness of the way our understanding is changing is important. Using this textbook alone, therefore, cannot guarantee success. What it can do, however, is point you in the right direction to find the resources that will enable you to keep your learning – and your assessment answers – up to date.

- Finally, remember that prenatal development is just one part of the developmental process. What happens during this period of life has implications for further development – physically, cognitively, socially and emotionally (see Figure 2.1). Good assessment answers will take account of this and will recognise that developmental psychology is just one element

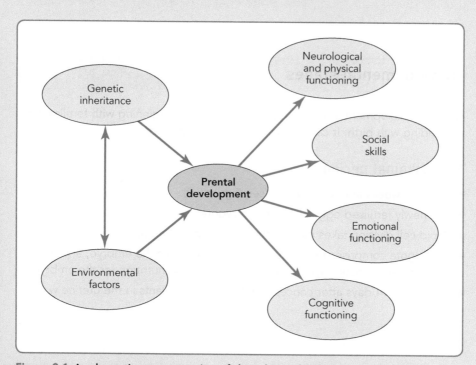

Figure 2.1 A schematic representation of the relationship between prenatal development and later functioning

of an extensive discipline. Making links between the different areas of psychology is an important part of the learning process; demonstrating such a synthesis of knowledge is also a feature of good assessment answers and will therefore be encouraged throughout this chapter.

Can you draw a similar diagram to demonstrate the relationship between developmental psychology and the other core areas of psychological study – for example, cognitive, social, individual differences and neuropsychology?

Sample question

Could you answer this question? Below is a typical essay question that could arise on this topic.

 Sample question   *Essay*

Critically evaluate the risks to development during the prenatal period.

Guidelines on answering this question are included at the end of this chapter, whilst further guidance on tackling other exam questions can be found on the companion website at: **www.pearsoned.co.uk/psychologyexpress**

Developmental stages

Prenatal development lasts approximately 266 days, beginning with fertilisation and ending with birth. It can be divided into three periods.

The germinal period

- First two weeks after conception (see Figure 2.2).
- The newly fertilised egg is known as a zygote.
- Rapid cell division takes place within the zygote by *mitosis*.
- The zygote comprises the blastocyst, which becomes the embryo, and the trophoblast, an outer layer of cells that will provide nutrition for the embryo.
- Finally, 10–14 days after conception the zygote implants in the uterine wall.

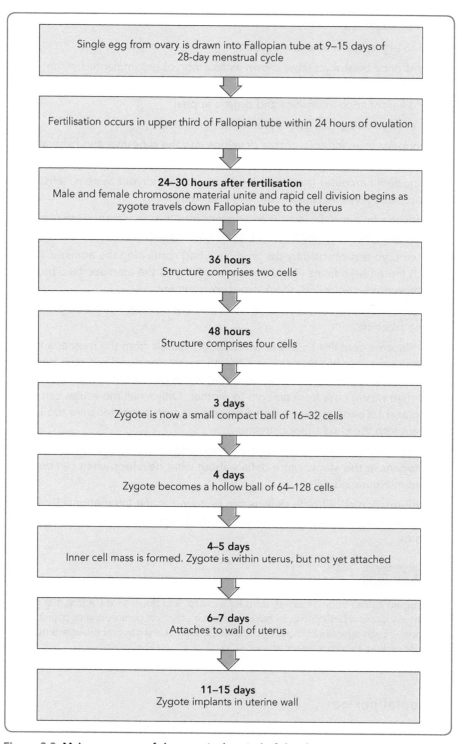

Figure 2.2 **Main processes of the germinal period of development**

The embryonic period

- Two to eight weeks after conception.
- Begins once blastocyst (now known as an embryo) has implanted in the uterine wall.
- Cell differentiation intensifies and organs appear.
- The embryo comprises three layers.
  - *endoderm*: an inner layer that develops into the digestive and respiratory systems.
  - *ectoderm*: an outer layer that develops into the nervous system, sensory receptors (eyes, ears) and skin, hair and nails.
  - *mesoderm*: a middle layer that develops into the circulatory system, bones, muscles, excretory system and reproductive systems.
- The embryo is protected by the *amnion*, a bag containing the amniotic fluid in which the embryo floats. Together the amnion and the amniotic fluid provide a temperature-controlled, shock-proof environment.
- The umbilical cord contains two arteries and one vein and connects the baby to the placenta.
- The placenta contains tissues in which blood vessels from the mother and offspring entwine but do not join. Oxygen, water, food and salt pass from the mother's bloodstream to the embryo, and waste products (carbon dioxide, digestive waste) pass from embryo to mother. Only small molecules can cross the placental barrier; many harmful substances such as bacteria are too large to pass into the child's bloodstream.
- Major organs are formed during this period and so are most vulnerable to teratogens at this stage. More details about what develops when can be found in Figure 2.3.

More information about birth defects can be found at the International Birth Defects Information System (IBIS) website: **http://www.ibis-birthdefects.org/index.htm**

Key term

Teratogen: comes from the Greek word for monster and refers to any agent that can potentially cause a birth defect or have a negative effect on behavioural or cognitive outcomes. Such agents include drugs, alcohol, maternal disease and environmental hazards such as exposure to radiation.

The foetal period

- Begins two months after conception and lasts on average for seven months.
- The organism is now known as a foetus.

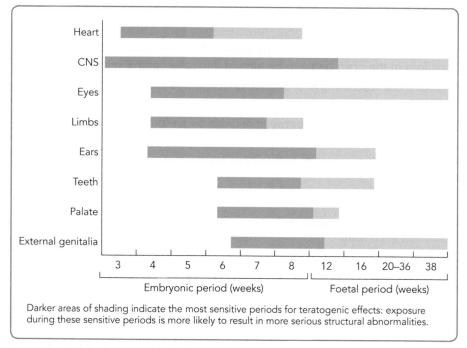

Darker areas of shading indicate the most sensitive periods for teratogenic effects: exposure during these sensitive periods is more likely to result in more serious structural abnormalities.

Figure 2.3 **Critical periods of development for the major organ systems**

- The foetus is active, moving arms and legs and opening and closing mouth.
- Facial features can be distinguished and genitals can be identified as male or female.
- By the end of the fourth month a growth spurt occurs in the lower body and the mother begins to feel the movement of her unborn child.
- Activity increases over the fifth month and preferences are shown for particular positions.
- Grasp reflex develops by the end of the sixth month and irregular breathing movements occur.
- At seven months the foetus is viable, but will need help breathing if born at this time.
- During the last two months of prenatal development fatty tissues develop and organ functioning improves.

Brain development

- The nervous system begins developing 18–24 days after conception with the formation of the neural tube.
- Once the neural tube has closed in approximately Week 5, a massive proliferation of new immature neurons begins to take place.
- This neurogenesis continues throughout the prenatal period.

- At the peak of neurogenesis approximately 200,000 neurons are generated every minute.
- Around 6–24 weeks after conception the different levels, structures and regions of the brain begin to be formed through neuronal migration.
- Once a cell reaches its final destination it matures and develops a more complex structure.
- At 23 weeks connections between neurons begin forming, a process that continues postnatally.
- By the time they are born, babies have approximately 100 billion neurons.

Key terms

Neural tube: the precursor to the central nervous system (CNS), which includes the brain and spinal cord.

Neuron: nerve cell that handles information processing. Neurons are the core components of the CNS. They form complex networks that communicate through the transmission of chemical and electrical impulses.

Neurogenesis: the process by which neurons are generated. During prenatal development, neurogenesis is responsible for populating the growing brain with neurons.

Test your knowledge

2.1 What are the three stages of prenatal development?

2.2 During which stage is the unborn child most vulnerable to outside influences?

2.3 Which organ system has the longest period of vulnerability to teratogens?

2.4 How does the placenta protect the unborn child?

2.5 At what age (in months) is the foetus viable?

2.6 What is neurogenesis?

Answers to these questions can be found on the companion website at: **www.pearsoned.co.uk/psychologyexpress**

Influences on development

Genes and heredity

The importance of genetics and inheritance for physical traits such as eye colour, height, etc. are well established. Likewise, it is known that chromosomal abnormalities can result in atypical development, as seen in Down's syndrome or Fragile X. Such syndromes are often associated with specific cognitive or behavioural deficits. However, the extent to which other cognitive or behavioural problems have a genetic basis is not known. Likewise, the importance of inheritance for psychological traits such as intelligence and personality remains highly controversial.

Key terms

Genes: units of hereditary information composed of DNA, the complex molecule that contains our genetic information. Each gene controls one hereditary characteristic. Genes direct cells to reproduce themselves and manufacture the proteins that maintain life.

Chromosomes: threadlike structures composed of bundles of genes. Chromosomes come in 23 pairs, a member of each pair coming from each parent. Chromosomal abnormalities occur when there are structural problems with the chromosome (for example, a portion is missing or altered) or where the number of chromosomes is atypical. Down's syndrome, for instance, results from an extra copy of chromosome 21.

Further reading Genes and heredity

Topic	Key reading
Behaviour and genetics	Kagan, J., Articus, D., Feng, W. Y., Snidman, N., & Hendler, J. (1994). Reactivity in infants: A cross-national comparison. *Developmental Psychology, 30*(3), 342–345.
Chromosomal abnormalities and atypical development	McGuffin, P., Riley, B., & Plomin, R. (2001). Genomics and behavior: Toward behavioral genomics. *Science, 291*, 1232–1249.

CRITICAL FOCUS

Are behavioural tendencies inherited?

In the paper 'Reactivity in infants: A cross-national comparison', Kagan et al. (1994) argue that behavioural traits such as the amount of motor activity seen in infants are innate. In this study, Kagan provides evidence for very different patterns of motor arousal in four-month-old infants in three different cultures: China, Ireland and the USA. The data suggests that Chinese infants are much calmer, quieter and less fretful than the American and Irish infants, which Kagan cites as evidence for *biological* differences in temperament between Caucasian and Asian infants.

As you are reading this paper, think very carefully about the evidence Kagan provides. Can we be certain that these differences are biological? He cites evidence of earlier studies showing this difference in younger infants. Does this therefore negate the experiential factor? At what point in development is experience relevant? For example, how might prenatal experiences have influenced the behaviours shown by these infants? How might this idea be tested further? For instance, would it be useful for studies to test Asian infants born in the USA?

▶

An important issue highlighted by this paper is the role of culture in development, which is one of the environmental factors discussed in this section. The social context of development is clearly important as it helps define beliefs and social practices. Remember, though, that culture is not defined by geography: culture refers to the attitudes and behaviour that are characteristic of a particular social group or organisation. These attitudes and behaviours may therefore be influenced by social and economic factors as well as ethnicity. Can you think of different cultural groups in the UK for example? This paper therefore highlights one of the links between social and developmental psychology.

Environmental factors

A range of environmental factors have been suggested to impact on human development, including culture, socio-economic status and family context. Such factors are relevant from before birth as they will impact on issues such as access to, and uptake of, prenatal care, maternal and paternal lifestyle choices, exposure to potential teratogens, etc. They may also confound some of the other factors thought to influence prenatal development, as described in the paper by Nebot, Borrell and Villalbi (1997).

Further reading Environmental factors

Topic	Key reading
Socio-economic factors influencing adolescent motherhood	Nebot, M., Borrell, C., & Villalbi, J.R. (1997). Adolescent motherhood and socio-economic factors: An ecological approach. *European Journal of Public Health, 7*, 144–148.
Factors influencing prenatal care	Scholl, T. O., Hediger, M. L., & Belsky, D. H. (1994). Prenatal care and maternal health during adolescent pregnancy: A review and meta-analysis. *Journal of Adolescent Health, 15*, 444–456.

Gene–environment interactions

There is evidence to support a role for both inheritance and environment in the development of a range of psychological functions, including intelligence and personality, as well as psychological disorders such as schizophrenia. In terms of intelligence and personality, it is suggested that, while the *genotype* (a given combination of genes) is inherited, the *phenotype* (that which is observed) develops over time in response to environmental factors. Likewise it may be that an individual inherits a particular genotype that predisposes them to developing schizophrenia, but whether the disorder is actually manifest in an individual will depend on the presence of environmental triggers (diathesis-stress model). While the relevance of genetics prenatally may be evident, the role of the prenatal environment should also be considered and factors such as maternal health and well-being should not be dismissed lightly. Indeed there is increasing evidence that prenatal stress combined with a genetic predisposition affects changes in brain development associated with schizophrenia.

Genotype: a person's actual genetic material.

Phenotype: the way that an individual's genotype is expressed in observed and measureable characteristics.

Diathesis-stress model: a psychological theory that explains behaviour as a result of both genetic factors and life experiences. The term 'diathesis' refers to a genetic predisposition towards a specific disorder. According to this model, this predisposition, in combination with certain kinds of environmental stress, results in atypical behaviour.

Further reading Gene–environment interactions

Topic	Key reading
Genes and prenatal environment in the development of schizophrenia	Koenig, J. I., Kirkpatrick, B., & Lee, P. (2002). Glucocorticoid hormones and early brain development in schizophrenia. *Neuropsychopharmacology, 27*, 309–318.

Test your knowledge

2.7 Which human characteristics are significantly affected by heredity?

2.8 How do environment and genetics work together to determine human characteristics?

2.9 How convincing is the evidence for the inheritance of behavioural tendencies?

Answers to these questions can be found on the companion website at: **www.pearsoned.co.uk/psychologyexpress**

Threats to development

A teratogen is any agent that has the potential to cause a birth defect or have a negative affect on cognitive and behavioural outcomes. The effects of teratogens may not always be evident at birth. Severity of damage is linked to a range of factors, including dose, developmental period during which exposure takes place (see Table 2.1) and genetic susceptibility. The most common teratogens are the following.

Maternal health

Illness in pregnancy can have devastating effects, depending on the timing. Rubella in the eleventh week of pregnancy can cause blindness, deafness, heart defects and brain damage as this is a critical developmental stage for organ development.

Rubella at later stages of pregnancy may, however, have no long-term impact on the unborn child. Other infections with the potential to harm include chickenpox, some sexually transmitted diseases (for example, syphilis) and AIDS. Table 2.1 lists other common diseases and their effects. An important issue here for psychologists is how these risks can be reduced. As noted earlier, strategies may be employed at either a social or an individual level. Once you have finished studying this section, create your own final column for this table – 'ways of reducing risk' – and enter as many different ways of reducing risk as you can think of, based on your reading.

Maternal diet and nutrition are also important, as the developing embryo or foetus relies solely on the mother for its own nutrition. Maternal malnourishment increases the risk of deformity, while maternal obesity has been linked to foetal death, stillbirth and CNS defects. Folic acid deficiency has been linked to neural tube defects such as spina bifida.

Table 2.1 Threats to prenatal development due to maternal health problems

Disease or health condition	Common effects for the unborn child	Impact of timing on teratogenic effect
Rubella	Blindness Deafness Cognitive deficits Heart defects Cerebral palsy Microencephaly	Infection in weeks 1–8 most likely to lead to deficits (60–85% of cases), reducing to 50% in weeks 9–12 and 16% in weeks 13–24
Chickenpox	Premature birth Slowed growth Limb, facial or skeletal malformation	Infection in weeks 1–12 most likely to lead to deficits. Infection up to four days before birth can also have implications for perinatal health, resulting in neonatal death in 30% of cases
AIDS	HIV infection	Infection is more likely during the birth process or perinatally than prenatally
Chlamydia	Premature birth Low birth weight Neonatal conjunctivitis Pneumonia in newborn infant	Of infants born to infected mothers, 25% contract pneumonia and 50% contract conjunctivitis. In both cases infection is transmitted during the birth process
Syphilis	Blindness Deafness Cognitive deficits Heart defects	Syphilitic organisms cannot cross the placental barrier until Week 18. Thus, if treatment can be given before this time teratognic effects are rarely seen
Herpes	Microencephaly Hydrocephalus Cognitive deficit Eye defects	Prenatal infection occurs in only 8% of cases. Infection is more likely to occur during the birth process
Toxoplasmosis	Blindness Deafness Cognitive deficit	Infection in weeks 1–8 most likely to lead to deficits

Key terms

Spina bifida: a developmental birth defect caused by the incomplete closure of the embryonic neural tube. Some vertebrae overlying the spinal cord are not fully formed and remain unfused and open. If the opening is large enough, this allows a portion of the spinal cord to protrude through the opening in the bones, leaving it vulnerable to damage or infection. In more severe cases, damage to the nervous system may result in a range of problems, including partial or total paralysis of the lower limbs, bowel and bladder incontinence or learning difficulties.

Further reading Maternal health

Topic	Key reading
Maternal nutrition	Derbyshire, E. (2007a). The importance of adequate fluid and fibre intake during pregnancy. *Nursing Standard, 21*, 40–43.
Maternal nutrition	Derbyshire, E. (2007b). Nutrition in pregnant teenagers: How nurses can help. *British Journal of Nursing, 16*, 144–145.
Herpes infection during pregnancy and birth	Avigil, M., & Ornoy, A. (2006). Herpes simplex virus and Epstein-Barr virus infections in pregnancy: Consequences of neonatal or intrauterine infection. *Reproductive Toxicology, 21*, 436–445.
Rubella	Dontigny, L., Arsenault, M. Y., Martel, M. J., Biriuger, A., et al. (2008). Rubella in pregnancy. *Journal of Obstetrics and Gynaecology Canada, 30*(2), 152–168.
AIDS	The Royal College of Obstetrics and Gynaecology (2004). Clinical green top guidelines: Management of HIV in pregnancy. Available online at www.rcog.org.uk/womens-health/clinical-guidance/management-hiv-pregnancy-green-top-39
Teratogens	Further information on teratogens and papers concerning this issue are available from the Organisation of Teratology Information Specialists (OTIS) website: www.otispregnancy.org

Maternal age

Delayed childbirth is increasingly common in Western societies and this can increase risks to the health of both mother and child. Risks to the infant include prematurity, low birth weight and certain chromosomal abnormalities such as Down's syndrome. Risks are thought to be greatest for mothers over 30 years of age and have been linked to the declining condition of a woman's eggs; however, there is some evidence that in women with no pre-existing maternal health difficulties the risk of problems in pregnancy are lower. There are also risks for the offspring of younger mothers: adolescent pregnancies are more likely to result in premature birth and infant mortality rates for this age group are higher than for any other. However, there are possible confounding factors here related to social circumstances and social support: teenage mothers are more likely to be from lower-income families and live in areas of greater deprivation.

Down's syndrome: a genetic abnormality that causes physical and intellectual impairments. Typical physical features include a flat facial profile, eyes that slant upwards, small ears, a flat back of the head and protruding tongue. People with the syndrome also tend to be shorter than average with poor muscle tone and have short, broad hands. Heart defects, intestinal problems and thyroid disorders are also common. People with Down's syndrome have varying degrees of learning disability, which may range from moderate to severe. Autistic spectrum disorders are also more common.

Further reading Maternal age

Topic	Key reading
Teenage pregnancy	Fraser, A. M., Brockert, J. E., & Ward, R. H. (1995). Association of young maternal age with adverse reproductive outcomes. *New England Journal of Medicine, 332*, 1113.
Older mothers	Jacobsson, B., Ladfors, L., & Milsom, I. (2004). Advanced maternal age and adverse perinatal outcome. *Obstetrics & Gynecology. 104*(4), 727–733.
Maternal age	Further information is also available from the Royal College of Obstetricians and Gynaecologists at: www.rcog.org.uk/what-we-do/campaigning-and-opinions/statement/rcog-statement-later-maternal-age

Maternal stress

Intense emotional states during pregnancy can affect the unborn child as the physiological changes experienced by the mother may have consequences for uterine blood flow and available oxygen levels. High levels of corticotrophin-releasing hormone (CRH) have been linked to maternal stress and subsequent premature birth and infant distress. Maternal stress may also have an indirect effect on the health of the unborn child by increasing the likelihood of maladaptive behaviours such as drug-taking, smoking and alcohol use.

Further reading Maternal stress

Topic	Key reading
Long-term effects of maternal stress in pregnancy	Talge, N. M., Neal, C., Glover, V., & the Early Stress, Translational Research and Prevention Science Network (2007). Fetal and neonatal experience on child and adolescent mental health: Antenatal maternal stress and long-term effects on neuro-development. How and Why? *Journal of Child Psychology and Psychiatry, 48*, 245–261.

Prescription and non-prescription drugs

Potentially harmful prescription drugs (see Table 2.2) include certain antibiotics (for example, streptomycin), anticonvulsants, antidepressants and synthetic hormones (for example, DES). Thalidomide prescribed for morning sickness in the 1960s is a commonly cited example of the disastrous effects of drugs on the unborn child. Non-prescription drugs with potential to harm include diet pills and aspirin.

Key terms

DES (diethylstilbestrol): a non-steroidal synthetic oestrogen, once prescribed for some women during pregnancy to prevent miscarriages. It was banned for such use when it was discovered that daughters born to mothers who took this drug had abnormally high rates of cervical and vaginal cancer.

Thalidomide: this drug was prescribed to pregnant women to prevent morning sickness in the late 1950s and early 1960s. Unfortunately the drug caused severe deformities in babies known as phocomelia, a condition in which the limbs either do not develop or present as stumps.

Table 2.2 **Drugs and their effects on prenatal development**

Drug	Drug type and use	Effects
Carbemazepine and phenytoin	Prescription drugs. Used to control seizures (anticonvulsants)	Cleft lip and palate Neural tube defects Kidney disease Restricted growth
Aspirin, ibuprofen and other non-steroidal anti-inflammatory drugs (NSAIDs)	Non-prescription pain relief. Occasional use is not problematic	Neonatal bleeding Raise the risk of delayed labour
Sotretinoin and etretinate	Prescription drugs used to treat chronic acne and psoriasis	They may cause chronic malformations during the stage of organ development
Ergotamine and methysergide	Prescribed for migraine attacks	Raise the risk of premature labour
Coumarin	Anticoagulant drugs used in the treatment of heart disease and stroke to slow blood clotting	Taken during early pregnancy, they are associated with facial malformations and mental retardation. Later on they raise the risk of uncontrolled bleeding
Tetracycline	Antibiotic. Safe to use in the first four months of pregnancy	Discolouration of teeth Reduced bone growth

Illegal drugs

Cocaine use in pregnancy has been linked to low weight, body length and head circumference at birth, as well as more long-term neurological and cognitive deficits, including impaired motor development at two years of age, lower arousal, poorer self-regulation, higher excitability and poorer reflexes at one month of age. However, confounding variables linked to the environment and lifestyle of drug users should also be considered (for example, poverty and malnutrition). Children born to heroin users have been found to show withdrawal symptoms immediately after birth, including tremors, irritability, abnormal crying, disturbed sleep and impaired motor control. Heroin use in pregnancy has also been linked to behavioural problems and attention deficits in later childhood.

Alcohol

Consistent heavy drinking in pregnancy can result in foetal alcohol syndrome (FAS), a cluster of abnormalities that include facial deformity, defective limbs, heart problems and cognitive impairment. Binge drinking has also been found to lead to cognitive impairment and behavioural problems in offspring. Some studies have suggested that even moderate drinking in pregnancy can result in reduced attention and alertness that lasts at least through early childhood (four years of age).

Tobacco

Smoking cigarettes during pregnancy reduces the oxygen content while increasing the carbon monoxide content of the mother's blood and this in turn reduces the amount of oxygen available to the unborn child. This has been shown to increase the chance of premature birth, low birth weight, foetal and neonatal death, sudden infant death syndrome (SIDS) and respiratory problems. Nicotine withdrawal has also been noted in neonates of smoking mothers. Links have also been made to attention deficit hyperactivity disorder (ADHD) in childhood. Second-hand smoke may also affect the mother's health and thus the health of her unborn child; father's smoking may therefore have negative consequences for the child's health.

KEY STUDY

Mattson et al. (2010). Toward a neurobehavioral profile of fetal alcohol spectrum disorders

Excessive prenatal alcohol exposure can result in a number of developmental difficulties, including problems with cognitive functioning and behaviour. However, not all infants exposed to large amounts of alcohol prenatally go on to develop FAS. A primary goal of recent research is to enable better and quicker diagnosis of problems in infants exposed to alcohol to enable more timely interventions. The study by Mattson and her colleagues is a good example of recent work that has attempted to use neuropsychological data to develop a battery of tests to identify and differentiate FAS. The researchers were able to distinguish children with FAS from a control group not exposed to alcohol prenatally with 92 per cent accuracy. More importantly, they were able to distinguish children with heavy prenatal alcohol exposure but without FAS and non-exposed controls with 84.7 per cent accuracy. Overall, the neuropsychological test battery was more successful at distinguishing the groups than IQ testing. Measures of executive function and spatial processing were found to be especially sensitive to prenatal alcohol exposure.

Mattson, S. N., Roesch, S. C., Fagerlund, A., Aulti-Ränö, I., Lyons Jones, K., May, P. A., Adnams, C. M., Konovalova, V., Riley, E. P. & the CIFASD (2010) Toward a neuro behavioural profile of fetal alcohol spectrum disorders. *Alcoholism: Clinical & Experimental Research, 34*(9), 1640–1650.

Further reading Drug, alcohol and tobacco use in pregnancy

Topic	Key reading
Alcohol	Sayal, K., Heron, J., Golding, J., & Emond, A. (2007). Prenatal alcohol exposure and gender differences in childhood mental health problems: A longitudinal population-based study. *Pediatrics, 119,* e426–e434.
FAS	Caley, L., Syms, C., Robinson, L., Cederbaum, J., Henry, M., & Shipkey, N. (2008). What human service professionals know and want to know about fetal alchohol syndrome. *Canadian Journal of Clinical Pharmacology, 15,* e117–e123.
Tobacco use	Shea, A. K., & Streiner, M. (2008). Cigarette smoking during pregnancy. *Nicotine and Tobacco Research, 10,* 267–278.
Alcohol, marijuana and tobacco	Faden, V. B., & Graubard, B. I. (2000). Maternal substance use during pregnancy and developmental outcome at age three. *Journal of Substance Abuse, 12,* 329–340.
Cocaine and/ or opiates	Lester, B. M., Tronick, E. Z., LaGasse, L., Seifer, R., et al. (2002). The maternal lifestyle study: Effects of substance exposure during pregnancy on neurodevelopmental outcome in 1-month-old infants. *Pediatrics, 110*(6), 1182–1192.

Environmental hazards

Radiation can cause gene mutations; chromosomal abnormalities are higher in the offspring of fathers exposed to high levels of radiation through their occupation. X-rays in the first few weeks of pregnancy (when expectant mothers often do not know they are pregnant) increases the risk of microencephaly, cognitive problems and leukaemia.

Other hazards include pollutants such as carbon monoxide, mercury (sometimes found in fish such as tuna), certain fertilisers and pesticides.

Further reading Environmental hazards

Topic	Key reading
Environmental hazards such as air pollution	Hertz-Picciotto, I., Park, H.- Y., Dostal, M., Kocam, A., Movec, T., & Sram, R. (2008). Prenatal exposure to persistent and non-persistent organic compounds and effects on immune system development. *Basic & Clinical Pharmacology & Toxicology, 102*(2), 146–154.

Your sister's best friend Lisa is pregnant with her first child at the age of 17. Lisa is not known for her healthy lifestyle – like many of her friends she smokes and drinks and says she 'hates' exercise. She is not keen on giving up her partying lifestyle now she is pregnant. In fact she thinks she should 'make the most' of her freedom before being 'tied down' by a baby. Your sister is worried that Lisa might be putting herself and her unborn baby at risk.

What sort of things could your sister encourage Lisa to do to make sure she gives birth to a healthy baby?

Paternal health

As noted earlier, fathers who smoke risk affecting the health of their unborn child through effects on the mother's health. However father's health preconception is also important and can directly influence the development of their child. Thus exposure to environmental pollutants, poor diet and drug and alcohol use have all been suggested to cause abnormalities in the father's sperm, resulting in miscarriage, childhood disease such as cancer and infant deformity. More recently father's age has been suggested to increase the risk of birth defects.

Further reading Paternal health

Topic	Key reading
Paternal exposure to environmental hazards	Cordier, S. (2008). Evidence for a role of paternal exposures in developmental toxicity. *Basic & Clinical Pharmacology & Toxicology, 102*, 176–181.
Paternal age	Yang, Q., Wen, S. W., Leader, A., Chen, X., Lipson, J., & Walker, M. (2007). Paternal age and birth defects: How strong is the association? *Human Reproduction, 22*, 696–701.

Test your knowledge

2.10 How can fathers ensure the health of their future child?

2.11 Which maternal diseases pose the greatest threat during the birth process or perinatally?

2.12 What are the main characteristics of FAS?

Answers to these questions can be found on the companion website at: www.pearsoned.co.uk/psychologyexpress

Discuss the importance of timing for ameliorating or enhancing the teratogenic effects of maternal disease, drug and alcohol use and environmental agents such as radiation.

Design a website for parents with information about the impact of environmental and other agents on the future cognitive and psychological health of their unborn child.

Prenatal learning and cognitive development

Evidence of prenatal learning is linked to infant auditory perception. Hearing develops at around the sixth month prenatally and it has been well established that the foetus can perceive and respond to sounds, such as speech and music. The recognition of, and preference for, their mother's voice shown by neonates is thought to be a learnt response based on prenatal experience. Research studies have also shown that neonates can recognise either music or prose they have been exposed to prenatally, suggesting the development of cognitive skills such as memory before birth. A burgeoning industry has also built up around the idea that prenatal sonic stimulation with classical music (for example, Mozart and Bach) can have a positive effect on prenatal development, although the evidence for this is equivocal.

Hormonal levels have been found to influence later cognitive skills, including sex differences. Increased levels of testosterone are thought to result in more rapid growth of neurons in the foetal brain and have been linked to enhanced spatial skills.

Further reading Prenatal learning and cognitive development	
Topic	*Key reading*
Prenatal learning	DeCasper, A. J., & Spence, M. J. (1986). Prenatal maternal speech influences newborns' perception of speech sounds. *Infant Behavior and Development, 9*, 133–150.
Prenatal learning	DeCasper, A. J., & Fifer, W. P. (1980). Of human bonding: Newborns prefer their mothers' voices. *Science, 280*(6), 1174–1176.
Prenatal/early influences on later cognitive development	Caulfield, R. (2002). Babytalk: Developmental precursors to speech. *Early Childhood Education Journal, 30*, 1573e–1707e.

> ### ? Sample question · *Problem-based learning*
>
> A pregnant neighbour has read about prenatal learning programmes and is wondering whether or not to invest in one. She asks for your opinion as a student of psychology. What would you tell her about the evidence for such systems and the pros and cons of her investment were she to make one in terms of time and money? Can you suggest anything else she could do to give her baby the best start in life?

CRITICAL FOCUS

DeCasper and Spence (1986). Prenatal maternal speech influences newborns' perception of speech sounds

In this study mothers read the Dr Seuss story *The Cat in the Hat* to their foetuses during the last six weeks of gestation. After birth, babies were given dummies linked to recordings of this and another story that were read aloud by their mother. Babies sucked more on the dummy linked to the recording of the Dr Seuss story, suggesting a preference for *The Cat in the Hat*. This indicates that newborns could recognise the story read aloud by their mothers prenatally and the study is therefore often cited as evidence for prenatal learning. However, it has also been used as evidence to support the burgeoning industry that has developed around prenatal learning programmes. See www.babyplus.com/WhatIsIt.php for one example of such a programme.

While reading this paper you should consider the following types of questions. Can you think of any problems with the way this study has been used? Just how much does it tell us about prenatal learning? Does the study provide *any* evidence to support the idea that education should begin prenatally?

Do a literature search using an academic search engine such as Psycinfo to find further evidence about prenatal learning and postnatal preferences. To what extent does the evidence fit the claims of those advocating prenatal learning?

DeCasper, A. J. & Spence, M. J. (1986). Prenatal maternal speech influences newborns' perception of speech sounds. *Infant Behavior and Development, 9,* 133–150

> ### ? Sample question · *Essay*
>
> To what extent does the evidence support the suggestion that prenatal experiences may affect postnatal preferences and behaviours?

Chapter summary – pulling it all together

→ Can you tick all the points from the revision checklist at the beginning of this chapter?

→ Attempt the sample question from the beginning of this chapter using the answer guidelines below.

→ Go to the companion website at www.pearsoned.co.uk/psychologyexpress to access more revision support online, including interactive quizzes, flashcards, You be the marker exercises as well as answer guidance for the Test your knowledge and Sample questions from this chapter.

Answer guidelines

 Sample question   Essay

Critically evaluate the risks to development during the prenatal period.

Approaching the question

Your answer should aim to provide an analysis of risks to psychological development, describing what these risks are and discussing how they will impact on later outcomes for the child. Remember to keep the focus on psychological impacts rather than purely physical outcomes.

Important points to include

- Begin by outlining the factors that are relevant, including genetics, environmental (teratogenic) agents and the possiblity of gene–environment interactions.

- Discuss the ways in which genetics can influence prenatal development and what impact this might have on future psychological functioning.

- Discuss some of the different types of environmental teratogens such as:
  - maternal infectious disease or malnutrition
  - impacts of maternal drug or alcohol use
  - noxious agents in the physical environment
  - paternal health.
- For each you will need to:
  - highlight how the vulnerability of the organism and different organ systems change at specific stages of development
  - demonstrate the importance of timing of exposure to potential hazards, and show how this differs for different teratogens
  - show what the effect of any damage to the organism might be for later psychological well-being.

47

Make your answer stand out

It is really easy to fall into the trap of simply describing a number of teratogens and how they affect human development during the prenatal period. A good answer will take a critical stance, evaluating the impact of the risk for later development and will focus clearly on psychological aspects of development, including cognitive, social and emotional elements. Linking your evaluation to what you know about other periods of development will demonstrate your ability to synthesise the information you have learnt. Evaluating the methodological approaches of any research studies cited will also make your answer stand out.

Explore the accompanying website at www.pearsoned.co.uk/psychologyexpress

→ Prepare more effectively for exams and assignments using the answer guidelines for questions from this chapter.

→ Test your knowledge using multiple choice questions and flashcards.

→ Improve your essay skills by exploring the You be the marker exercises.

Notes

3

Motor, sensory and perceptual development

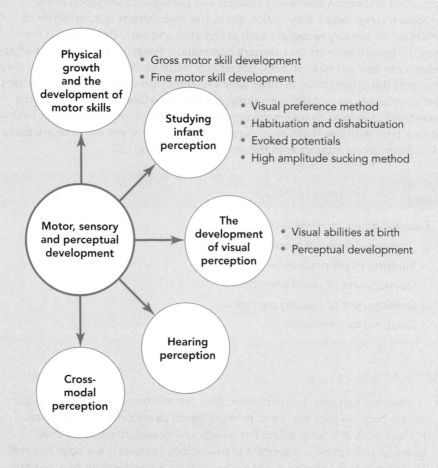

A printable version of this topic map is available from
www.pearsoned.co.uk/psychologyexpress

Introduction

In this chapter we consider important aspects of physical and neurological growth that take place during infancy and early childhood. Physical growth progresses at an astounding rate during the first two years of life and the infant increasingly gains control over physical functioning, in particular *gross* and *fine motor skills*. This motor control enables the infant to begin to explore their environment, which in turn facilitates the development of cognitive skills. These skills continue to develop over the next few years.

Perception is an important cognitive process that has been referred to as the 'beginning of knowing' (Gibson & Spelke, 1983). Psychologists make an important distinction between sensation and perception. *Sensation* is the process through which information about the environment is transmitted to the brain via sensory receptors such as the eyes and ears. *Perception* is the way the brain interprets that sensory information. Research has taught us what infants can see and hear at birth, but what is much harder to assess is how they interpret this information; in other words how they perceive the world. Perhaps not surprisingly, one of the main questions that developmental psychologists have tried to answer concerns the nature of infant perceptual abilities at birth – are we born with the ability to understand and interpret our world or are these skills learnt as we interact with the environment around us?

→ *Revision checklist*

Essential points to revise are:
❏ Changes in fine and gross motor skills
❏ Studying infant perceptual skills
❏ Development of visual perception
❏ Development of hearing perception
❏ Cross-modal perception

Assessment advice

● It is evident that one reason psychologists are interested in increasing motor skills is because they are linked to neurological development, so increases in these skills in infancy reflect the growth and development of the brain. Likewise, perception is important to psychology because it is a cognitive skill. However, simply knowing this is not enough for a good answer to a question on this topic.

● It is important to realise that motor and perceptual skills are also significant for developmental psychologists because of the way that they enable the infant to explore their world.

- Gross and fine motor skills provide the infant with the ability to manipulate objects and move around the environment, while perceptual skills help the infant to see and understand objects and the people around them. These two skills therefore work together to enable increasing psychological development; as you will learn in Chapter 7, according to constructivist accounts of cognitive development, early learning relies on the child's active engagement with the environment around them. In addition, object perception provides a window into the development of mental representations of the world.

- It is therefore important to be able to make the links between the skills described here and higher-level functioning.

- Pointing and other gestures, for example, need good motor skill development and are important for establishing joint attention, which in turn aids language development as you will learn in Chapter 5.

- You will therefore find it useful to link your learning in this chapter to other topics in developmental psychology, in particular language (Chapter 5) and cognition (Chapter 7). However, you should also consider the importance of these skills for social functioning such as attachment (Chapter 4) and play (Chapter 6).

Sample question

Could you answer this question? Below is a typical essay question that could arise on this topic.

 Sample question   **Essay**

Evaluate the role of emerging motor and perceptual skills for later development.

Guidelines on answering this question are included at the end of this chapter, whilst further guidance on tackling other exam questions can be found on the companion website at: **www.pearsoned.co.uk/psychologyexpress**

Physical growth and the development of motor skills

Humans grow from the moment of conception until they attain adult height around the age of 20 years. This process of growth is not regular and one of the periods of most rapid growth is infancy. For example, by the end of the first year of life, a typical infant has achieved around three times his or her birth weight. This increase in weight and height continues through the first few years, before slowing down until puberty when there is another growth spurt. Increases in overall body size are also accompanied by changes in bodily proportions: in infancy the head accounts for a quarter of the baby's height, but by adulthood this proportion has reduced to one-sixth.

However, physical growth is not just about increases in weight and height; it also involves developing control over the muscles of the body and increasing physical co-ordination. Human motor control is a relatively slow process and, by the end of the first two years of life, infants have achieved mastery of only the basics of mobility and co-ordination as shown in Table 3.1.

Table 3. 1 **Fine and gross motor development in the early years**

Age (years)	Gross motor skills	Fine motor skills
2	Walks well Runs Goes up and down stairs alone Kicks ball	Uses spoon and fork Turns pages of a book Imitates circular stroke Builds tower of 6 cubes
3	Runs well Marches Rides tricycle Stands on one foot briefly	Feeds self well Puts on shoes and socks Unbuttons and buttons Builds tower of 10 cubes
4	Skips Standing broad jump Throws ball overhand High motor drive	Draws a person Cuts with scissors (not well) Dresses self well Washes and dries face

Gross motor skill development

- Gross motor skills involve the large muscles of the body and include *locomotor functions* such as sitting upright, walking, kicking and throwing a ball.
- Gross motor skills depend on both muscle tone and strength. This motor development proceeds from the head down (cephalocaudal) and from the centre outwards (proximodistal).
- Activities involving the head and upper extremities therefore develop before those involving the lower extremities, and those involving the trunk and shoulders develop before those involving hands and fingers (see Figure 3.1 on page 63).
- Motor skills evolve in a definite sequence, and age norms are often used to gauge an infant's developmental progress (Bayley, 1993).
- This distinct pattern of motor skill development led early theorists to propose that it represents the unfolding of a genetically programmed sequence of events in which the nerves and muscles mature in a downward and outward direction (Shirley, 1933).

- Individual variation is common in the development of these skills and the timing of motor skills development may vary by as much as two to four months without being indicative of atypical development.
- Evidence suggests that environmental factors influence the timing of motor skills development. For example, the early motor development of African and Jamaican infants has been linked to parenting behaviours.
  - Parents in African cultures have been shown to promote the development of motor skills by providing opportunities for infants to develop muscle tone and strength by, for example, by placing them in an upright position (Cintas, 1989).
  - Jamaican mothers traditionally expect early motor development and work to promote this development by massaging and stretching their baby's limbs (Hopkins, 1991).
  - Jamaican infants born and raised in the traditional way in the UK continue to show this accelerated development.
  - Jamaican infants not raised in the traditional way show no difference in the age at which they acquired these skills when compared to their non-Jamaican peers.
  - This demonstrates clearly that this difference is not genetic, but experiential.
- Infants may also miss out milestones.
  - In the African Mali tribe most infants never crawl (Bril, 1999).
  - Adolph (2002b) describes infants in the USA who also bypass the crawling phase, either moving around by rolling or not engaging in locomotion until they are upright.
  - Environmental factors such as parenting behaviours are likely to be important here as well: the reduction in the number of American infants crawling coincided with late twentieth-century recommendations to lie babies to sleep on their backs to reduce the risk of SIDS (Davies, et al., 1998).
- Current evidence therefore supports a greater role for the environment in the development of these skills.
- Maturational processes are believed to place some limits on the age at which an infant will be able to sit up, crawl or walk, but the experiences and opportunities to practise each child encounters are very important in influencing the actual age at which these milestones are reached.
- Modern theories of motor skill development emphasise the interactive process between nature and nurture.
- For example, the dynamic systems theory (Thelen, 1995) is a constructivist approach to motor skill development.
  - Both nature and nurture are believed to contribute to development.
  - The child takes an active role in its own development.
  - Motor skills are constructed by the infant as they actively reorganise existing motor capabilities into new and more complex actions.

- At first, motor actions rely on innate reflexes – for example, grasping, sucking and rooting.
- Gradually these reflexes are reorganised into new and more complex motor configurations.
- Initial action systems are likely to be tentative, disjointed and unco-ordinated; however, they are progressively modified and refined until the components mesh, resulting in smooth, well co-ordinated systems.
- Development is seen as a self-organising system, whereby the inquisitive infant actively develops more complex motor skills in order to achieve new goals. Interesting sights and sounds in the environment, for example, provide motivation for locomotion, especially where the target is just out of reach.
- Improving physical strength, increases in neurological connections, sensory stimuli and parenting behaviours all contribute to the development of these motor skills.
- This theory therefore integrates action, perception and thought, as the infant has to think about how to organise locomotion in order to achieve their goals (von Hofsten, 2007).

Fine motor skills development

- Fine motor skills involve the small muscles of the body that enable functions such as grasping and manipulating small objects.
- Functions such as writing, drawing and fastening clothing rely upon our fine motor skills.
- These skills involve strength, fine motor control and dexterity.
- The ability of the infant to reach out and manipulate objects changes considerably over the first year of life.
- Voluntary reaching and grasping usually develops at three months of age; prior to this, infants engage in unco-ordinated, often unsuccessful, swipes at objects in the visual field that rarely result in capture of the object in question.
- The onset of reaching and grasping marks a significant accomplishment for an infant's capacity to interact with their environment.
- By four or five months, infants are able to transfer objects from hand to hand and the reflexive *palmar* grasp is replaced by the voluntary *ulnar* grasp.
- Clumsy and claw-like, this grip nevertheless provides an increased ability to engage in the tactile exploration of objects.
- Gradually, greater proficiency is gained in manipulation of objects, so that by the end of the first year of life infants are able to use the far superior *pincer* grasp.

- This is a crucial development in terms of dexterity, as this finger and thumb grip provides the basis for our more sophisticated manual skills such as writing, using scissors and cutlery, turning the pages of a book, etc.

- Throughout the second year of life infants become increasingly dexterous and co-ordinated.

- At 16 months of age they are able to hold a pencil and make rudimentary scribbles.

- By the age of 24 months they are able to copy simple vertical or horizontal lines.

- Building blocks, buttons, dials and other objects can also be manipulated easily by 24 months.

- Consistent with dynamic systems theory, infants are gaining control over simple movements and gradually reorganising them into increasingly complex systems (Fentress & Mcleod, 1986).

Key term

Pincer grasp: Using the thumb and forefinger to pick up small objects. This is an important developmental milestone, demonstrating that the infant's brain, muscles and nervous system are becoming highly synchronised and capable of increasingly sophisticated co-ordination. The pincer grasp will eventually allow a child to button a shirt, use a pencil, tie shoelaces. When it first emerges between the ages of 8 and 12 months, it opens up a whole new world for the infant to explore. It is a very precise movement that progresses slowly and steadily. At around six months, a baby will begin to pick up objects by pushing their hand over a toy and curling fingers around it (*ulnar* grasp). Between seven and nine months, the infant will start to grasp things using fingers and thumb. Lifting up small objects with just two fingers becomes possible around nine months, but the pincer grasp is only truly refined by the end of the first year. Once this forefinger – thumb co-ordination kicks in, children begin to lift and place things with accuracy, practising the dexterity they'll need for jigsaw puzzles, drawing, writing and even turning the pages of a book.

CRITICAL FOCUS

Cephalocaudal pattern of motor development

If you have ever observed a young infant of just a few months old, you might have noticed that leg kicking is a common feature of motor behaviour. These kicking movements present a problem for the cephalocaudal principle of motor development, so are usually dismissed as unintentional movements generated by the CNS (Lamb & Yang, 2000). However, new evidence suggests that this is an inaccurate assumption and infants gain voluntary control of their legs far earlier than the cephalocaudal theory would predict (Galloway & Thelen, 2004).

Galloway and Thelen carried out two experiments with infants of two to three months of age and found that these infants made contact with an object held within reach with their feet earlier than with their hands. Contact was made using feet at 12 weeks and using hands at 16 weeks.

Sample question **Problem-based learning**

Read the paper by Galloway and Thelen (2004). Answer the following review questions.

- What methods did the study employ?
- What evidence is provided to support the hypothesis presented by Galloway and Thelen that purposive leg movements are seen in infants of only a few months of age?
- How strong is the evidence against the cephalocaudal theory of motor development? Should we reject this 'rule'? Might the proximodistal principle also be incorrect?

Galloway, J. C., & Thelen, E. (2004). Feet first: Object exploration in young infants: *Infant Behavior and Development, 27*, 107–1112

Test your knowledge

3.1 What are gross motor skills?

3.2 How are fine motor skills useful for psychological functioning in later life?

3.3 Briefly describe the main principles of Dynamic Systems Theory.

Answers to these questions can be found on the companion website at: www.pearsoned.co.uk/psychologyexpress

Further reading Motor development

Topic	Key reading
Gross motor development	Adolph, K. E. (2002b). Babies' steps make giant stride towards a science of development. *Infant Behaviour and Development, 25*, 86–90.
Motor development and later cognitive skills	Piek, J. P., Dawson, L., Smith, L. M., & Gasson, N. (2008). The role of early fine and gross motor development on later motor and cognitive ability. *Human Movement Science, 27*, 668–681.

Studying infant perception

The biggest challenge when studying infant perception is communication. How can the pre-verbal infant tell us what they can see and understand about the world around them? They cannot tell us through words or even sign language, so sophisticated research methods have been developed to allow psychologists to study the abilities of infants (Slater, 2004). The important thing to remember about these techniques is that they rely on the interpretation of infant behaviour; researchers make inferences about how infants respond to stimuli, so they can only ever be a 'best guess'.

Visual preference method

- This approach was pioneered by Robert Fantz in the 1960s.
- Fanz noticed that infants look at different things for different lengths of time.
- Fantz laid infants down in a looking chamber, which had two visual displays above the infant's head.
- An experimenter would watch the infant's eyes through a peephole.
- If the infant fixated on one of the displays, the experimenter could see the display reflected in the infant's eyes and so could determine how long they looked at each display.
- If the infant spent more time looking at one of the stimuli, it was said that they had shown a preference for that stimuli.
- This method therefore assumes that infants can tell the difference between the two stimuli and therefore prefer to look at one rather than the other.
- One problem with this method is that no difference is shown in looking time. It is therefore impossible to know whether the infant is unable to discriminate between the two images or finds them equally interesting.

Habituation and dishabituation

- In this method infants are presented with a stimulus such as an image or a sound several times.
- If the infant decreases its response to the stimulus after several presentations, it is said that the infant is no longer interested in the stimulus – they have become *habituated*.
- If a new stimulus is then presented and the infant's interest recovers, it is said that the infant has been able to discriminate between the old and new stimulus and has become *dishabituated*.
- Researchers measure habituation and dishabituation in a number of ways:
  - *sucking behaviour*: this stops when the infant pays attention to a stimuli
  - *heart rate and respiration*: these decrease when the infant pays attention to a stimuli
  - *looking at a visual stimuli*: the infant stops looking so often when habituated.
- Infants habituate to a range of stimuli so stimuli are used to test perception of sight, sound, smell, touch and taste.
- However, distinguishing between habituation and preference can be difficult: infants display preference when they are familiar with, but not too familiar with, a stimulus. When first shown two stimuli, infants will show no preference.

When one stimulus does capture their interest they will look at it more often and for a short time will look at this partially familiar stimulus in preference to an unfamiliar stimulus. When they become thoroughly familiar with this stimulus they will, however, habituate and so spend less time looking at this stimulus. In order to categorise looking behaviour properly researchers need to pay careful attention to each infant's familiarisation timeline (Houston-Price & Nakai, 2004)

Evoked potentials

- Electrodes are placed on the infant's scalp above the brain centres that process the sensory information of interest.
- If the infant senses the stimuli presented, a change will be seen in brainwaves or evoked potential.
- Stimuli not detected show no change in evoked potential.
- This can also be used to test discrimination, because two stimuli that are sensed as different will produce different patterns of electrical activity.

High amplitude sucking method

- Infants are given a non-nutritive nipple or dummy to suck, which is connected to either a slide projector or a sound sytem.
- Baseline sucking rate is established before the procedure begins.
- Each time the infant sucks harder than the baseline rate, they trigger the sound system or slide projector, which then delivers some sensory stimulus.
- If the infant detects this stimulus and finds it interesting, they can make it last by maintaining bursts of high amplitude sucking.
- Once interest decreases and sucking returns to baseline, the stimulus stops.
- At this point a new stimulus can be introduced and if the rate of sucking increases it is inferred that the infant has been able to discriminate the two stimuli.
- A modification of this procedure is to have two stimuli, one activated by high amplitude sucking, the other by low amplitude or no sucking.
- It is inferred that the infant prefers one stimulus over the other if they behave so as to activate one stimulus more than the other. This technique was used by DeCaspar and Spence (1986) to test infants' recognition of material they had heard prenatally (see Chapter 5).

Problems with these techniques

- There are a number of general problems related to working with young infants that make applying these techniques difficult:
  - infants are easily distracted

- they need to sleep often and can fall asleep during testing
- they become irritable and upset if hungry, thirsty or uncomfortable
- measuring and interpreting changes in heart rate, head turning, etc., can be difficult
- individual differences mean that some infants are in an alert, attentive state for 9 hours out of 24, while for others this is closer to 1 hour in 24.

Test your knowledge

3.4 What are the main methods used to study perceptual development in infancy?

3.5 Define habituation and dishabituation.

3.6 What are the main difficulties when studying perception in infancy?

Answers to these questions can be found on the companion website at:
www.pearsoned.co.uk/psychologyexpress

? Sample question   *Essay*

Critically evaluate the methods used to study perceptual abilities in infancy.

? Sample question   *Problem-based learning*

Research using the high amplitude sucking method have shown that babies prefer to listen to their mother's voice over those of other women. However infants show no preference for their father's voice over that of another man. It has been suggested that this preference is linked to the familiarity of the mother's voice, which develops prenatally. Design an experiment to test this idea empirically.

Further reading Studying perception

Topic	Key reading
Habituation	Domsch, H., Thomas, H., & Lohaus, A. (2010). Infant attention, heart rate, and looking time during habituation/dishabituation. *Infant Behaviour and Development, 33,* 321–329.
High amplitude sucking	Vouloumanos, A., & Werker, J. F. (2007). Listening to language at birth: Evidence for a bias for speech in neonates. *Developmental Science, 10,* 159–164.

The development of visual perception

Visual abilities at birth

Infant visual abilities are very limited when compared to those of an adult.

- At birth, an infant can only focus on objects 20 to 25 cm (8 to 10 inches) from their face (around about the distance to the parent's face when being held).
- *Acuity* (the ability to see fine detail) is limited. It is estimated to be approximately 20/600 (that is, an object 6 m (20 feet) away is seen as if it were 183 m (600 feet) away as 20/20 vision is not achieved until around 12 months of age.
- The eyes are almost mature at birth, although the retinas continue to develop until the child is around 11 years of age.
- The optic nerve is completely developed, but not fully myelinated.
- Most of the neurons in the visual cortex have developed, but are poorly interconnected; these connections develop rapidly over the first six months of life.

Perceptual development

Early debates about perceptual development focused on the influences of heredity and environment. According to William James (1890), sensory experience for infants is one of 'blooming buzzing confusion' and infants have to learn to discriminate between sensations. In contrast, psychologists from the Gestalt school argued that the infant was born with the ability to create order in what they could perceive. Experimental psychology has made an important contribution to our understanding of what infants perceive at birth and the question is no longer do they have perceptual skills but, rather, what are those skills?

- Early studies by Fantz (1963) showed that infants of only two days of age prefer to look at patterns such as a face or bullseye rather than plain, coloured disks.
- Fantz also found that two–three-week-old infants prefer to look at a normal face rather than one with scrambled features.
- Infants 12 hours old prefer looking at their mother's face rather than that of a stranger (Bushnell, 2003).
- This is sometimes thought to be a familiarity preference as the preference gets stronger with experience.
- Babies prefer attractive faces to those judged by adults to be less attractive (Hoss & Langlois, 2003), and this effect is seen in infants as young as three days (Slater & Johnson, 1998).
- Studies such as this have confirmed the importance of the face as a visual stimulus for infants and have often been cited as evidence of an innate preference for faces.

- This has been further reinforced by studies that have shown infants can imitate an adult's facial expression only a few minutes after birth (Reissland, 1988).

- Facial imitation is thought to show that babies have an innate knowledge of their own face and can match what they can see to their own behaviour.

- Meltzoff and Moore (2000) suggested that this is a useful skill as it allows infants to engage in social interaction from early in life, which is an important skill in the development of relationships and bonding with carers (Quinn & Slater, 2003).

- Infants are also able to discriminate faces on the basis of gender (Quinn et al., 2002).

- However, socialisation also appears to play an important role in this skill as infants raised by a female primary carer show better memory for female faces, while those raised by male primary carers show better recognition for male faces (Quinn et al., 2002).

- It is therefore suggested that infants are born with the ability to recognise individual faces – another important skill for early relationship development – but this is further refined through experiences after birth.

- Other abilities, such as perception of depth, seem to be present at birth to an extent, but develop more over time so that by around five–six months an understanding of depth cues is demonstrated (Sen, Yonas, & Knill 2001).

- This development is thought to be linked to the development of locomotion. A classic experiment by Gibson and Walk (1960) showed that infants would not cross a visual cliff even though it was safe to do so (see Figure 3.1).

- Campos, Bertenthal and Kermoian (1992) showed that when infants first start to crawl they will cross the visual cliff, suggesting that some experience is necessary for wariness of heights to develop.

Figure 3.1 The visual cliff
Source: after Gibson and Walk (1960)

Key term

Visual cliff: this is a classic piece of equipment developed by Gibson and Walk to investigate depth perception in human infants and animals. The visual cliff is created by connecting a transparent glass surface to an opaque patterned surface. The floor below has the same pattern as the opaque surface. This apparatus creates the visual illusion of a cliff, while protecting the infant from injury. In the test, a child is placed on one end of the platform and the carer stands on the other side of the clear surface. It was thought that if a child had developed depth perception, they would be able to perceive the visual cliff and would be reluctant to crawl across it to the carer.

Test your knowledge

3.7 What is the evidence to support the idea that facial recognition is innate?

3.8 Why might facial recognition be important for later development?

3.9 Name three pieces of evidence that support a role for learning in the development of perceptual skills.

Answers to these questions can be found on the companion website at:
www.pearsoned.co.uk/psychologyexpress

? Sample question   Information provider

Design a mobile that will be attractive to a newborn infant. Write a brief to go with the mobile that provides the evidence to support the benefits of including the different components of your mobile.

Further reading Visual perception

Topic	Key reading
Depth perception	Campos, J. J., Bertenthal, B. I., & Kermoian, R. (1992). Early experience and emotional development: The emergence of wariness of heights. *Psychological Science, 3,* 61–64.
Face perception	Quinn, P., Yahr, J., Kuhn, A., Slater, A. M., & Pascalis. O. (2002). Representation of the gender of human faces by infants: A preference for female. *Perception, 31*(9), 1109–1121.

Hearing perception

Hearing develops around the sixth month prenatally and at birth the anatomical structures are more mature than in the visual system. The auditory nerves are fully myelinated at birth, but, as with the visual cortex, interconnectivity in the auditory neural pathway is not complete until adolescence. However, in general, the evidence is that infant hearing is very sophisticated from birth.

- Infants show a preference for some sounds over others and will turn their heads towards child-directed speech (see Chapter 5) in preference to normal speech patterns (Fernald, 1985).

- One characteristic of child-directed speech is that it usually suggests happy emotions. Singh, Morgan and Best (2002) found that infants prefer happy, child-directed speech, suggesting that the preference was for speech that showed positive emotion.

- Newborn infants show a preference for their mother's voice (DeCasper & Fifer, 1980).

- However, this is probably linked to prenatal learning as the unborn baby can hear their mother's voice from around six months and, as described in Chapter 2 DeCasper and Spence (1986) showed that babies recognise prose read to them during prenatal development.

- Infants are also able to discriminate between a range of speech sounds, including ones that are not from their native language; this is a skill lost by adults, suggesting it is an innate ability that becomes gradually attuned to the language heard every day (Werker, 1989).

- Infants are able to discriminate their own language from others' by the age of four–five months, respond to their own name at seven-and-a-half months and attach meaning to word sounds by eight months (Jusczyk, 2002).

Test your knowledge

3.10 At birth, how is the development of hearing different from that of vision?

3.11 Describe infant sound preferences.

Answers to these questions can be found on the companion website at: **www.pearsoned.co.uk/psychologyexpress**

Further reading Hearing perception

Topic	Key reading
Child-directed speech	Fernald, A. (1985). Four-month-old infants prefer to listen to motherese. *Infant Behaviour and Development, 8*, 181–195.
Happy talk	Singh, L., Morgan, J., & Best, C. (2002). Infants' listening preferences: Baby talk or happy talk? *Infancy, 3*(3), 365–394.

Cross-modal perception

Our perception of the world usually involves the integration of different modes of perception: we use sight and sound together. For example, during conversations we co-ordinate the sounds of voices with the movement of mouths and faces. Can infants integrate sound and vision from birth or is this a skill that we learn through experience?

- The evidence suggests that infants can integrate sound and vision, but the sound and vision must be synchronised (Slater, 1999).
- From around two months of age, infants are able to match correctly the vowel they hear with the appropriate mouth/face movement.
- Integration of perceptual pathways is complex, but there is evidence from evoked potential studies that brain functioning is sophisticated enough to sustain cross-modal perception by ten weeks of age (Bristow, Dehaene-Lambertz, & Mattout 2008).
- Learning about cross-modal relationships becomes more sophisticated as infants aged 11 weeks expect a single object to make a single sound, and a compound object (made up of several small objects) to make a complex sound when they hit a surface (Bahrick, 2001).
- Cross-modal processing includes using feedback from movement as well as vision and hearing.
- There is evidence that posture and body position feedback are used by the infant from birth; each new motor development, from sitting through to crawling and walking, has an impact on the infant's perceptual world. This is clearly demonstrated in the work of Gibson and Walk (1960) and Campos et al. (1992; 2000), which has shown how learning locomotion affects understanding of depth.

CRITICAL FOCUS

The role of action in perception

We tend to believe that we have only five senses: touch, taste, smell, hearing and vision. However, we have two other senses that are often forgotten: the sense of bodily posture and balance, which is controlled by the semi-circular canals in the inner ear (the *vestibular system*), and feedback from the nerves throughout our bodies telling us where our body parts are (*kinaesthetic feedback*).

Try these two tasks.

- Stand on one leg and close your eyes.
- With your eyes closed, touch the tip of your nose with your right hand.

Touch, smell, taste, hearing and seeing contribute little to these tasks, but you should have been able to do the first task without falling over and, with the second, you should have been able to touch your nose with ease. In both cases this was because of vestibular and kinaesthetic feedback.

Test your knowledge

3.12 How does cross-modal perception develop?

3.13 What is the link between motor development and perception?

Answers to these questions can be found on the companion website at:
www.pearsoned.co.uk/psychologyexpress

Further reading Cross-modal perception

Topic	Key reading
Brain and behaviour	Bristow, D., Dehaene-Lambertz, G., & Mattout, J. (2008). Hearing faces: How the infant brain matches the face it sees with the speech it hears. *Journal of Cognitive Neuroscience* 21(5), 905–921.
Link between motor and perceptual development	Campos, J. J., Anderson, D. I., Barbu-Roth, M. A., Hubbard, E. M., Hertenstein, M. J., & Witherington, D. (2000). Travel broadens the mind. *Infancy*, 1(2), 149–219.

Chapter summary – pulling it all together

→ Can you tick all the points from the revision checklist at the beginning of this chapter?

→ Attempt the sample question from the beginning of this chapter, using the answer guidelines below.

→ Go to the companion website at www.pearsoned.co.uk/psychologyexpress to access more revision support online, including interactive quizzes, flashcards, You be the marker exercises as well as answer guidance for the Test your knowledge and Sample questions from this chapter.

Answer guidelines

 Sample question   *Essay*

Evaluate the role of emerging motor and perceptual skills for later development.

Approaching the question

Your answer should provide a critical evaluation of what develops in terms of motor and perceptual skills in infancy, linking these to later developments in cognitive and psychosocial functioning. You should aim to consider as wide a range of functions as possible, placing this within a theoretical model such as that provided by dynamic systems theory.

Important points to include

- Begin by defining dynamic systems theory as a modern theoretical approach that brings together seemingly disparate areas of development into a single system.
- You should then consider the skills that develop in infancy such as:
  - fine motor skills
  - gross motor skills
  - visual perception
  - hearing perception.
- For each one, show how later skills are supported by these early developments. For example, fine motor skills help independent skills, such as feeding and dressing, and cognitive functions, such as writing; gross motor skills aid locomotion, which in turn aids depth perception. Perception of faces and voices aids the development of language and interpersonal relationships.
- This should lead you to a discussion of how these different skills and abilities are integrated in cross-modal perception.

Make your answer stand out

It is really easy just to take a descriptive approach in which you describe motor and perceptual skills separately. A good answer, however, will take an integrative approach, showing how skills that seem to be mainly physical, such as crawling and walking, may play a role in later cognitive development. Showing the possible advantages of innate skills and how these are adapted in response to experiences is essential for a high-level answer. Linking your evaluation to complex contemporary theories such as Thelen's (1995) dynamic systems theory will also make your answer stand out.

Explore the accompanying website at www.pearsoned.co.uk/psychologyexpress
→ Prepare more effectively for exams and assignments using the answer guidelines for questions from this chapter.
→ Test your knowledge using multiple choice questions and flashcards.
→ Improve your essay skills by exploring the You be the marker exercises.

Attachment and relationship formation

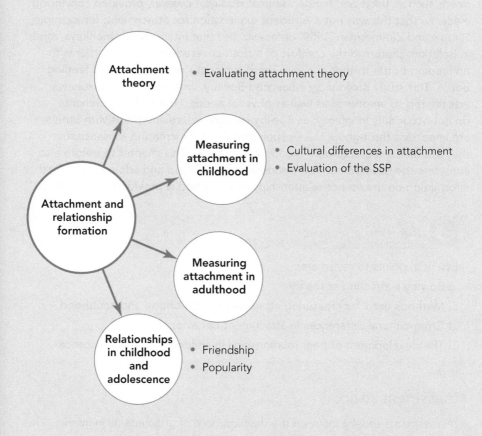

- **Attachment theory**
  - Evaluating attachment theory

- **Attachment and relationship formation**

- **Measuring attachment in childhood**
  - Cultural differences in attachment
  - Evaluation of the SSP

- **Measuring attachment in adulthood**

- **Relationships in childhood and adolescence**
  - Friendship
  - Popularity

A printable version of this topic map is available from
www.pearsoned.co.uk/psychologyexpress

Introduction

This chapter focuses on the development and measurement of our emotional bonds or attachments to others. Early emotional development typically takes place in a clearly defined social context: the family. It is in this context that early relationships have therefore traditionally been studied, with most emphasis placed on the parent–child dyad and in particular the mother–child relationship. One of the dominant and enduring theories of parent–child relationships was put forward by Bowlby (1969) in his theory of attachment, which is described later in this chapter. Early theories suggested that attachment in infancy was primarily based on physical needs; Freud, for instance, proposed that the infant develops a relationship with their mother because the mother satisfies basic needs such as thirst and hunger. Animal studies, however, provided convincing evidence that this was not a sufficient explanation for attachment: for example, Harlow and Zimmerman (1959) demonstrated that infant rhesus monkeys, raised in isolation, preferred the comfort of a cloth-covered surrogate mother with no feeding bottle to that of a wire-mesh surrogate with an attached feeding bottle. This study profoundly influenced Bowlby, who believed that survival was related to emotional as well as physical needs. However, attachments do not occur only in infancy; as Bowlby recognised, relationships with others are important throughout the lifespan and there is increasing evidence that they are fundamental to our emotional well-being. This chapter therefore also considers the development of friendships in childhood and adolescence. Further information on the role of relationships in adulthood is provided in Chapter 10.

> **➡ *Revision checklist***
>
> *Essential points to revise are:*
> - ❏ Bowlby's attachment theory
> - ❏ Methods used for measuring attachment in childhood and adulthood
> - ❏ Cross-cultural differences in attachment behaviours
> - ❏ The development of peer relationships in childhood and adolescence

Assessment advice

- Assessments usually focus on the development of attachments in infancy. This is because we learn about relationships with others from early attachments to our carers. This period of development is therefore very important to future emotional and social development.

- However, relationships may also be important for other areas of development and a good student will remember to consider evidence from topics such as:
  - *language development* (Chapter 5): infants and children learn about communication and social interactions through early relationships with carers
  - *play* (Chapter 6): play behaviour and relationship formation in childhood is often linked in current literature
  - *identity development* (Chapter 9): social relationships at both an individual as well as a group level are thought to play an important role for identity development in a number of ways.
- Finally a word of caution related specifically to the theory of infant attachment. This is a very emotive topic and anecdotal evidence about early infant bonding, parental roles and the impact of care by non-family members is easily come by. However, it is very important to put aside any personal beliefs and focus on academic evidence only; as with all your work in psychology you must ensure that any ideas you put forward, whether in an essay, poster or information sheet, are clearly supported by sound evidence provided by peer-reviewed papers.

Sample question

Could you answer this question? Below is a typical essay question that could arise on this topic.

 Sample question   *Problem-based learning*

Discuss the importance of early relationships for later psychological development.

Guidelines on answering this question are included at the end of this chapter, whilst further guidance on tackling other exam questions can be found on the companion website at: **www.pearsoned.co.uk/psychologyexpress**

Attachment theory

According to Bowlby, the survival value of attachment is not just physical. A psychoanalyst by training, he believed that attachment provided 'lasting psychological connectedness between human beings' (Bowlby, 1969: 194). He also believed that the earliest bonds formed by children with their carers have an impact on relationship formation that continues throughout life.

- Attachment is believed to be an evolutionary mechanism designed to ensure the survival of the vulnerable and dependent infant.
- Infants and their primary carers (usually the mother) are therefore biologically predisposed to form attachments.
- Infants are born with the ability to elicit attachment behaviour from the carer through reflex behaviours such as clinging, crying and proximity-seeking behaviours, which keep the carer nearby and attentive to the offspring's needs, thus maximising survival rates.
- Although biologically based, attachments are not automatic and maternal responsiveness and sensitivity to a child's needs is suggested to be the key to the development of secure attachments.
- Infants who are unable to develop a relationship with a mother or permanent mother substitute are said to be suffering from *maternal deprivation*; according to Bowlby this can have a profound negative impact on future psychological well-being.
- Specific attachments develop gradually as carers become more proficient in interpreting and responding to infant signals, and the infant begins to recognise different individuals and their behaviours.
- Once specific attachments have developed at around six months of age, infants begin to demonstrate other attachment behaviours such as fear of strangers and *separation anxiety*.
- Early relationships provide a prototype for later relationships in adolescence and adulthood through the development of an *internal working model* (IWM).
- The IWM can be modified as the infant develops new types of relationship: contact with a greater variety of people with whom infants can form attachments can therefore lead to a more fully developed IWM, better preparing the child for forming relationships with a wider range of people later on in life.
- The IWM is thought to influence the child's responses to others even in adulthood (Bretherton & Mulholland, 2009). Therefore a child whose IWM is based on maladaptive relationships is likely to repeat this pattern of behaviours through life.

Bowlby based his theory on evidence from a number of research studies carried out in the 1940s and 1950s.

- Goldfarb (1947) studied the extreme cognitive, language and social dysfunction commonly seen in children raised in orphanages at the time. Bowlby believed that these problems were a direct result of a lack of a permanent attachment figure.
- Robertson and Robertson (1967–1973) documented the inconsolable despair demonstrated by young children separated from their mothers when placed in hospital for short-term care (Robertson & Robertson, 1989).

- Harlow and Harlow (1958; 1966) found that young rhesus monkeys raised in isolation showed social maladjustment when placed with other monkeys.
- Bowlby (1944) carried out his own research study, often referred to as the 'Forty-four thieves'. In this study he linked adolescent delinquency to some form of maternal separation experience in childhood such as hospitalisation or parental divorce.

Evaluating attachment theory

While attachment theory remains an important construct within the study of early relationship formation, there have been some criticisms of this approach, especially with regard to the notion that mothers should be a child's primary carer. Feminist psychologists have objected to the idea that female identity is tied to child-rearing and believe there is a high price to pay for maternal sensitivity (for example, Woollett & Phoenix, 1991). However, while Bowlby talks primarily about mother–child relationships, it should be remembered that this theory was developed in the 1950s when social convention dictated that mothers took the main parenting role. It should also be noted that Bowlby does not write exclusively about mothers; he does recognise the notion of a permanent mother substitute.

The evidence surrounding the notion of maternal deprivation has been discussed extensively by a number of authors.

- Rutter (1991) argued that it is the discord surrounding separation that results in behaviour problems, not the separation per se. Subsequent work, which has shown that children from divorced families do not develop behavioural problems when the separation is handled in a sensitive way, supports this view.
- Re-evaluation of the work into the effects of institutional rearing have shown that the orphanages concerned were poorly equipped with a high staff turnover. Children raised in these institutions had very little sensory stimulation and only limited social interaction. It is therefore perhaps not surprising that they showed delayed language, social and cognitive development. Subsequent work has shown that improved institutional care has fewer harmful effects (Hodges & Tizard, 1989; Tizard & Hodges, 1978). Consistency of care seems to be more important than whether or not a child is cared for by their biological parents.

Bowlby's work has been instrumental in changing the way in which parent and child separations are dealt with in today's society including:

- improvements in the standard of institutional care
- phasing out of much institutional care in favour of fostering
- encouraging parents to stay in hospital when a child undergoes medical care.

Internal working model (IWM): This is a central premise of attachment theory and is essentially an internalised set of expectations about how relationships work based on a mental model of the self, the carer and the relationship between these two (Bowlby, 1969). The IWM is thought to provide a prototype or model for future relationships. Although believed to develop early in infancy, the IWM can change over time as children encounter new experiences and different types of relationship.

The circle of security

The circle of security intervention protocol is a 20-week, group-based, parent education and psychotherapy intervention based on attachment theory. It is designed to shift patterns of attachment in high-risk carer–child dyads to a more appropriate developmental pathway. Carers are shown videotapes of their interactions with their children and encouraged to increase their sensitivity and appropriate responsiveness to the child's needs. They are also encouraged to reflect on their own experiences of relationships as children and how this may have affected their own care-giving patterns. Preliminary evaluation findings have been positive (Marvin, Cooper, Hoffman, & Powell, 2002). For more information go to the intervention website at: www.circleofsecurity.org

CRITICAL FOCUS

Factors influencing early attachment

Key question: *How might transactional models of development explain differences in the attachment process?*

Traditional attachment theory suggests that the carer's behaviour, in particular their responsiveness to the child's needs, is an important factor in the development of a good relationship. However, as you probably realise, this is not the only factor involved in relationship development. The sociocultural context of development, including expectations and beliefs about behaviour, is also relevant. In addition, it is important to remember that relationships by definition involve more than one person and it is essential to ask what influence the child brings to the developing relationship. Sameroff (1991) describes a transactional model of development (see Chapter 1) in which the mutual effects that children and adults have on modifying each other's behaviour is emphasised. In this model the dynamic interactions between child and social environment are seen to be at the heart of developmental progression. Furthermore, the response of each individual to the other at a given time point fundamentally changes each individual's future response. In this way patterns of interaction develop. Sameroff (1991:174) provides the following example.

> A complicated childbirth may have made an otherwise calm mother somewhat anxious. The mother's anxiety during the first months of the child's life may have caused her to be uncertain and inappropriate in her interactions with the child. In response to such inconsistency, the infant may have developed some irregularities in feeding and sleeping patterns that give the appearance of a difficult temperament. This difficult temperament decreases the pleasure that the mother obtains from the child and so she

tends to spend less time with the child. If there are no adults interacting with the child, and especially speaking to the child, the child may not meet the norms for language development and score poorly on preschool language tests. In this case the outcome was not determined by the complicated birth or by the mother's consequent emotional response. If one needed to pick a cause it would be the mother's avoidance of the child, yet one can see that such a view would be a gross oversimplification of a complex developmental sequence.

Read the following case studies and, drawing on the information presented above, reflect on how the different experiences of the two children's carers may impact on how they respond to their child and how this in turn may have further influenced the child's development and the relationship between parent and child.

Case study 1: Anna, aged two years, lives in a three-bedroom semidetached house with her two parents and her older sister Laura, who is four years of age. When Anna was born she suffered from severe anoxia as a result of a difficult birth. However, she seemed to show no lasting physical effects and was discharged home with a clean bill of health. Although initially worried, her parents were reassured by the positive attitude of the midwife and hospital consultant. Anna's mum felt her second-born child initially fussed more than her sister Laura had done, but used the same calm, consistent approach that had worked with Laura and found that she was soon able to settle her. Early developmental checks were normal and the family soon forgot about the more alarming aspects of Anna's birth. At age two she is able to walk alone, kick and throw a ball. She understands spoken language and is a good communicator, able to use sentences of two–three words. At this stage her preferred activities are 'drawing' (undefined scribbles) and 'reading' (turning the pages in her favourite picture book). Her mother, a part-time florist, takes her to a mother-and-toddler group twice a week, where she socialises well with the other children. Attachments appear to be secure. On the days when her mother is working she is cared for either by her maternal grandmother or by her father, who works shifts in a local factory.

Case study 2: Maria is also two years of age. An only child, she lives in a two-bedroom terraced house with her mother, a single parent. Maria also suffered from severe anoxia at birth, which seemed to show no lasting physical effects. However, Maria seemed to be a difficult, fretful child who was hard to settle. As a small baby she cried frequently, which her mother found very distressing. Maria's mother works full-time to support herself and her child and feels constantly tired. The emotional and physical stress experienced by Maria's mother makes it harder and harder for her to enjoy interacting with Maria – even caring for her physical needs always seems an uphill struggle. When her mother is at work Maria is cared for by her aunt, a caring but busy mum herself, who has three children of her own aged ten months, three years and five years. Maria therefore experiences very little social interaction with adults, either at home or with her aunt. Early developmental checks suggested some delayed development and this seems to have continued. The health visitor who did Maria's two-year health check noted that Maria has a vocabulary of only about 20 words rather than the 50 words that would be expected by this stage. She also noticed that Maria shows little concern when her mother leaves her with her aunt and shows little interest when her mother returns from work. According to her mother, Maria actively avoids interaction and ignores her bids for interaction when she goes to fetch her: 'She doesn't bother if I am here or not. In fact I think she punishes me for leaving her sometimes – she runs away when I get back and refuses to speak to me. I think she'd rather be here with my sister.'

Test your knowledge

4.1 Why is attachment important for human infants?

4.2 Describe the processes of attachment that have evolved to ensure species survival.

4.3 Which attachment behaviours develop at around six months of age?

4.4 What is the importance of the IWM?

Answers to these questions can be found on the companion website at: **www.pearsoned.co.uk/psychologyexpress**

 Sample question   *Information provider*

Design a poster for social workers, health visitors or other childcare professionals that shows the importance of attachment for emotional development. How can they promote healthy attachment relationships? Remember to write in an appropriate voice for your audience and to provide evidence to support your argument.

Further reading Attachment theory

Topic	Key reading
The role of fathers	Pleck, J. H. (2007). Why could father involvement benefit children? Theoretical perspectives. *Applied Developmental Science, 11*(4), 196–202.
Maternal/paternal sensitivity	Schoppe-Sullivan, S. J., Diener, M. L., Brown, G. L., Mangelsdorf, S. C., McHale, J. L., & Frosch, C. A. (2006). Attachment and sensitivity in family context: The roles of parent and infant gender. *Infant and Child Development, 15*(4), 367–385.

Measuring attachment in childhood

Individual variation has been noted in the development of attachments. The standard method for assessing attachment type in infancy is the strange situation procedure (SSP) developed by Ainsworth and Bell (1970).

- This 20-minute procedure has 8 episodes, designed to expose infants to increasing amounts of stress.
- Carers (typically mothers) and their one-year-old infants are observed in a playroom through a two-way mirror and their attachment behaviours when in an unfamiliar environment are recorded.

- Observers are particularly interested in separation anxiety, willingness to explore, stranger anxiety and response to mother following separation (reunion behaviour).
- The procedure is as follows.
  1 Mother and infant enter the room, which looks like a typical GP's waiting room with chairs, magazines and some toys.
  2 Mother and infant are left alone. Mother sits quietly on a chair, responding if the infant seeks attention. Infant usually plays with available toys.
  3 A stranger enters the room, talks to the mother, then gradually approaches the infant with a toy.
  4 Mother leaves the stranger alone in the room with the infant. The stranger tries to engage the infant with toys. If the infant becomes distressed the scenario ends here.
  5 Mother returns and waits to see how the infant greets her. The stranger leaves quietly and the mother waits until the infant settles, then she leaves again.
  6 The infant is left in the room alone. If the infant becomes distressed the scenario ends here.
  7 The stranger returns and again tries to engage the infant with toys.
  8 Mother returns, the stranger leaves and reunion behaviour is noted.
- Attachment is classified in one of four ways, depending on the child's behaviours during separation and reunion.
  - *Secure* children use their mother as a secure base from which to explore the novel environment. The stranger's entrance inhibits the infant's exploration, causing them to draw a little closer to their mother. The infant will be distressed by the mother's departure and attempt to bring them back by crying or searching behaviours. Infants should seek to re-engage in interaction on the mother's return. If distressed, they may also want to be cuddled and comforted.
  - *Insecure–avoidant* children show little concern at their mother's absence. Instead of greeting their mother on reunion, they actively avoid interaction and ignore their mother's bids for interaction.
  - *Insecure–resistant* children are distressed by their mother's absence and behave ambivalently on reunion, both seeking contact and interaction and angrily rejecting it when it offered.
  - *Insecure–disorganised* children show contradictory behaviour patterns and seem to be confused or apprehensive about approaching their parents This behaviour has been found to be associated with children who have been abused or who have had severely depressed mothers. However, the causes of disorganised attachment are still not clear and research continues on this topic.

Cultural differences in attachment

- In most cultures the majority of attachments are rated secure, suggesting the meaning of attachment relationships are universal.
- However, cross-cultural research has highlighted variations in attachment classifications, as shown in Table 4.1. In Germany, for example, more infants are categorised as avoidant, while in Japan more infants are categorised as resistant.
- It is suggested this cultural variation illustrates how different care-giving patterns lead to varying percentages of secure and insecure attachments.

Table 4.1 Cross-cultural patterns of attachment

Country	Secure (%)	Insecure–avoidant (%)	Insecure–resistant (%)
USA	65	21	14
Germany	57	35	8
Japan	68	26	27
UK	75	22	3

Source: based on data provided in Van IJzendoorn and Kroonenberg (1988)

- An alternative interpretation is that what qualifies as secure or insecure attachment varies across cultures and while attachment is a universal feature of human relationships the meaning of attachment and what constitutes a healthy relationship is not. Thus, in some cultures dependence is valued as a necessary element in attachment.
  - In Japan mothers strive to *anticipate* their infant's needs rather than *react* to infant cries as Western mothers tend to do (Rothbaum, et al., 2000).
  - The aim of attachment is to promote a state of total dependence on the mother and presumption of the mother's love and indulgence known as *amae* (ah-MY-ay). Social routines and independent exploration are thus given less emphasis than in the West.
  - In Japan this state of total dependence and resistance to separation from the mother is considered healthy, secure attachment.
  - This is thought to set the stage for the development of a culturally valued community orientation in which individuals are interdependent, accommodating to others' needs, co-operating and working towards group goals (Rothbaum et al., 2000).

Evaluation of the SSP

- The SSP classification has become the accepted methodology worldwide for measuring attachment (Van IJzendoorn & Kroonenberg, 1988).
- This technique achieves consistent results and so has good *reliability*: for example, a study conducted in Germany found 78 per cent of the children were classified in the same way at one and six years of age (Wartner et al., 1994).

- The *validity* of the SSP as a measure of global attachment has been challenged: the strange situation only measures attachment to one individual (usually the mother) and it has been shown that the child may have a different type of attachment to others such as the father or grandmother (Lamb, 1977).

- The strange situation has also been criticised for being ethnocentric in its approach and assumptions, as it does not take into account the diversity of socialising contexts that exist in the world.

  - Attachment patterns may be influenced by cultural expectations about infant independence as described earlier.

  - Choice of care-giver will also influence attachment patterns. In Nigeria, for example, Hausa infants develop attachments to a large number of carers because they are cared for by the grandmother and siblings as well as the mother (Harkness & Super, 1995). Separation from the mother may therefore not provoke distress.

  - Likewise, in Western cultures increasing numbers of children spend time either in daycare or being looked after by a relative other than the mother (Hochschild & Machong, 1989), which could influence their response to maternal separation.

- The ecological validity of the SSP has been challenged because of the artificial environment and the use of a carefully predefined script.

- Finally, the SSP has also been criticised on ethical grounds, because the child is deliberately put under stress through maternal separation and stranger anxiety.

Measuring attachment in adulthood

Attachment in adults is usually measured either through the adult attachment interview (AAI) or self-report questionnaires:

- The AAI (Main & Goldwyn, 1988) is a semi-structured interview comprising 20 questions and lasting for about an hour.

- The focus of the AAI is attachment to parents in childhood and adolescence. Interviewees are asked about past and current relationships with parents and significant others, how they think past relationships have influenced their personality and relationships with their current partner and/or their own children.

- As with SSP, this technique achieves consistent results when repeated and so has good reliability (Bakermans-Kranenburg, Van IJzendoorn, & Juffer, 2003).

- A strong association has been found between AAI classifications of parents and the quality of attachment relationships with their infants as measured by the SSP (Van IJzendoorn, 1992), suggesting some validity for this measure.

- However, this notion of validity can be contested on the basis that it relies on the validity of the SSP as a measure of attachment.

- In contrast, most self-report questionnaires focus on current adult relationships – in particular, romantic relationships.
- The best-known self-report questionnaire is the adult attachment questionnaire (Hazan & Shaver, 1987; 1990). The questionnaire was designed to classify adults into the three attachment styles originally identified by Ainsworth.
  - *Secure* – the individual finds it relatively easy to get close to others and feels comfortable depending on others/being depended on. No concerns about being abandoned or about someone getting too close.
  - *Avoidant* – the individual has difficulty being close to or depending on others and trusting them. Feels nervous when anyone gets too close.
  - *Anxious/ambivalent* – the individual feels others are reluctant to get as close as they would like. Concerns that partner doesn't really love them. Intensity of need can sometimes scare people away.
- The measure shows good *convergent validity,* with factors such as passion, intimacy and commitment (Levy & Davis, 1988), loneliness and relationship duration (Hazan & Shaver, 1987) and relationship satisfaction (Kirkpatrick & Davis, 1994; Pistole, 1989).
- However, the reliability of this measure has not as yet been clearly established (Garbarino, 1998).
- Contemporary questionnaires take a multidimensional approach to measuring attachment, the main dimensions being closeness/dependency and fear of rejection/abandonment. Most continue to focus on adult romantic attachment – for example, see experiences in close relationships revised (ECR-R), in Fraley, Waller & Brennan (2000). However, relationships with others such as parents and friends are sometimes assessed (for example, experiences in close relationships-relationship structures (ECR-RS).
- One criticism of these self-report measures is that they are more likely to be measuring the state of current relationships than be a global attachment type.

Test your knowledge

4.5 Briefly describe the SSP.

4.6 What behaviours do babies with secure attachments demonstrate?

4.7 What are the three patterns of insecure attachment described by Ainsworth and others?

4.8 What are the advantages and disadvantages of using self-report measures to assess attachment?

Answers to these questions can be found on the companion website at: **www.pearsoned.co.uk/psychologyexpress**

CRITICAL FOCUS

Assessing the validity of the SSP

Use the information provided in Table 4.2 to decide how valid and reliable Ainsworth's 'strange situation' is when used in different cultures.

Table 4.2 **Cross-cultural patterns of attachment**

Country	Secure (%)	Insecure–avoidant (%)	Insecure–resistant (%)
USA	65	21	14
USA	67	21	12
USA	71	17	12
Germany	77	18	5
Germany	42	54	5
Sweden	75	21	4
Japan	70	0	30
Israel – kibbutz	69	14	17
Israel – daycare	86	4	11
Netherlands	66	34	0
Netherlands	75	20	5

Source: based on data provided in Van IJzendoorn and Kroonenberg (1990)

The data in Table 4:2 shows different patterns of attachment types in a number of cultures. What can you say from this table about different patterns of attachment in these different cultures? Thinking back to the earlier discussion of the strange situation, what does this data suggest about the reliability of the strange situation when used cross-culturally? Is it possible to say anything about the validity of this test on the basis of these figures? What other information would be useful when interpreting these figures?

To find out more about this data set and the use of the strange situation cross-culturally, read the paper by Van IJzendoorn and Kroonenberg (1990), available online from the University of Leiden at: https://openaccess.leidenuniv.nl/bitstream/1887/1435/1/168_101.pdf

Further reading Measuring attachment

Topic	Key reading
Adult attachment interview strange situation	A number of papers and other useful resources can be found at: www.psychology.sunysb.edu/attachment
Self-report measures	Fraley, R. C., Waller, N. G., & Brennan, K. A. (2000). An item response theory analysis of self-report measures of adult attachment. Journal of Personality and Social Psychology, 78(2), 350–365.

Topic	Key reading
Cross-cultural issues in measurement	Rothbaum, F., Pott, M., Azuma, K., & Weitz, J. (2000). The development of close relationships in Japan and the United States: Paths of symbiotic harmony and generative tension. *Child Development, 71*(5), 1121–1142. Available online at: www.wjh.harvard.edu/~jweisz/pdfs/2000b.pdf

Relationships in childhood and adolescence

It has been estimated that in middle childhood, 30 per cent of a child's social interactions involve peers – 3 times more than in early childhood (Rubin, Bukowski, & Parker, 1998). This trend continues throughout adolescence (Csikszentmihalyi & Larson, 1984). Most of this interaction takes place in a school setting and there is evidence that these experiences have both an educational and a social value for development (Blatchford et al., 2002). According to Blatchford, even apparently negative interactions may have a value for social development.

- Blatchford, Creeser & Mooney (1990) found that a child-governed break-time culture from which adults are excluded exists in the playground.
- While this culture is not always a benign one, it is nevertheless extremely important to children, because of the freedom from adults that it affords.
- The developmental advantage is that, without adult intervention, children have to learn to regulate playground games and space themselves. They must also discover how to manage teasing and bullying. In so doing, Blatchford argues, they are able to develop a sophisticated set of social understandings.

Friendship

In early childhood, a friend is defined as someone you play with or share some other activity. Friendships are usually:

- transient in nature
- rooted in proximity
- with others of similar age and background.

In middle childhood, relationships still tend to be with others who are similar to themselves, partly because children are more likely to come into proximity because of similarities such as age, socio-economic status, ethnicity, etc. However, there is also evidence that children become increasingly similar to their friends as they interact (Hartup, 1996). 'Fair-weather friends' are common in this age group as friendships are often unable to survive periods of conflict or disagreement (Rubin, Bukowski, & Parker, 1998).

However, during middle childhood children begin to identify some of the special features of friendship (for example, Azmitia, Kamprath, & Linnet, 1998; Parker & Seal, 1996; Selman, 1980) including:

- companionship
- help
- protection
- support
- reciprocity
- trust and loyalty
- longevity.

By the end of middle childhood, friendships are becoming intimate, characterised by an enduring sense of trust in each other. The ability to engage in mutual role-taking and collaborative negotiation develops throughout this period, leading to greater loyalty, trust and social support. For example, girls' expectation that friends would keep secrets rose from 25 per cent in 8–9-year-olds, to 72 per cent in 11–12-year-olds (Azmitia, Kamprath & Linnet, 1998). The ability to form close, intimate friendships becomes increasingly important as children move towards early adolescence (Buhrmester, 1990). However, there are gender differences in the nature of friendships in this age group:

- expectations of trust and intimacy develop slightly later in boys than girls
- triads are more common in the friendships of school-age girls than boys and this can cause one member of the group to feel left out
- boys are quicker to resolve friendship breakdowns, typically working through the problem and renewing the friendship in one day, whereas girls take about two weeks (Azmitia, Kamprath, & Linnet, 1998).

It has been suggested that some of these differences continue into adolescence, with boys forming larger, more status-orientated social networks than girls, who are thought to form more tight-knit relationships with other girls. However, recent research has challenged these assumptions (Guest et al., 2007).

Friendships gradually become more stable in adolescence (Epstein, 1986), although they may be disrupted by transitions such as changing class or school (Waro Aikins, Bierman, & Parker, 2005). However, high-quality friendships, which are marked by intimacy, openness and warmth, are more likely to be maintained despite such transitions (Waro Aikins, Bierman, & Parker, 2005). Indeed, there is an increased emphasis on intimacy and self-disclosure throughout adolescence (Zarbatany, McDongall, & Hymel, 2000), although there is some evidence to suggest that greater levels of intimacy are reported by girls than boys (Buhrmester, 1996). This increasing intimacy and self-disclosure has been suggested to be fundamentally important for the adolescent's developing sense of self as described in Chapter 9 (Parker & Gottman, 1989).

Popularity

Popularity or social status is a central concern for most school-age children or adolescents. A relationship has been found between children's popularity levels and their social behaviours:

- *popular children*: demonstrate high levels of positive social behaviour and cognitive ability and low levels of aggression and withdrawal compared with average children
- *rejected children*: are more aggressive and withdrawn and less sociable and cognitively skilled than average children – they tend to be perceived as 'different' by their peers
- *neglected children*: demonstrate less social interaction and disruptive behaviour but more withdrawal than average children
- *controversial children*: are less compliant and more aggressive than average children.

According to Newcomb, Bukowski and Pattee (1993), it is popular children's competencies that make them the recipients of positive peer nominations. However, another explanation is that popularity leads to increased opportunities for interaction with others, which, in turn, lead to an increase in social skills. For example, peer acceptance might influence friendships by determining the amount of choice that children have for making friends (Azmitia, Kamprath, & Linnet, 1998). It has also been suggested that, in adolescence, style or image provide a crucial means of sustaining and defining group boundaries (Croghan et al., 2006):

- Milner (2004) proposes that adolescents use their chosen style and identity to gain a sense of acceptance and belonging with their peer group (see Chapter 8, Identity development, for more details).
- However, the flip side of this is that failing to maintain such an identity can lead to problems such as teasing, social exclusion and loss of status (Blatchford, 1998; Crogan et al., 2006).
- Since style is often linked to particular brands, economic disadvantage might therefore impact upon adolescent popularity. Some evidence suggests that not having enough money to afford the 'right' brands leads to social exclusion as brand items serve as markers of group inclusion that have to be genuine and cannot be faked (Croghan et al., 2006).
- Alternatively, rather than engaging in conflicts around style, young people may express solidarity with these cliques by modelling themselves on the popular groups, but resisting the consumption of brand-name goods, thereby establishing a new, less high-status, group (Milner, 2004).
- Conformity and conflict over style groups become less marked after the age of about 16 years, with older adolescents claiming they no longer feel pressured into buying and wearing particular items (Miles, 2000).
- It is suggested that this is part of maturing as a teenager, which may imply a developmental progression in thinking and identity.
- An alternative explanation is that young people's relative powerlessness at school makes them particularly prone to focus on status hierarchies that are highly dependent on consumption; at age 16 young people in the UK are leaving compulsory education, which brings with it a change in social status and context.

Key terms

Popularity: in developmental research, this is usually defined by the number of children who name a target child as 'liked', 'disliked', 'friend' or 'best friend' (Newcomb, Bukowski, & Pattee, 1993):

- children with the most 'liked' nominations are popular
- children with the most 'disliked' nominations are rejected
- children with very few (or even no) nominations are neglected
- children who are both nominated frequently by some and actively disliked by others are considered controversial.

Status hierarchy: refers to levels of social dominance commonly seen within adolescent social networks. Social hierarchies exist between, as well as within, friendship groups or cliques: a higher social status is associated with belonging to certain cliques rather than others.

Clique: a small, exclusive group of friends. Group size averages around five or six, although larger groups may be seen. These groups have a shared identity and are often based on a shared interest or style.

Test your knowledge

4.9 How does the nature of friendship change from childhood to adolescence?

4.10 How is popularity defined in the developmental literature?

4.11 Name three factors that might influence an individual's popularity in adolescence?

Answers to these questions can be found on the companion website at: **www.pearsoned.co.uk/psychologyexpress**

 Sample question   *Problem-based learning*

You have recently taken up a job as a part-time teaching assistant in the reception class of a local school. You have noticed that one of the girls in the class rarely plays with the other children. They are not unkind to her, but even so you have observed that they rarely respond to her bids for interaction during free play in the classroom. At break time she is usually the last to leave the classroom and her peers all seem to ignore her.

What do you think you should do? Should you share your concerns with the class teacher or the child's parents? Should you try to help the girl to be accepted by her peers and, if so, how?

Are you right to be worried or is this just a normal stage of development?

KEY STUDY

Dwyer et al. (2010). Attachment, social information processing, and friendship quality of early adolescent girls and boys

Social information processing (SIP) theory attempts to explain social behaviours through cognitive processes, using an information-processing approach (see Chapter 7, Cognitive development, for an overview of information-processing models of cognition). SIP theory suggests that people come to social situations with a set of biologically determined capabilities and a 'database' of past experiences. Our interpretation of other people's intentions and motivations during an interaction is therefore influenced by the information contained within this database. According to this theory, the IWM influences later relationships because it provides the database of rules and emotion processes that guide the processing of attachment-related information. This questionnaire study explored the relationship between attachments to parents, the ways that young adolescents think and feel about situations with their closest friends (SIP) and the quality of these friendships.

A sample of 114 boys and 109 girls aged 11–12 years completed a battery of validated questionnaires that asked about their security in their relationships with their mothers and fathers, their attributions, emotional responses and coping strategies regarding challenging social situations with their closest friend and the quality of the relationship with that friend. It was found that more maladaptive attributions, emotions and coping strategies were significantly related to higher levels of insecurity. This provides some evidence that attachment to parents and relationships with friends are related. In particular, it indicates that children's IWM may impact on how they think about conflict situations with close friends.

Dwyer, K. M., Fredstrom, B. K., Rubin, K. H., Booth-La Force, C., Rose-Krasnor, L., & Burgess, K. B. (2010). Attachment, social information processing, and friendship quality of early adolescent girls and boys. *Journal of Social and Personal Relationships, 27*(1), 91–116

Further reading Friendships

Topic	Key reading
Social status in adolescence	Guest, S. D., Davidson, A. J., Rulison, K. L., Moody, J., & Welsch, J. A. (2007). Features of groups and status hierarchies in girls' and boys' early adolescent peer networks. *New Directions for Child and Adolescent Development, 118,* 43–60.
Rejection and friendship	Pedersen, S., Vitaro, F., & Barker, E. D. (2007). The timing of middle-childhood peer rejection and friendship: Linking early behavior to early-adolescent adjustment. *Child Development, 78,* 1037–1051.
Friendship in childhood and early adolescence	Rubin, K. H., Bukowski, W. M, & Parker, J. G. (2006). Peer interactions, relationships, and groups. In W. Damon, R. M. Lerner, & N. Eisenberg (Eds.), *Handbook of child psychology: Vol. 3: Social, emotional, and personality development* (6th ed., pp. 571–645). New York: Wiley.

Chapter summary – pulling it all together

→ Can you tick all the points from the revision checklist at the beginning of this chapter?

→ Attempt the sample question from the beginning of this chapter using the answer guidelines below.

→ Go to the companion website at www.pearsoned.co.uk/psychologyexpress to access more revision support online, including interactive quizzes, flashcards, You be the marker exercises as well as answer guidance for the Test your knowledge and Sample questions from this chapter.

Answer guidelines

 Sample question   *Problem-based learning*

Discuss the importance of early relationships for later psychological development.

Approaching the question

Your answer should aim to provide an analysis of aspects of early relationships such as attachment and discuss which areas of development might be influenced by the quality of these early relationships. You will find it useful to think beyond attachment and relationship formation. Read Chapter 5, for example, which looks at language development.

Important points to include

● Begin by outlining the importance of early relationships for human survival; make it clear this is psychological as well as physical.

● Discuss different aspects of early relationships and which areas of psychological functioning they may impact upon. Remember to include the child behaviours as well as parental ones. You might want to consider features such as:
  ● maternal/paternal responsiveness
  ● child temperament/responsiveness, etc.
  ● joint action formats
  ● security of attachment and development of IWM.

● You will need to show how these different features of early relationships are related to each other. A transactional model would be useful here to show how both members of the dyad contribute to the relationship's development.

● You should also consider other factors such as the environment and cultural expectations and how they might affect developing relationships.

85

Make your answer stand out

It is really easy simply to focus on the obvious link between attachment, IWM and later relationships when answering this question. A good answer will take a much broader view than this and for example consider the importance of early relationships for the development of language and cognition. According to Vygotsky, social interactions are central to our cognitive development, so early relationships must be vital as well. Remember to take a critical stance, evaluating any causatory mechanisms that have been proposed in this area and the methodological approaches of any research studies cited. Reinterpreting some of the traditional theories of attachment in light of new models such as the transactional model or SIP will also make your answer stand out.

Explore the accompanying website at www.pearsoned.co.uk/psychologyexpress

→ Prepare more effectively for exams and assignments using the answer guidelines for questions from this chapter.

→ Test your knowledge using multiple choice questions and flashcards.

→ Improve your essay skills by exploring the You be the marker exercises.

Notes

5

Language development

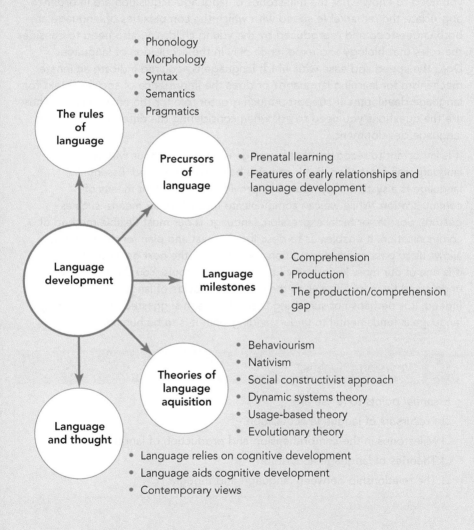

- Phonology
- Morphology
- Syntax
- Semantics
- Pragmatics

The rules of language

Precursors of language
- Prenatal learning
- Features of early relationships and language development

Language development

Language milestones
- Comprehension
- Production
- The production/comprehension gap

Theories of language aquisition
- Behaviourism
- Nativism
- Social constructivist approach
- Dynamic systems theory
- Usage-based theory
- Evolutionary theory

Language and thought
- Language relies on cognitive development
- Language aids cognitive development
- Contemporary views

A printable version of this topic map is available from
www.pearsoned.co.uk/psychologyexpress

Introduction

Language is a central part of human intelligence. As a student of psychology, it is important that you understand how and when language is acquired and what social, cognitive and neurological factors underpin early language development. You might also ask yourself how these different aspects of development are linked. For example, what is the relationship between cognitive and language processes?

In addition to a basic understanding of the rules and structure of language, you need to know what the milestones of language acquisition are in order to appreciate the remarkable speed with which the complexities of language are both understood and reproduced by the young child. You also need to consider the roles that biology and experience play in the acquisition of language. Does the speed and ease with which language is acquired indicate an innate mechanism for learning language? or does the importance of social context for language development support a much greater role for the environment? These are the questions you need to ask when considering the different theories of language development.

It is important to recognise that language is not synonymous with speech; language can be spoken, but it can also be written or signed. Essentially, language is a system of symbols that provides an important means of communication. While we can communicate through other means, such as gesture, posture or facial expression, language is our most flexible method of communication. It enables us to describe the past and plan for the future. It allows us to pass on ideas, tradition and values to the next generation. As such, it is one of our most important cultural and social tools. You therefore need to understand the social as well as the cognitive aspects of language acquisition. Indeed, it is perhaps not surprising that it has been suggested understanding language is fundamental to understanding what it is to be human.

➡ *Revision checklist*

Essential points to revise are:
❏ Precursors of language acquisition
❏ Milestones in the comprehension and production of language
❏ Theories of language acquisition
❏ The relationship between language and thought

Assessment advice

- Tasks related to language development often refer to some of the fundamental issues in developmental psychology described in Chapter 1.

- The issue of whether language is innate or learnt continues to occupy both linguists and psychologists. While it is generally accepted that both nature and nurture play a role in language acquisition, the extent to which each matters and the specific role each plays is debated by contemporary theorists. These include Steven Pinker, who takes an evolutionary stance, and Michael Tomasello, who argues that language learning is based on usage (sometimes called a social-pragmatic approach).

- When answering questions about the origins of language, it is important to ensure that you are able to support your answer with reference to both empirical evidence and theoretical argument. It is easy to fall into the trap of simply describing and comparing both approaches. The good student will recognise that this is not sufficient and a critical, evaluative, evidence-based response is required.

- Another common question concerns the relationship between cognition and language. Does the acquisition of language promote our cognitive skills or do we need symbolic thinking in order to acquire language? Is there another common process or function that underpins both language and cognitive development?

- Given the important relationship between cognition and language on the one hand and language and social development on the other, a good student will consider material on cognitive development and early relationships when answering a question on language development in order to demonstrate synthesis of understanding.

Sample question

Could you answer this question? Below is a typical essay question that could arise on this topic.

 Sample question   *Essay*

Critically evaluate the role of the environment in early language development.

Guidelines on answering this question are included at the end of this chapter, whilst further guidance on tackling other exam questions can be found on the companion website at: **www.pearsoned.co.uk/psychologyexpress**

The rules of language

Phonology: the sound system of a language. Includes the sounds used and rules about how they are combined. A *phoneme* is the smallest sound unit in a language. For example, 'cat' has three phonemes: /c/ /a/ /t/.

Morphology: the rule system that governs how words are formed in a language. *Morphemes* are the smallest sound units that have meaning. For example, 'girl' is one morpheme – it cannot be broken down further and still have meaning.

Syntax: the ways words are combined to form acceptable phrases and sentences. Word order can change meaning in language – for example, 'David drove the car' has a different meaning from 'The car drove David'.

Semantics: the meanings of words and sentences. Semantic restrictions affect the ways words can be used in sentences. For example, the following sentence is syntactically correct, but semantically wrong: 'The bike talked John into going for a ride'. The sentence violates our semantic knowledge that bikes cannot talk.

Pragmatics: the system of using appropriate conversation – knowing how to use language effectively in context. For example, turn-taking in conversation; school-aged children addressing the teacher 'Ben Smith' by his title and second name 'Mr Smith', rather than by his first name, 'Ben'.

Precursors of language acquisition

Prenatal learning

- Hearing develops at around the sixth month prenatally and the foetus responds to sounds.
- The recognition of, and preference for, their mother's voice shown by neonates is thought to be a learnt response based on prenatal experience.
- Research studies have also shown that neonates can recognise either music or prose they have been exposed to prenatally, suggesting prenatal learning of 'acoustic cues' (the patterns of speech and language).
- This skill is the precursor to developing an understanding of what words mean; the ability to recognise and remember speech sounds; and to segment words from the speech stream – in other words, to identify where words begin and end from the flow of sounds people make when they speak.
- Prenatal linguistic experience therefore provides a sensory and perceptual bridge into postnatal life so that newborn infants:
  - have already learnt to identify their native language
  - can recognise different speech patterns within that language – for example, they can differentiate 'happy talk' from other patterns of speech (Mastropieri & Turkewitz, 1999).

- this prenatal learning is thought to influence infants' responsiveness to speech and voices, which in turn provides a foundation for later language acquisition.

Features of early relationships and language development

In addition to providing a basis for social and emotional development, early relationships also have a role to play in the development of cognitive functioning and, in particular, the acquisition of language. There are particular features of early relationship that have been noted as being important precursors to language development.

Child-directed speech

This is a distinctive speech pattern that uses a lot of repetition, simplified short utterances, raised pitch and exaggerated expression (see Table 5.1). This form of speech has also been called 'baby-talk' and 'motherese' (Matychuk, 2005). These adaptations are shown not only by parents but also by women who have not had children (Snow, 1972), fathers (Berko Gleason, 1973) and even four-year-old children (Shatz and Gelman, 1973). This type of speech is very widespread and has been identified in a range of cultures including:

- the !Kung Bushmen of the Kalahari
- forest-dwellers in the Cameroons
- the Yanomami of the Amazon Basin
- the Eipo of New Guinea (Fernald, 1989).

However, it is not a universal feature of language and in cultures where it is not used language development follows the same progress although more slowly (Lieven, 1994), suggesting that such speech is useful but not essential for language development. Child-directed speech is thought to make language learning easier because:

- it simplifies language (Thiessen, Hill, & Saffron, 2005)
- it is more effective than standard speech in getting an infant's attention
- it is preferred by infants (Singh, Morgan, & Best, 2002).

Table 5.1 **Features of child-directed speech**

Phonological characteristics	Semantic characteristics
• Higher pitch	• Limited range of vocabulary
• Exaggerated and more varied intonation	• 'Baby-talk' words
• Lengthened vowels	• More words with concrete referents
• Clear enunciation	

Meshing

This describes the smoothly integrated interactions seen when two people get on well together, with each person's contribution to the interaction fitting in with the other's. This feature is particularly evident in conversations where one partner waits until the other has finished speaking, picks up the signals that they have finished, then gives their input, while their conversational partner takes their turn in the listening role, waiting for their turn to speak to come round again and so on. In the 1970s ,observations of mother–child interactions during infant feeding (breast or bottle) demonstrated that both the baby's and the mother's behaviour are closely meshed (Kaye & Brazelton, 1971):

- human infants feed with a 'burst–pause' rhythm, in which they suck for a while, then pause for a few seconds before starting to suck again
- mothers usually synchronise their own behaviour to this rhythm from the very first feed
- mothers speak to or jiggle their baby during a pause rather than while the baby is feeding.

Mothers typically say that jiggling 'wakes up' their baby and helps to keep them sucking. However, the evidence suggests jiggling actually lengthens the pause and inhibits sucking behaviours, which only recommence once the jiggling stops (Kaye & Brazelton, 1971). Once the mother stops jiggling, the baby is more likely to start a new burst of sucking.

Synchronised turn-taking behaviour

This is a 'conversation-like' interaction between mother and child, often referred to as a pseudo-dialogue. The mother's response is both predictable and contingent on the child's behaviour and, as such, is believed to provide the child's first experiences of relatedness, by showing how their behaviour has meaning and is responded to by the other. The infant learns that interactions with others can be predictable and they can play an active part within the relationship. Turn-taking behaviour includes the feeding behaviours described above, as well other parent–child interactions such as peek-a-boo (Kaye & Fogel, 1980). Initially controlled by the adult, these turn-taking episodes are progressively driven by the infant and their own active, appropriately timed, inputs. In this way pseudo-dialogue gradually metamorphoses into 'proto-dialogue', still without the meaningful language content that will come later, but with a clearly defined turn-taking framework.

Joint attention formats

The mother creates simplified and stereotyped sequences of actions with objects. Mothers structure interactions with their infant so that knowledge about what can be done and how to do it can be transmitted. Initially, such interactions may only involve the carer and child. Gradually, however, other objects are introduced into the interactions. For example, building blocks into a tower or using a spoon for feeding. Sequences are repeated over and over, which enables the infant to learn how to re-enact the sequence alone. According to Bruner (1975; 1983; 1993) because these shared sequences are also talked about, this provides the foundation for the development of language. Bruner argues that the social context of language is very important for the infant because people generally talk to them about familiar events and objects. Evidence that the first words to be understood by an infant are typically the child's own name, the names of other family members and the names of familiar objects such as clock, drink and teddy, supports this view (Harris et al., 1995a).

Infants' vocalisations

Crying, babbling and cooing are all recognised as important precursors to speech (see Table 5.2). Gestures such as pointing, waving and nodding are also seen in the pre-linguistic child and, as well as providing tools for communicating, may aid the development of language (Harris et al., 1995a).

Table 5.2 **Developmental sequence of pre-linguistic communication skills**

Age	Method of communication
Birth	Crying
1–2 months	Cooing begins
6 months	Babbling begins
8–12 months	Use of gestures begins

Key term

Joint attention: refers to the complex of social skills through which partners in an interaction incorporate a common referent in their exchange. Pointing to an object or following another's gaze are among common non-verbal ways of achieving joint attention. Once language is acquired, words can perform the same function. Joint attention is also thought to be important for relationship formation as it helps individuals to develop awareness of each other's thoughts and feelings and reach a state of mutual understanding and awareness referred to as *intersubjectivity*. Intersubjectivity develops initially through joint attention, which focuses on referents such as facial expressions and gestures but will later incorporate the verbal communications of the child and others. Thus language development is both embedded in developing relationships as well as instrumental in the development of relationships. There is some evidence that increasing joint attention can improve language acquisition in cases of atypical development such as autism where language development is delayed. Evidence to support this is described in the key study provided in this chapter.

Aldred et al. (2004). A new social communication intervention for children with autism: Pilot randomised controlled treatment study suggesting effectiveness

Interventions that focus on the psychosocial aspects of development form the core of autism treatments in the UK. Interventions often target aspects of social communication such as joint attention; however, the evidence for effectiveness of such interventions is limited. This UK-based study used a randomised control trial (RCT) design to test a social communication intervention for the treatment of autism. RCT – in which participants are randomly assigned to either the intervention or the control group – is accepted as the gold standard for evaluating the effectiveness of interventions. The intervention in this study involved parents of children with autism undertaking a 12-month training programme to learn how to use a technique called adapted communication. This technique focuses on joint attention, parental sensitivity and responsiveness to the child. The results of the trial demonstrated statistically significant improvement for children in the intervention group in terms of a range of skills, including expressive language, when compared with the control group. These findings are important because they provide sound evidence that interventions using joint attention can be effective for increasing language use in children with autism. In addition, the use of the RCT method provides a model for future research that aims to increase the evidence-base in this area.

Aldred, C., Green, J., & Adams, C. (2004). A new social communication intervention for children with autism: Pilot randomised controlled treatment study suggesting effectiveness. *Journal of Child Psychology and Psychiatry*, 45, 1420–1430.

Further reading Precursors of language development

Topic	Key reading
Prenatal learning	Krueger, C., Holditch-Davis, D., Quint, S., & DeCasper, A. (2004). Recurring auditory experience in the 28- to 34-week-old fetus. *Infant Behavior and Development*, 27, 537–543.
Turn-taking/social relationships	Ratner, N., & Bruner, J. (1978). Games, social exchange and the acquisition of language. *Journal of Child Language*, 5, 391–401. Available online at: http://web.media.mit.edu/~jorkin/generals/papers/33_ratner_bruner.pdf

Test your knowledge

5.1 What are the five rules of language?

5.2 How does prenatal linguistic experience seem to influence later language development?

5.3 Describe the relevance of child-directed speech, meshing, turn-taking and joint action to language acquisition.

Sample question   *Information provider*

Design a webpage for new parents that gives them advice on how to use play and one-to-one interactions with their baby to promote good language development.

Language milestones

Comprehension

- Most infants begin to comprehend their first words when they are around 8 months old, and the total number of words understood grows slowly up to about 12 months of age when there is a sudden increase in vocabulary size (Fenson et al., 1994).
- Harris et al. (1995b) found that the age at which infants first showed signs of understanding the names of objects was ten months and this development was highly correlated with the development of pointing.
  - This close relationship between the development of pointing and understanding object names suggests that these are closely linked processes with a common origin.
  - Pointing has an important role to play in ensuring joint attention during joint action formats. For example, when reading picture books with their carers, joint attention to individual objects is maintained through pointing. This suggests a role for social factors in language development.
  - Evidence that blind children produce significantly fewer words for discrete objects than sighted infants (Norgate, 1997) lends further support to the importance of pointing for acquiring object names.
- Changes in sound recognition may also be important for this development.
  - The neonate is born with the ability to recognise acoustic cues and can make distinctions between phonemes in any language (Kuhl et al., 2006).
  - Between the ages of 6 and 12 months they become better at perceiving the changes in sound in their native language, gradually losing the ability to detect differences that are not important. For example, the sounds *r* and *l* are important in spoken English, distinguishing words such as *rake* and *lake*. No such sound distinction exists in Japanese. Iverson et al. (2003) demonstrated that six-month-old infants from English-speaking homes could detect the change from *ra* to *la* and gradually improved in detecting this change over the following few months. In contrast, infants from Japanese-speaking homes were as good as the infants from English-speaking homes at 6 months, but by 12 months had lost this ability.

- It is likely that this recognition of distinct sounds and speech patterns develops over the first year of life into recognition and comprehension of words.
- Understanding of language also begins around the same time that this change from universal linguist to language-specific listener occurs.

Production

- Language production develops after comprehension.
- Precocious talkers may produce their first word as early as nine or ten months, but many children do not produce their first word until well into their second year.
- There is some evidence to support the idea that social interactions and adult responsiveness play an important role in language development (Tamis-LeMonda, Bornstein, & Baumwell, 2001).
- First words are limited in number and *over-extension* and *under-extension* are both commonly seen in the use of first words (Woodward & Markman, 1998).
- Infants express various meanings by simply altering the intonation of a single word. For example, 'Milk' could mean, 'I want my milk', 'Where is the milk?' and even 'I've spilt my milk!' Interpretation relies on the contexts in which they are uttered and, in the absence of environmental cues (such as spilt milk), carers may not always get the meaning right first time. These single-word sentences are known as *holophrases*.
- Word production increases gradually until around the end of the second year, when there is a vocabulary spurt (Bloom, Lifter, & Broughton, 1985). At around the same time, a qualitative change in language use can be seen as infants begin to use two-word phrases.
- Two-word utterances, or *telegraphic* speech, provides a more effective means of communication and is a universal feature of language development (Boysson-Bardies, 1999). However, the child still has to rely heavily on gesture, intonation and context for conveying meaning.
- Class work by Slobin (1972) identified a range of functions for these telegraphic utterances, as demonstrated in Table 5.3.

Table 5.3 **Functions of early telegraphic utterances**

Utterance	Function
See doggie	Identification
Book there	Location
More milk	Repetition
All gone	Non-existence
My candy	Possession
Big car	Attribution
Mama walk	Agent action
Where ball?	Question

- Once the telegraphic speech stage has been reached, young children move rapidly from producing two-word utterances to creating three-, four- and five-word combinations and so begin the transition from simple to complex sentences (Bloom, 1998).

- Utterances also become more grammatical and the transition from early word combinations to full-blown grammar is rapid. By the time children reach their fourth birthday, they have mastered an impressive range of grammatical devices, seemingly assimilating the structures of their native language without explicit instruction or correction (Brown & Hanlon, 1970). This is often cited as evidence for language acquisition being driven by an innate process.

The production/comprehension gap

- One reason for the lag between comprehension and production of language is that changes in the anatomy of the vocal tract are necessary for the production of the complex range of movements that speech requires.

  - At birth the infant vocal tract is very different from that of an adult. It is designed to enable strong, piston-like movements, which are essential for sucking.

  - The infant's *larynx* is positioned high up so that the epiglottis nearly touches the soft palate at the back of the mouth.

  - The tongue is large in relation to the size of the mouth, nearly filling the oral cavity, while the *pharynx* is very short compared to that of an adult, allowing little room for manipulation of the back part of the tongue.

  - Once sucking becomes less of a priority, at around four months of age, the vocal tract gradually takes on a more adult form.

- This physical change is accompanied by neural maturation of the related motor areas in the brain.

- Together these physical and neurological developments provide infants with control over the fine motor movements that are essential for producing the full range of speech sounds.

- There is evidence that production of sign language follows a similar sequence to the acquisition of spoken language, but the first word is seen two–three months earlier (Bonvillian, Orlansky, & Novack, 1983). The earlier development of signing may link to the reliance on gross motor skills, which develop sooner than the fine motor skills needed for speech.

Example of application of theory: the case of baby sign

The earlier acquisition of signing has led to increasing interest in teaching signing to babies (see **www.babysign.co.uk** for more information). There is some evidence that signing speeds up rather than hinders the speech process (Acredolo & Goodwyn, 1998), and the links to gesture and object labelling are clear. However, one question to ask is whether signing per se speeds language acquisition or whether this reflects an increase in parental responsiveness.

CRITICAL FOCUS

The vocabulary spurt

Read the article by Nazzi and Bertoncini (2003), which tries to account for the vocabulary spurt that occurs at around 18 months of age. Now answer the following questions.

● How do the authors attempt to explain the sudden increase in language learning at 18 months?

● To what extent does the evidence they present support this view? What are the disadvantages of using patterns of atypical development as evidence?

Nazzi and Bertoncini suggest that before the age of 18 months infants are not acquiring words which have meaning, but, rather, sounds they use to label objects. If this is true, what do you think might be the implications for infant comprehension of language? Does this view negate the impact on social factors for language development or do you think it makes them even more pertinent?

Nazzi, T. & Bertoncini, J. (2003). Before and after the vocabulary spurt: Two modes of word acquisition? *Developmental Science*, 6(2), 136–142. Available online at: http://lpp.psycho.univ-paris5.fr/pdf/1381.pdf.

Further reading Language milestones

Topic	Key reading
Social interactions	Tamis-LeMonda, C. S., Bornstein, M. H., & Baumwell, L. (2001). Maternal responsiveness and children's achievement of language milestones. *Child Development, 72*(3), 748–767.
Sign language	Bonvillian, J. D., Orlansky, M. D., & Novack, L. L. (1983). Developmental milestones: Sign language acquisition and motor development. *Child Development, 54*, 1435–1445.
Developmental delay	Leung, A. K. C., & Kao, C. P. (1999). Evaluation and management of the child with speech delay. American Academy of Family Physicians. Family Physician Website. Available online at: www.aafp.org/afp/990600ap/3121.html
Gestures and spoken language development	Iverson, J. M., & Goldin-Meadow, S. (2005). Gesture paves the way for language development. *Psychological Science, 16*(5), 367–371.

Test your knowledge

5.4 At what age do infants begin to understand spoken language?

5.5 What factors affect the emergence of language comprehension?

5.6 At what age does the production of language develop?

5.7 What are the main milestones of language production?

5.8 Why does production of language lag behind language comprehension?

Answers to these questions can be found on the companion website at:
www.pearsoned.co.uk/psychologyexpress

Sample question   *Essay*

Describe the main milestones of language acquisition. What factors influence this development?

 Sample question   *Problem-based learning*

Christopher is concerned that his son Peter, who is 18 months of age, can only say 3 or 4 real words. He seems to prefer to use gestures and signs to communicate his needs. Christopher is concerned that his son is showing language delay because of an over-reliance on the baby signing that he was taught at a local mother and baby group. This is causing friction between the parents as Peter's mother, Jill, believes that the signing has really helped her communicate with her son and Christopher is worrying over nothing. What advice would you give to Christopher and Jill? Should Jill stop signing as Christopher believes or is he worrying over nothing? Remember to support your answer with evidence from the literature.

Theories of language acquisition

One of the predominant debates in theories of language development concern the question 'Is language innate or learnt'? Traditionally, the debate has been between behaviourists such as Watson and nativists such as Chomsky.

Behaviourism

- States that language is learnt through a process of reinforcement and imitation.
- As the infant babbles, it happens to say 'dada'. This is interpreted by the mother as the baby trying to say 'daddy'. Hugs, kisses and praise given to the child reinforce this behaviour, making it more likely that the sound will be repeated.
- Gradually the infant will learn to associate a particular sound with an object or person.
- They have begun to learn how to label objects and what was initially meaningless babbling has become meaningful language.
- In addition, children are said to learn through imitating the sounds made by others.
- For example, during play a mother may use the word 'teddy' to her child, while giving them the teddy.
- Gradually the child learns the association between the word and the object and tries to imitate the sounds made by the mother, which results in reinforcement, repetition, etc.

Nativism

- Argues that this is too simple an explanation for what is essentially a complex behaviour.
- In particular, learning theory cannot explain how children are able to construct novel sentences or the ease with which children learn the rules of grammar.
- There is evidence, for example, that parents do not reinforce or explicitly correct syntax or other grammatical errors (Brown, 1973).
- Chomsky argues that there must therefore be an innate mechanism for learning language. He calls this the *language acquisition device* (LAD).

Most contemporary theories of language development tend to be less extreme. Both sides have modified their position, so that nativists recognise the environment has a role to play in language acquisition and environmentalists accept imitation and reinforcement are insufficient to explain the child's entry into the complex world of language.

Social constructivist approach

- J. S. Bruner's theory provides a good example of an interactional framework for thinking about language development.
- He maintains that while there *may* be a LAD as suggested by Chomsky, there must also be a *language acquisition support system* (LASS).
- In this support system he is referring to the features of early relationships described above.
- Parents and other carers (unknowingly) provide ritualised scenarios – the ritual of having a bath, eating a meal, getting dressed or playing a game – in which the phases of interaction are rapidly recognised and predicted by the infant. It is within these social contexts that the child first becomes aware of the way in which language is used.
- The utterances of the carer are themselves ritualised and accompany the activity in predictable and comprehensible ways.
- Gradually, the child moves from a passive to an active position, taking over the movements of the care-giver and, eventually, the language as well.
- Bruner cites the example of a well-known childhood game, peek-a-boo, in which the mother, or other carer, disappears and then reappears. Through this ritual, which at first may be accompanied by simple noises or 'bye-bye', ... hello' and later by lengthier commentaries, the child is both learning about separation and return and being offered a context within which language, charged with emotive content, may be acquired.
- It is this reciprocal and affective nature of language that Bruner suggests Chomsky neglects to consider.

Dynamic systems theory

The importance of shared activities for language development is supported by current research (for example, Liebal et al., 2009) and theorists from different schools now agree that the social context plays an important role in language development.

- Dynamic systems theorists (for example, Evans, 2006; Gershkoff-Stowe & Thelen, 2004) would agree with Bruner's proposition that features of the social environment are important for language development.
- They would also concur with the idea that development happens as a result of an interaction between this environment and the child's innate predispositions.
- However, they would disagree with the idea that there is an innate language-specific mechanism; according to this theory, language emerges from the same general processes as all other behaviours.
- In this way, language and cognitive development are linked rather than separate processes.

Usage-based theory

Tomasello (2006) also sees the social context as important for language development.

- However, he argues that the essence of language is its symbolic dimension, not its grammatical construction.
- Language is learnt as a specific tool for conversation and communication.
- Concrete words are learnt initially, with no grammatical rules at all.
- All the child has is a collection of useful concrete speech units, which form the basic building blocks of language.
- Gradually the ability to construct longer and more complex utterances emerges.
- Initially children do not possess the fully abstract categories and schemas of adult grammar. Children construct these abstractions only gradually and in piecemeal fashion.
- According to Tomasello, children construct their language using the following general cognitive processes:
  - intention-reading (for example, joint attention), by which they attempt to understand the communicative significance of an utterance
  - pattern-finding (categorisation, schema formation), by which they are able to create the more abstract dimensions of linguistic competence.

This implies that language development follows on from the development of our thinking processes.

Evolutionary theory

According to Pinker (1994), Chomsky is correct in saying that language is an innate faculty of mind, albeit one that has evolved by natural selection as a Darwinian adaptation for communication.

- The ability to acquire language is therefore hard-wired into our system.
- Pinker does, however, guard against extreme determinism, noting that even though we have evolved a specialisation for grammar, language itself must be shared if it is to be an effective means of communication, so the specifics of a language (such as vocabulary and pragmatics) must be learnt.

Key terms

LAD: according to Chomsky, the LAD is an innate mechanism by which children are able to construct the grammar of their native language. Through the LAD the child is hard-wired to recognise the grammar of whatever language they are exposed to in infancy. This LAD matures over time, allowing the child to use increasingly complex language. According to Chomsky, there are certain rules of grammar that all languages have in common. He calls these rules *universal grammar* (UG). Such rules include structures such as the use of past, present and future; designation of categories such as nouns and verbs. These implicit rules are 'known' by children from birth. However, the more complex and specific rules of a given language are learnt through experience: the speech children hear is filtered by the LAD, which extracts language regularities (such as adding 'ed' to a verb for the past tense) in order to construct language rules, thereby providing children with the guidelines needed to communicate in their native tongue.

LASS: according to Bruner, language development takes place in a social context, which includes parents and carers. The concept of the LASS refers to this social context and encompasses all the techniques used by adults to give a meaning to language, so making it easier for children to acquire.

Further reading **Key developmental theories**

Topic	Key reading
Evolutionary theory	Pinker, S., & Jackendof, R. (2005). The faculty of language: What's special about it? *Cognition, 95,* 201–236. Available online at: http://pinker.wjh.harvard.edu/articles/papers/2005_03_Pinker_Jackendoff.pdf
Usage-based theory	Tomasello, M. (2006). Acquiring linguistic constructions. In D. Kuhn & R. Siegler (Eds.), *Handbook of child psychology: Vol.2: Cognition, perception and language* (5th ed., pp. 255–298). New York: Wiley. Chapter available online at: http://email.eva.mpg.de/~tomas/pdf/tomasello_HoCP2005.pdf

5.9 How is language acquired according to behaviourist theory?

5.10 What is Chomsky's LAD?

5.11 What are the main factors involved in language acquisition according to Bruner?

5.12 What is a dynamic systems theory of language development?

5.13 To what extent does usage-based theory rely on cognitive mechanisms for language development?

5.14 What is the evolutionary perspective on language acquisition?

Answers to these questions can be found on the companion website at: **www.pearsoned.co.uk/psychologyexpress**

 Sample question   *Essay*

Critically discuss the advantages of interactionist approaches to language development.

Language and thought

The link between thought and language development deserves some consideration. This is another classic debate in psychology: Does language merely reflect thought or do we need to be able to think (for instance, categorise, understand concepts, etc.) before language can develop? The traditional arguments are as follows.

Language relies on cognitive development

Piaget claimed that although language and thought are closely related, language depends on thought for its development. Language is not possible until children are capable of symbolic thought; they have to understand that one thing can stand for another before they can use words to represent objects, events and relationships. He based this claim on a range of evidence, including development in infancy, in which fundamental principles of thought (for example, understanding concepts) are displayed well before language, and the simultaneous emergence of language and other processes explored later in this book, such as *symbolic play*, which suggests that language is just one of a number of outcomes of fundamental changes in cognitive ability.

Language aids cognitive development

In contrast, Vygotsky (1986) saw thought as dependent on language. According to Vygotsky, language is one of our most important cultural tools and the medium through which most, if not all, learning takes place. Mental operations are believed to be embodied in the structure of language and cognitive development results from the internalisation of language as follows.

- Initially thought and language develop as two separate systems.
- Before the age of about two years, children use words socially – that is, to communicate with others. Up to this point, the child's internal cognition is without language.
- At around two years of age, thought and language merge. The language that initially accompanied social interaction is internalised to give a language for thought. This internalised language can then guide the child's actions and thinking.

Vygotsky (1978) identified self-talk as a critical part of the child internalising previously external social speech. In early childhood, especially between the ages of three and four, children often talk out loud to themselves. Over time, this self-talk seems to disappear. Piaget (1923) called this self-talk *egocentric* speech and suggested it reflects some of the limitations of young children's cognitive skills (see Chapter 7). In contrast, Vygotsky argued that all speech, including self-talk, is 'social' and therefore does not disappear; it simply becomes internalised. He argued that to believe self-talk disappears would be like believing that children stop counting when they stop using their fingers to do so. Vygotsky alleged that even when internalised, self-talk continues to guide a child's actions. This idea is given some support by the way in which the conscious use of self-talk intensifies when children are presented with tasks of increasing difficulty. Perhaps you can even think of examples of adults using self-talk as an aid for learning?

Contemporary views

There is some evidence of related activity between cognitive and language development (Oates & Grayson, 2004) and some theorists still argue for a need to understand cognitive concepts before language can emerge (Gopnik & Meltzoff, 1997). However, it seems possible that language and cognition develop in a parallel but disassociated fashion (Cromer, 1987). Evidence in support of this view comes from studying atypical development – for example, deaf children with no language (verbal or signed) perform as well on problem-solving tasks as their same-age peers (Furth, 1973). Thus, while thought may eventually influence language and vice versa, the current view is that the development of language and cognition takes place in separate modules rather than in a single system.

Test your knowledge

5.15 How is cognitive development necessary for language acquisition according to Piaget?

5.16 Describe Vygotsky's theory of language internalisation.

5.17 How do contemporary views explain the interface between language and cognitive development?

Answers to these questions can be found on the companion website at:
www.pearsoned.co.uk/psychologyexpress

CRITICAL FOCUS

What is the relationship between language and thought?

Read the following newspaper article, which discusses the relationship between thought and language, using spatial knowledge as an exemplar. Does language shape our thoughts or is it the other way around? Available online at: **www.guardian.co.uk/ science/2002/may/16/languages.medicalscience**

Now answer the following questions.

- To what extent do you think the research cited provides good evidence in support of the idea that thought shapes language rather than the other way around?
- Can all of the findings presented be explained in terms of differences in social context?
- Which developmental theorists does this call to mind?

Social context is cited by a number of theorists as having a role in cognitive and language development, including Tomasello, Bruner and Vygotsky. In comparison, Piaget placed little emphasis on this issue. Indeed it is an important criticism of his theory, as you will see in Chapter 7 when you study cognitive development.

Chapter summary – pulling it all together

→ Can you tick all the points from the revision checklist at the beginning of this chapter?

→ Attempt the sample question from the beginning of this chapter using the answer guidelines below.

→ Go to the companion website at www.pearsoned.co.uk/psychologyexpress to access more revision support online, including interactive quizzes, flashcards, You be the marker exercises as well as answer guidance for the Test your knowledge and Sample questions from this chapter.

Answer guidelines

 Sample question   *Essay*

Critically evaluate the role of the environment in early language development.

Approaching the question

Your answer should aim to provide an analysis of the different features of the environment that may impact on language development. You should consider both theoretical and empirical evidence to support your answer.

Important points to include

- Begin by outlining the opposing theoretical approaches to language acquisition – that is, biological, environmental, interactionist.
- Discuss the ways in which the majority of contemporary theories acknowledge both biological and environmental factors in language development, but how the relative contributions of each are still contested.
- Discuss some of the different types of environmental features of relevance. For example:
  - prenatal environments
  - joint action formats
  - meshing
  - child-directed speech.
- Discuss possible biological limitations on language development, such as motor skills and physiological development.
- For each you will need to:
  - discuss the theoretical rationale for each feature
  - provide empirical evidence in support/against these features
  - evaluate the evidence.

> *Make your answer stand out*

It is really easy to fall into the trap of either simply describing the opposing nature–nurture arguments or focusing solely on environmental factors. A good answer will take a critical stance, evaluating the theoretical propositions as well as the available evidence. Linking your evaluation to what you know about other areas of development, such as cognitive and social development, will demonstrate your ability to synthesise the information you have learnt. Including prenatal environments will also show the ability to think creatively. Evaluating the methodological approaches of any research studies cited will also make your answer stand out. You might also consider including more global theories of development (for example, dynamic systems, bio-ecological models) to help frame your answer.

6

Play

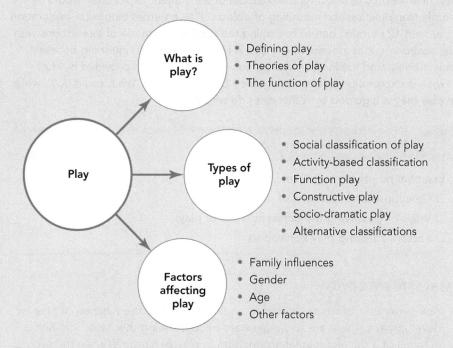

- **What is play?**
  - Defining play
  - Theories of play
  - The function of play

- **Play**

- **Types of play**
  - Social classification of play
  - Activity-based classification
  - Function play
  - Constructive play
  - Socio-dramatic play
  - Alternative classifications

- **Factors affecting play**
  - Family influences
  - Gender
  - Age
  - Other factors

A printable version of this topic map is available from
www.pearsoned.co.uk/psychologyexpress

Introduction

What is play? What role does it have in children's development? What factors influence the play that children engage in? These are the sorts of questions you need to be able to address when studying the topic of children's play. Play has long been considered a hallmark of childhood and many theorists have seen the value of play as being in the development of skills and abilities for adulthood. Play, it has been suggested, helps develop social, cognitive and psychological functions and, for this reason, you will need to link your study of this chapter to other areas of development. You also need to be aware that, in developmental terms, play is different from exploration. Exploration is seen as an information-gathering venture that allows children to get to know their environment and the objects within it. This knowledge is important because it provides the basis for play. Exploration therefore precedes play, dominating infant behaviour for the first nine months of life; a typical example of early infant exploration would be the simple manipulation and mouthing of objects. Play emerges alongside exploration at around 12 months, before becoming the dominating mode of interactions with the environment at around 18 months. A useful way of distinguishing between object-orientated exploration and person-orientated play is provided by Hutt (1966): in exploration children are guided by the question 'What can *it* do?', while in play they are guided by 'What can *I* do with it?'

→ *Revision checklist*

Essential points to revise are:
❏ Definitions and functions of play
❏ Ways of classifying the different types of play
❏ Factors affecting play behaviours

Assessment advice

- Assessments in this area tend to focus on the issue of the function of play for development. There are two main ways of considering this issue. The first is in terms of a developmental progression in play behaviours, while the second is concerned more with the importance of play for developing specific skills and abilities.

- Attempts have been made to show a developmental progression in play behaviours. However, more recent work has demonstrated limitations to such approaches. Far more focus is now given over to the way that play helps development to progress, so your task is to ensure that you have a very clear and detailed picture of how play behaviours reflect and enhance learning in other areas of development.

- Play is most often linked to relationship development in contemporary texts, with the emphasis on the interactive component of play behaviours. Play is therefore often presented as assisting relationship formation.

- A good student will recognise that in some instances play may reflect the current status of relationships rather than influencing them; it is important to remember that simply being able to link two behaviours does not mean one must cause the other.

- Finally, a good student will remember to look beyond the obvious and consider the ways in which all aspects of development – for example, motor skills, cognition and language – may interact within a play setting.

Sample question

Could you answer this question? Below is a typical essay question that could arise on this topic.

 Sample question   *Essay*

Play is essential to a child's development. Discuss.

Guidelines on answering this question are included at the end of this chapter, whilst further guidance on tackling other exam questions can be found on the companion website at: **www.pearsoned.co.uk/psychologyexpress**

What is play?

Defining play

The complexity of play means that definitions of play are notoriously difficult and it is generally considered that no one definition of play is necessary or sufficient (Smith & Pellegrini, 1998). One of the most commonly agreed criteria for defining play is behaviour that does not seem to serve an apparent immediate purpose. According to this definition, children are less concerned with the outcome of the behaviour than the behavioural processes per se. In dispositional terms, what matters is 'means over ends'. Although, as you will see in the next section, this does not mean that play has no purpose, simply that its purpose is neither explicit nor consciously recognised by the players.

Play has also been defined according to the circumstances that elicit and support play. Rubin, Fein and Vandenberg. (1983) suggest that the context must be familiar (in terms of objects and people), safe and friendly if play is to occur and children must be free from stress, hunger and fatigue in order to play. According to Martin and Bateson (1993), spatial relations can also categorise behaviour as play – thus behaviours in the playground are generally considered play, because of the specific setting they take place in.

In the same way, play has been defined depending on consequences. For example, a behaviour may be categorised as play-fighting because the children stay together afterwards; the same behaviour may be defined as aggression if the children separate afterwards (Smith & Pellegrini, 1998).

Theories of play

Early theories of play focused on the possible origins of play.

- The surplus energy theory (Spencer, 1873) suggests that play originates from the build-up of excess energy in the body that needs to be expelled. Play is possible only when the biological system builds up an excess or surplus of energy. After such an accumulation of energy within the system, the organism engages in play behaviour to dissipate or release this surplus energy

- Preparation for life (Groos, 1898). Children play to imitate adult life and practise what it may be like. Many manufacturers sell toys designed on this premise – for example, toy ovens, construction tools, phones, dolls, dressing-up clothes, etc.

- Recapitulation theory (Hall, 1904) suggested that we play to replicate earlier stages of human history. The development of infants and their play re-enact elements representative of the historical development of all humanity.

Twentieth-century theories focused more on the importance of play to development.

- **Psychoanalytic theories of play** (for example, Freud, 1856–1939) emphasise the importance of play in a child's social and emotional life. Psychoanalysis believes that play allows the child to gain mastery over objects and social situations by manipulating them in play. Play also allows the child to gratify wishes and desires that are not possible to fulfil in reality. So a little boy can 'kill' an action figure that is a soldier and then bring him back to life.

- **Cognitive theories of play** Piaget (1962) described three stages of play that were later elaborated by Smilansky (1968). These range from simple (that is, not intellectually challenging) to complex (that is, requiring understanding of rules and logic).

  - **Functional play** involves simple, repetitive movements that do not require constructing reality in symbolic ways. The infant who continues to drop objects from the highchair and laughs at the sound each one makes is participating in functional play. Piaget calls these repetitive behaviours, from which the young child derives pleasure, *circular reactions*.

  - **Constructive play** involves manipulation of physical objects to build or construct something. Constructive play may occur with peers. Most often its importance is in teaching the child the mastery motive or that he or she can conquer a challenge.

- **Dramatic or symbolic play** appears in the preoperational stage of development and is when the child substitutes imaginary situations or objects for real ones. It is a direct result of the child acquiring figurative thought. Often during this stage of development children's creative energy and fantasies create imaginary playmates.

- **Games with rules** appear in middle childhood, as children enter Piaget's concrete operational stage. Negotiating the rules is often as enjoyable as the social interaction of the game.

- It is important to note that while Piaget believed play can facilitate intellectual development, he did not think it is not synonymous with it. For true cognitive development to take place, both assimilation and accommodation have to occur; in play, assimilation dominates over accommodation (see Chapter 7 for a definition of assimilation and accomodation).

- According to Vygotsky, through play children learn to give meaning to objects, to tease out relationships, to try and practise different roles.

- Play can also help meet children's needs for immediate gratification. Vygotsky gives the example of a child who wants to go horse riding but cannot, so instead uses a stick to represent a horse and plays at riding.

- Play also leads to development because during play children acquire and invent rules and, in this way, the child's conceptual abilities are expanded.

- Play also serves as a means through which children attain abstract thought. Initially, children's play involves games that are based on memories and recreating real situations. Then through the use of imagination and adhering to rules, children acquire abstract thought.

- According to Vygotsky, play creates a zone of proximal development (ZPD) in which the child can feel a sense of mastery, as in play they are able to function at the very top of the zone (see Chapter 7 for a definition of ZPD).

The function of play

Play has an integral relationship to early social, cognitive and linguistic development. It has been described as essential to mental and physical health and social and emotional well-being. Key theorists in psychology have ascribed many different roles to play.

Psychological well-being

- Freud and Erikson believed play helps master anxiety and conflict. Play relieves tension, allowing children to cope with life's problems.

- Play therapy is based on this idea and allows children to work off excess energy and release pent-up emotions. In therapy, play also provides an opportunity to analyse children's conflicts and ways of coping. Children may also feel less threatened and more likely to express their true feelings.

Cognitive development

- Piaget (1962) maintained that symbolic play advances cognitive development. Through play, children are able to practise their competencies and skills in a relaxed and pleasurable way. You can find out more about the importance of understanding symbolism for cognitive development in Chapter 7.

- Vygotsky (1962) also saw a value in symbolic play for cognitive development, especially during the preschool years. Imaginary play drives creative thinking.

- Play is also thought to be of value for language development, which it supports because play with others involves communication. In addition, play with language, although understudied (Crystal, 1996), seems to have a useful purpose. Children enjoy nursery rhymes and word games, which help them learn about the rhythm and patterns of spoken language. Young children have been observed engaged in playing with language through repetition of sounds, making up nonsense rhymes and generally practising manipulating language sounds and meaning (Garvey, 1990). More sophisticated language play, including puns and jokes, are seen as children grow older and start to understand the semantic and pragmatic aspects of language (Crystal, 1996). (Language development is dealt with in more detail in Chapter 5.)

- Conflicts in play and discussion and negotiation of rules when playing games have been suggested to influence the development of moral reasoning (Piaget, 1932). This topic is explored in Chapter 8.

Social and emotional development

- Play is often described as reflecting social competence, although there is also a suggestion that play in fact promotes social competence (Creasey, Jarvis, & Berk, 1998).

- Play increases affiliation with peers by raising the probability that children will interact and communicate, leading to the development of friendships. Peer relationships and group affiliation are also important for the development of self-identity. The development of peer relationships is also described in Chapter 4, Attachment and relationship formation.

- Play may also reinforce gender roles, another aspect of identity development. Martin and Fabes (2001) found that the more time boys spent playing with other boys, the more their activity level and rough and tumble play increased. In contrast, the more time girls spent with other girls, their aggression and activity levels decreased. For both sexes, increased contact with same-sex peers was linked to an increase in sex-typed, toy/game choice. Gender role is explored in more depth in Chapter 9.

- Play (particularly socio-dramatic play) has also been linked to the development of self-regulation, which is the ability to control your own thoughts, feelings and behaviours.

Key terms

Social competence: this term usually refers to an individual's ability to get on with others, read social situations and interact appropriately with peers. Lack of social competence is often seen as a marker of maladjustment or atypical development. Social competence is an umbrella term that covers a diverse set of behaviours and skills, meaning that definitions vary depending upon the focus of a particular study. Thus researchers interested in the child's behaviour tend to define social competence in terms of behavioural competence, while others interested in cognitive processes may define it in terms of a child's perception of others. Social competence should be thought of in terms of the effectiveness of a child's interaction with others, as assessed in relation to the child's age, culture setting and social situation.

KEY STUDY

Elias and Berk (2006). Self regulation in young children: Is there a role for sociodramatic play?

This study tested the idea that socio-dramatic play can contribute to the development of self-regulation. A longitudinal design was used in which 51 three- and four-year-olds were observed playing in their preschool classrooms. Children were observed at the start of the school year (Time 1) then again, four–five months later (Time 2). Standardised measures were used to record the children's involvement in socio-dramatic play and self-regulatory skills. Child temperament and verbal abilities were also assessed. Children who were involved in more episodes of socio-dramatic play at Time 1 showed better self-regulation by Time 2. In contrast, those engaged in more solitary pretend play were less likely to show self-regulation at Time 2. The longitudinal nature of this study strengthens its predictive validity and strongly suggests that socio-dramatic play influences the development of self-regulation. Furthermore, because the researchers also measured each child's verbal ability, they were able to show that more interaction with others and self-regulation were not simply a function of better communication skills. This is important because there is evidence that verbal ability can influence both socio-dramatic play and self-regulation. Finally, it was found that the benefits of socio-dramatic play for increasing self-regulation were greatest for children rated as having an impulsive temperament. This suggests a potential interventional role for socio-dramatic play as impulsive children have been demonstrated to have less well-developed self-regulatory skills when compared with their peer group. However, there are limitations to the generalisability of the study, which was based on a small sample of white American children, all from middle- to upper-income families.

Elias, C. & Berk, L. (2006). Self regulation in young children: Is there a role for sociodramatic play? *Early Childhood Research Quarterly, 17,* 216–238

Physical development

- Play also allows children to practise their developing motor skills. During the ages of two–four years, impressive gains in gross motor development and fine motor skills are seen (see Table 6.1 overleaf). More information on motor skill development can be found in Chapter 3.

- Better control of their bodies allows children to run, skip, ride a tricycle, enjoy the slides and swings in the park. Engaging in this type of play also has implications for physical growth in terms of strength, stamina and general health.
- Fine motor skills development allows children to draw, colour and construct and make things. Although this play can be a solitary activity, it can also be a social activity, especially in the preschool years.

Table 6.1 **Fine and gross motor development in the early years**

Age (years)	Gross motor skills	Fine motor skills
2	Walks well Runs Goes up and down stairs alone Kicks ball	Uses spoon and fork Turns pages of a book Imitates circular stroke Builds tower of 6 cubes
3	Runs well Marches Rides tricycle Stands on one foot briefly	Feeds self well Puts on shoes and socks Unbuttons and buttons Builds tower of 10 cubes
4	Skips Standing broad jump Throws ball overhand High motor drive	Draws a person Cuts with scissors (not well) Dresses self well Washes and dries face

Example of application of theory: play therapy

Play therapy is one of the most common applications of psychodynamic theory to child therapy in the UK and Europe. In the UK, play therapy follows the guidelines established by Axline (1971). These guidelines are based on the person-centred approach of Carl Rogers, which views the therapist as a facilitator who guides their client towards finding their own solution. In the same way, play therapists usually take a non-directive role during therapy, being guided by the child. The British Association of Play Therapists (BAPT, 2008) defines play therapy as:

> the dynamic process between child and Play Therapist in which the child explores at his or her own pace and with his or her own agenda those issues, past and current, conscious and unconscious, that are affecting the child's life in the present. The child's inner resources are enabled by the therapeutic alliance to bring about growth and change. Play Therapy is child-centred, in which play is the primary medium and speech is the secondary medium.

Although play therapy has been in use since the early 1900s, it was not until the late twentieth century that systematic attempts were made to collect robust evidence of the therapeutic effectiveness of play. Studies are often limited by sample size, leading to a reliance on meta-analysis, a technique in which the results of a number of studies are combined and re-analysed. Results from recent meta-analyses (for example, Bratton et al. 2005; Ray et al. 2001) have shown moderate to strong effects for play therapy in improving children's emotional and social well-being. Findings have also indicated that including parents in the therapeutic process by teaching them to facilitate play sessions (filial therapy) has the greatest benefits (Bratton et al., 2005).

More information about play therapy can be found at: **www.playtherapy.org.uk**

CRITICAL FOCUS

Learning through play: a view from the field

According to Hewes (2010), many play advocates believe that play is 'under siege'. Educators are striving to secure a greater focus on play in the development and implementation of early years curricula. A major concern for all is that the decline of opportunities for unstructured free play in the early years may be a contributing factor in rising childhood obesity levels, as well as increased levels of anxiety and stress in young children.

Hewes is writing from a Canadian perspective, yet much of what she says holds true for the UK as well.

Do a literature search, using an academic search engine such as Psycinfo to find further evidence about learning and play. To what extent does the evidence support the importance of play for learning? Can you find any evidence to support the idea that free play is declining in today's society and being replaced by more structured activities – or even by computer games as is sometimes suggested?

A useful review of UK research and policy: S. Lester and W. Russell (2008). *Play for a change: Play, policy and practice: A review of Contemporary Perspectives.* London: National Children's Bureau. Available online **www.education.gov.uk/research/data/uploadfiles/DCSF-RBX-09-06.pdf**

The original article: J. Hewes (2010). Voices from the field – learning through play: A view from the field. In R. E Tremblay, R. G Barr, R. De V. Peters, & M. Boivin, (Eds.), *Encyclopedia on early childhood development* [online]. Montreal, Quebec: Centre of Excellence for Early Childhood Development) Available online at: **www.enfant-encyclopedie.com/pages/PDF/HewesANGps.pdf**

 Sample question — Essay

Play has been defined as 'activity without a purpose'. To what extent is it accurate to say that play has no purpose or value to development?

Test your knowledge

6.1 How can we define play?

6.2 Describe the psychoanalytical, cognitive and learning theories of play.

6.3 What are the main cognitive, social and psychological advantages of play?

6.4 How do fine and gross motor developments allow children to try new play experiences?

6.5 How might motor skill development, play and cognitive development be linked?

Answers to these questions can be found on the companion website at: **www.pearsoned.co.uk/psychologyexpress**

> **Further reading The function of play**
>
> | Topic | Key reading |
> |---|---|
> | Physical play | Pellegrini, A. D. & Smith, P. K. (1998). Physical activity play: The nature and function of a neglected aspect of play. *Child Development*, 69(3), 577–598. |
> | Motor skills and self-esteem | Bunker, L. K. (1991). The role of play and motor skill development in building children's self-confidence and self-esteem. *Elementary School Journal*, 91, 467–471. |
> | Cognitive development | Vygotsky, L. (1933). Play and its role in the mental development of the child. *Psychology and Marxism Internet Archive*. Available online at: **www.mathcs.duq.edu/~packer/Courses/Psy225/ Classic%203%20Vygotsky.pdf** |
> | Cognitive development | Tamis-LeMonda, C. S., Shannon, J. D., Cabrera, N. J., & Lamb M. E. (2004). Fathers and mothers at play with their 2- and 3-year-olds: Contributions to language and cognitive development. *Child Development, 75*(6), 1806–1820. |
> | Functions of play | Smith, P. & Pellegrini, A. (2008). Learning through play. *Encyclopedia on Early Childhood Development*. Available online at: www.pre-kventura.org/Portals/48/Learning%20Through%20 Play.pdf |

Types of play

A number of theorists have advanced elaborate classifications of play. Perhaps the most well-known is that of Parten (1932).

Social classification of play

In this model, based on observations of play during the preschool years, Parten describes six different types of play (see Table 6.2).

It used to be thought that these categories were developmental – children progressed from solo to more social play. Recent research, however, suggests that this is far from the case. All these types of play are seen in the preschooler; five-year-olds spend more time in solitary or parallel play than in co-operative or associative play; parallel play is as common at five years as it is at three years of age (Rubin, Bukowski, & Parker, 2006). Furthermore, there is evidence that parallel play is not an immature form of play but a sophisticated strategy for easing your way into an ongoing game; successful integration into co-operative play involves observation of others at play, followed by playing alongside before interacting with other players (Rubin et al., 2006).

Table 6.2 Classification of play behaviours

Type of play	Description of play behaviour
Unoccupied play	Child is relatively stationary and appears to be performing random movements with no apparent purpose. A relatively infrequent style of play.
Solitary play	Child is completely engrossed in playing and does not seem to notice other children.
Onlooker play	Child takes an interest in other children's play, but does not join in. May ask questions or just talk to other children, but the main activity is simply watching.
Parallel play	Child mimics other children's play, but doesn't actively engage with them. For example, they may use the same toy.
Associative play	Child now more interested in other children than the toys they are using. This is the first category that involves strong social interaction between the children while they play.
Co-operative play	Some organisation enters children's play. For example, the playing has some goal and children often adopt roles and act as a group.

Source: adapted from Parten (1932)

Activity-based classification

It has also been argued that this model is limited by neglecting the cognitive aspects of play (Bergen, 1988). A more useful way of classifying play may be to focus on the type of activity rather than the social aspects. Rubin et al. (1998) describe three main activity types emerging from this way of thinking, as shown in Table 6.3. The different levels of social interaction described by Parten can be seen in each of these activity types – solitary play may be functional (for example, bouncing a ball) or constructive (for instance, building with Lego). All these activities are popular throughout early childhood, but the social play that is seen most often in the preschool years is socio-dramatic play. Indeed, many experts in play consider this period of development the peak time for make-believe or fantasy play (Fein, 1986).

Table 6.3 Types of play activity

Activity type	Description of play behaviour
Functional play	Physical activities such as bouncing a ball, rough and tumble
Constructive play	Building and making things, drawing, colouring
Socio-dramatic play	Role play or 'let's pretend'

Functional play

- Includes activities such as 'practice play', as it involves the repetition of behaviour when new skills are being learnt or mastered. Practice play can be engaged in at any age (practising a new sport in secondary school, for example), although it is most popular in preschool years, then declining in the primary school years.

- The sensorimotor play described by Piaget and which refers to play in infancy is functional. In this type of play, infants engage in exploration of objects from about three months of age. By nine months they will select novel objects for exploration and play, especially responsive toys that make a noise or move.

Constructive play

- This occurs when children engage in the self-regulated creation of a product or solution. It increases in the preschool years as sensorimotor play decreases and is also very common in the primary school years. It can include creative activities such as painting as well as jigsaw puzzles, building blocks, etc.

Socio-dramatic play

- Socio-dramatic is perhaps the most complex form of play as it involves sharing a fantasy world with others. Children need to negotiate roles ('I want to be the mummy' – 'No it's my turn'), agree on the development of the narrative ('my baby is poorly and needs to go to the doctor'), rules ('my Power Ranger can jump over houses, but yours can't') and symbolism ('the chair is my car').

- Socio-dramatic play is thought to reflect a high level of cognitive skill, including meta-cognition.

- It requires a sophisticated level of interaction and is thought to foster children's understanding of other minds (Dunn, 1988) because of the opportunities present for discussing thoughts, feelings and motivations. It also helps the child develop their sense of who they are as they practise different social roles and learn about how others see them.

Key terms

Socio-dramatic play: is probably the most studied type of play. It is sometimes also labelled as pretend play, because it involves an element of make-believe or pretence. However, strictly speaking, pretend or make-believe play does not have to involve other people and therefore it seems more appropriate to consider socio-dramatic play as a specific type of pretend play. You may also come across the term 'symbolic play' used to describe socio-dramatic play. This is because children may use one object to represent another during socio-dramatic play, thereby demonstrating symbolism. However, symbolic play can also take place without involving others. For example, Sammy sits alone in a cardboard box, pretending that the box is a

▶

car that he is driving to town. This play involves symbolism and pretence, but is not socio-dramatic play until Jessica comes along and joins in the game. The difference between socio-dramatic play and other forms of pretend play is that the child shares their intentions with another person.

Alternative classifications

Authors often define their own categories of play, although it is usually possible to see how they fit into Rubin's typology. Smith and Pellegrini (2008), for example, define the following types of play:

- locomotor play
- social play
- object play
- language play
- pretend play.

Test your knowledge

6.6 How did Parten classify play? What are the problems with this scheme?

6.7 What are the advantages of a classification based on activity?

Answers to these questions can be found on the companion website at: **www.pearsoned.co.uk/psychologyexpress**

Further reading Types of play

Topic	Key reading
Functional play	Bober, S. J., Humphry, R., Carswell, H. W., & Core, A. J. (2001). Toddlers' persistence in the emerging occupations of functional play and self-feeding. *American Journal of Occupational Therapy*, 55(4), 369–376. Available online at: http://ajot.aotapress.net/content/55/4/369.full.pdf+html
Socio-dramatic play	Bergen, D. (2002). The role of pretend play in children's cognitive development. *Early Childhood Research and Practice*, 4(1), 193–483. Available online at: http://teacher.edmonds.wednet.edu/aecc/arecato/documents/rolepretendplay.pdf

---

 Sample question   *Information provider*

You have been asked to develop a short marketing film for your local preschool nursery. They want to show the parents of current and prospective pupils the high-quality teaching and learning that takes place in the nursery. The headteacher's ethos is that young children learn best through play and she is very keen to promote the school's 'outdoor classroom' as well as the other work the school does. Write a short brief, explaining what type of activities you would expect to include in your video and why. Are there any ethical issues to deal with before making the film? If you would like more information about the outdoor classroom in the UK, Teacher's TV has some interesting resources (at: www.growingschools.org.uk).

Factors affecting play

Family influences

- A recent study found that children living in low socio-economic status (SES) neighbourhoods in the USA were significantly more likely to be video game users than those living in high SES neighbourhoods. They also found that girls living in low SES neighbourhoods watched more TV than girls living in high SES neighbourhoods. The same relationship was not observed for boys. (Carson et al., 2010).

- However, this may relate in part to access to appropriate facilities for other types of play. A positive association has been found between the proximity of parks and playgrounds to the home and children's engagement in physical activity (for example, Sallis et al., 2001).

- Ellaway et al. (2006) suggested that outdoor play is more limited in areas of deprivation in Glasgow, not because these areas lack facilities but because the quality of play areas is poor.

- Parental perception of danger (for example, the number of roads to cross, the volume of traffic) has also been found to influence children's use of outdoor play areas (Timperio et al., 2004).

- Securely attached children engage in more sophisticated socio-dramatic play, which also tends to have more positive themes (Roggman, Langlois, & Huhhs-Tait, 1987).

- Mothers play an important supportive role in the development of early pretend play interactions (Haight & Miller, 1993).

Gender

- Gender differences in toy play have been documented among preschool children with studies indicating that, by age three, children prefer to play with toys deemed appropriate for their own gender (for example, O'Brien & Huston, 1985; Smetana & Letourneau, 1984).

- It has been proposed that these early behaviours may affect later skills and abilities. For example, play with masculine toys has been suggested to affect the development of spatial skills and interests (Linn & Peterson, 1985; Signorella, Jamison, & Krupa, 1989).

- Parents (particularly fathers) have been noted to engage in more rough and tumble with their sons than with their daughters (MacDonald & Parke, 1986).

- As noted above, girls are often observed to engage in more sedentary activities than boys. In a school-based study it was found that primary school-aged girls engaged in 13.8 per cent more sedentary activity and 8.2 per cent less vigorous activity than their male peers during break time (Ridgers, Fairclough, & Stratton 2010).

- Socio-dramatic play is seen in both males and females, but is more frequently seen in females (Pellegrini & Smith, 1998).

- Girl's pretend play tends to revolve around domestic themes, while boys engage in more fantasy-type play involving superheroes (Pellegrini & Perlmutter, 1987).

- Boy's play with female-typed toys such as dolls is less sophisticated than it is with male-typed toys such as blocks (Pellegrini & Perlmutter, 1989).

Age

- As you learnt in the previous section, children engage in all types of play at different ages. However, there is some evidence that different types of play are more popular in different age groups:
  - Physically vigorous play such as rough and tumble play peaks in early childhood, both in the home (MacDonald & Parke, 1986) and in school contexts (Pellegrini, 1990).
  - Practice play is most often seen in preschool years.
  - Constructive play is popular in the primary school years.
  - Socio-dramatic play is usually first seen in the second year of life, peaking during the late preschool years and then declining (Pellegrini & Smith, 1998).
  - Computer/video game play increases during the early school years (Case-Smith, 2008).

Other factors

- Pretend play is more sustained and complex when playing with friends rather than acquaintances (Howe, Moller, & Chambers, 1994), suggesting that the emotional commitment of friends motivates sustained co-operation.

- Children with developmental delays show higher preference for rough and tumble play and object exploration (Case-Smith 2008).

- Children with developmental delays show lower preference for drawing and colouring, construction and doll and action figurine play than typically developing children. (Case-Smith 2008).

- 'Rejected' children are less likely to engage in play with same-age peers at school, tending to seek out younger play partners (Ladd & Price, 1993). These children also show less consistency in play partners and have play preferences that are less likely to be reciprocated (see Chapter 4, Attachment and relationship formation, for a definition of 'rejected children').

- 'Popular' children are often 'key players' who suggest, maintain and terminate playground games (Blatchford, 1998). Boys tend to be viewed as key players because of physical prowess, whereas girls dominate because of social skills and imagination. (See Chapter 4, Attachment and relationship formation, for a definition of 'popular children'.)

Test your knowledge

6.8 What are the main factors that influence the types of play behaviours children engage in?

6.9 Describe how age influences play.

6.10 What are the differences in play behaviours of boys and girls?

6.11 To what extent does family background affect play?

Answers to these questions can be found on the companion website at: **www.pearsoned.co.uk/psychologyexpress**

? Sample question   Essay

Is there a developmental sequence in play behaviours or do factors other than age influence children's play?

Further reading Factors affecting play

Topic	Key reading
Gender	Ridgers, N. D., Fairclough, S. J., & Stratton, G. (2010). Variables associated with children's physical activity levels during recess: The A-CLASS project. *International Journal of Behavioral Nutrition and Physical Activity, 7*:74. The electronic version of this article is the complete one and is available online at: www.ijbnpa.org/content/7/1/74
Family	Veitch, J., Bagley, S., Ball, K., & Salmon, J. (2006). Where do children usually play? A qualitative study of parents' perceptions of influences on children's active free-play. *Health & Place, 12*(4), 383–393.

Chapter summary – pulling it all together

→ Can you tick all the points from the revision checklist at the beginning of this chapter?

→ Attempt the sample question from the beginning of this chapter using the answer guidelines below.

→ Go to the companion website at www.pearsoned.co.uk/psychologyexpress to access more revision support online, including interactive quizzes, flashcards, You be the marker exercises as well as answer guidance for the Test your knowledge and Sample questions from this chapter.

Answer guidelines

 Sample question *Essay*

Play is essential to a child's development. Discuss.

Approaching the question

Your answer should aim to provide an analysis of the main functions of play that have been described in the literature. A discussion of the possible threats to play that have been suggested in recent times will help illustrate the importance often placed on play in contemporary Western society.

Important points to include

- Begin by defining play and discussing the difference between immediate and delayed purpose for activities such as play.
- Discuss the theoretical approaches to play, comparing classic views, which considered the origins of play, to more current approaches, looking at the benefits of play to development.
- Discuss the ways in which play behaviours might benefit later functioning such as:
  - cognition
  - peer relationships
  - gender identity
  - psychological well-being.
- For each you will need to:
  - highlight the different types of play
  - explain the possible consequences of play behaviours
  - include other factors that will influence children's engagement in play activities.

Make your answer stand out

It is important to remember to take a critical approach to this question. While there is a lot of theory surrounding the purpose of play for development, the empirical evidence is more limited. This does not, however, mean that the ideas cannot be critiqued and a good student will approach this question with an inquiring eye. Can we be sure, for example, that play enhances cognitive skills or does it simply reflect a child's current abilities? Does play help relationships flourish or do other factors (such as a child's motor skills or verbal abilities) mediate both play behaviours and acceptance by peers? The importance of linking your answer to other areas you have studied cannot be highlighted enough. Introducing some of the current debates happening across the Western world concerning the rights of children to play and the impact of government-imposed curricula will demonstrate your ability to apply your theoretical understanding of psychology and make your answer stand out.

Explore the accompanying website at www.pearsoned.co.uk/psychologyexpress
→ Prepare more effectively for exams and assignments using the answer guidelines for questions from this chapter.
→ Test your knowledge using multiple choice questions and flashcards.
→ Improve your essay skills by exploring the You be the marker exercises.

Notes

Cognitive development

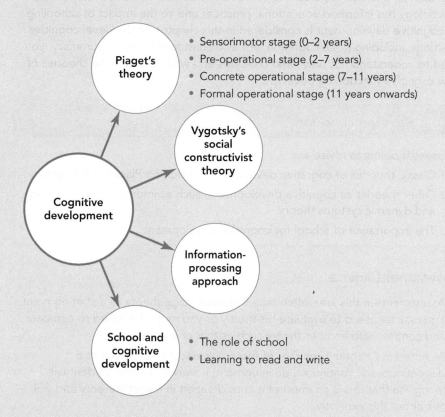

- Piaget's theory
  - Sensorimotor stage (0–2 years)
  - Pre-operational stage (2–7 years)
  - Concrete operational stage (7–11 years)
  - Formal operational stage (11 years onwards)

- Vygotsky's social constructivist theory

- Cognitive development

- Information-processing approach

- School and cognitive development
  - The role of school
  - Learning to read and write

A printable version of this topic map is available from
www.pearsoned.co.uk/psychologyexpress

Introduction

Cognition is an important area of developmental psychology. Much of the focus in this area concerns understanding how a child conceptualises the world. Piaget remains one of the key figures in this area, even though many of his claims have been criticised. However, his constructivist approach and his description of the way in which development moves from being dependent on actions and perception in infancy, through reasoning based on concrete examples in early childhood to the ability to use abstract rules and principles in adolescence, is still generally accepted. Moreover, research continues into many of the phenomena he described. You also need to be aware of alternative theories, including Vygotsky's social constructivist theory and information-processing approaches. It is also important to remember that this field of developmental psychology has informed educational practices and so the impact of schooling on cognitive development is considered in this chapter. Higher-level cognitive functions, including meta-cognition, are also considered here. In summary, you need to understand not only what develops and when but also the theories of how cognitive functioning develops.

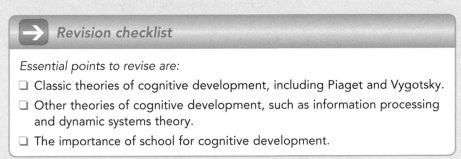

Revision checklist

Essential points to revise are:

❏ Classic theories of cognitive development, including Piaget and Vygotsky.

❏ Other theories of cognitive development, such as information processing and dynamic systems theory.

❏ The importance of school for cognitive development.

Assessment advice

● Assessments in this area often take Piagetian stage theory as a starting point. You may be asked to evaluate his theory or you might be asked to compare and contrast with another theory such as that of Vygotsky.

● As noted in Chapter 1, neither of these approaches has mentioned discontinuous v. continuous development; however, a good student will recognise that this is an important consideration in Piaget's theory and will talk about this explicitly.

● The nature–nurture issue is also relevant and consideration of the importance of environmental factors for development is often essential when considering cognitive development.

● A lot of cognitive development in childhood takes place at school and so some understanding of the relationship between these two things will demonstrate the ability to make links between theoretical and applied psychology.

- This chapter outlines the main issues regarding the theories of cognitive development, but you should also refer to Chapter 1 to remind yourself of the relevance of major themes to this topic.

Sample question

Could you answer this question? Below is a typical essay question that could arise on this topic.

 Sample question   **Essay**

Critically evaluate the importance of the social context to the development of cognitive functioning in childhood.

Guidelines on answering this question are included at the end of this chapter, whilst further guidance on tackling other exam questions can be found on the companion website at: **www.pearsoned.co.uk/psychologyexpress**

Piaget's theory

As you saw in Chapter 1, Piaget believed that children gradually develop an understanding of the world through active and motivated exploration, which leads to the development of mental structures called *schemas*. Thinking is qualitatively different at each stage as follows.

Sensorimotor stage (0–2 years)

- Development depends upon the infant using senses and motor skills to explore and learn about the world. This stage is further subdivided into six substages (see Table 7.1).
- According to Piaget, the most important achievement of this stage of development is *object permanence*.
- According to Piaget, in the early months of life infants behave as if an object that they can no longer see has ceased to exist. He tested this in the hidden toy experiment as follows:
  - the infant is shown an attractive toy
  - the toy is left within reach and covered with a soft cloth
  - despite having the abilities needed to retrieve the toy, infants do not search for a toy that is completely hidden until around eight or nine months of age.

Table 7.1 Substages of the sensorimotor stage of development

Substage (age)	Exploratory actions	Understanding of objects
Reflex schemas (0–1½ months)	Involuntary responses to stimuli, e.g. sucking	Makes no attempt to locate objects that have disappeared
Primary circular reactions (1½–4 months)	Attempts to repeat chance pleasurable actions, on or near the body, e.g. bringing thumb to mouth	Makes no attempt to locate objects that have disappeared
Secondary circular reactions (4–8 months)	Attempts to repeat chance pleasurable actions in the environment, e.g. hitting a mobile, picking up a cup	Begins to search for objects that are partially hidden
Co-ordinated secondary circular reactions (8–12 months)	Can put 'secondary circular reactions' together to solve new problems, e.g. uncover, then grasp	Searches for completely hidden objects, but makes the A-not-B error
Tertiary circular reactions (12–18 months)	Will deliberately vary an action pattern to discover the consequences, e.g. dropping ball from different heights	Can follow visible displacements of an object
Beginnings of symbolic representation (18–24 months)	Can solve problems using representation, e.g. opening and closing mouth	Can follow invisible displacements of an object

- However, it is possible that even though infants under nine months of age can both reach and grasp, it may be difficult for them to retrieve the toy because they cannot co-ordinate the actions necessary to remove the cloth.

- Experiments using visual gaze and habituation techniques (see Chapter 3) to overcome the motor co-ordination problem confirm this idea, demonstrating that infants two-and-a-half months old understand object permanence (Aguiar & Baillargeon, 2002; Baillargeon et al., 1985).

- However, a lack of motor co-ordination cannot explain another phenomenon noted by Piaget, known as the A-not-B error.
  - Two cloths are placed side by side in front of infants aged 9–12 months and they are shown an attractive toy.
  - The toy is hidden under one of the cloths (location A).
  - Infants older than nine months typically find the toy.
  - After a number of trials, the toy is hidden under the other cloth (location B).
  - Despite watching the toy being hidden in the new location (B), infants under the age of 12 months continue to look for the toy under the first cloth (location A).

- According to Piaget, this suggests infants do not understand that objects can exist independently of their own actions. The infant connects the rediscovery of the object in location A with his or her own actions in lifting the cloth and reasons that, 'If I wish to find the toy again I must do what I did before'.

- This is clearly incompatible with the idea that the understanding of object permanence develops in the first few months of life. However, other explanations include:

  - the fragility of infant memory (Harris, 1989)

  - habit perseveration (Diamond, 1985)

  - changes in neurological functioning (Munakata, 1998)

  - no single cause adequately explains this behaviour and multi-causal theory has been proposed (Smith et al., 1999); the ability to search for the toy under the correct cloth is the result of a combination of cognitive, perceptual and motor skills, which unfold over time at different rates – only once all have developed fully can the correct search behaviour occur.

Key terms

Schemas: a schema is a basic cognitive structure that individuals use to make sense of the world. According to Piaget, a schema includes both a category of knowledge and the process of obtaining that knowledge. New information gathered through experience is used to modify previously existing schemas. This takes place through two processes described in Chapter 1, **assimilation** and **accommodation**. For example, a child may have a schema about animals. If the child's sole experience has been with small domestic animals such as dogs and cats, a child might believe that all animals are small, furry and walk on four legs. On a trip to the zoo the child then encounters an animal that does not fit this schema, such as a kangaroo. The child will need to take in this new information – that not all animals are small and walk on four legs – and modify their animal schema accordingly. Piaget believed that we try to strike a balance between assimilation and accommodation. This is achieved through a mechanism called **equilibration**. According to Piaget, when we first encounter new information that does not fit into our existing schemas, this creates a state of disequilibrium as we realise our current level of knowledge is deficient. This is unpleasant and produces tension or cognitive conflict that motivates us to change our schemas and so progress to a new, more advanced level of understanding. We therefore adapt our existing schemas to include the new information encountered so as to once again achieve equilibrium. Equilibration is therefore one of the most important mechanisms in cognitive development according to Piaget, as it is the means by which children progress through the four stages of development.

Object permanence: the understanding of objects and the realisation that objects continue to exist even when we cannot see them. According to Piaget, object permanence is one of an infant's most important accomplishments as it demonstrates that the child has developed a mental representation of an object. Without mental representations, cognitive functions such as memory, symbolic thinking and later abstract reasoning would not be possible.

Multi-causal explanations of the A-not-B error

In revisiting the A-not-B error, Smith et al. (1999) take a new approach, attempting to explain what infants do in the A-not-B task rather than what they cannot do. Their explanation focuses on performance and ultimately raises profound questions about what it means to know. The idea of knowledge as an enduring mental structure that exists independently of behaviour dominates in the study of cognitive development. Indeed, this idea of mental structures that gradually develop over time underlies Piaget's seminal theory of cognitive development. Thus achieving the AB task has always been taken to represent a qualitative change in infant thinking; the task can only be successfully completed once the infant has developed a new schema: the object concept. Smith et al. challenge this idea. They argue that although successful completion of the A-not-B task suggests a *qualitative* change in infant behaviour, this change in behaviour in fact represents a number of *quantitative* changes in a complex dynamic system. The A-not-B error is explained in terms of general processes of goal-directed reaching; the erroneous reach back to A is seen as the *behavioural* product of a number of graded processes, including those involved in looking, in discriminating locations, in posture control and in motor planning. All these processes are brought together and self-organised by the task of reaching for a particular object in a particular context. In this perspective, behaviour and cognition are not separate and there are no causal mechanisms such as an object concept that generates a thought or a behaviour. Thus what we commonly and casually call knowledge and concepts are distributed across and embedded in behavioural processes.

This model represents a major shift in thinking and is known as dynamic systems theory. How easy do you think it is to explain human cognition and behaviour with reference to function only? Should we no longer aim to explain psychological functioning by the study of mental structures? Might it be useful to retain these ideas as a shorthand, a convenient way to describe common human thought and behaviour?

Pre-operational stage (2–7 years)

- So called because children cannot yet perform mental operations (logical thinking tasks), although the beginnings of logical reasoning and symbolic thinking can be seen, especially towards the end of this stage.
- This period is subdivided into two substages:
  - symbolic functioning (two–four years)
  - intuitive thinking (four–seven years).
- A key feature of the symbolic functioning substage is the ability to represent mentally an object that is not present (symbolic thinking). This is necessary for language development.
- This is demonstrated by children's pretend play.
  - Two- and three-year-old children engage in 'symbolic play', using one object to represent another that they do not have access to at the time – for example, a Lego block used as a hairbrush, a finger as a toothbrush (Boyatzis & Watson, 1993).

- The ability to pretend that a particular object can be something else not present shows the child has a mental representation of the object not present.
- By the age of four years children no longer need to use an object to symbolise another object that is not present – they can use an imaginary representation – for example, pretend to be holding a toothbrush.

- Children's mental reasoning is limited by *magical thinking and animism*, which limits understanding of how the world works and so reduces the ability to think logically.

- However, some theorists disagree with the idea that children's thinking is more magical than adults, arguing it is social context which determines magical thinking, not age (for example, Woolley, 1997).
  - Adults have been found to be just as likely as children to engage in magical thinking, especially when they do not have the knowledge to explain phenomena.
  - Many of the fantastical ideas children believe in – Father Christmas, the tooth fairy and the Easter bunny – are all actively encouraged by the adults around them.

- Another limitation to logical thinking at this age is *egocentrism*, the inability to distinguish between your own perspective and someone else's, as demonstrated by the three mountains task (Piaget & Inhelder, 1969).
  - The child walks around a model of mountains (see Figure 7.1) to see what the mountains look like from different perspectives.
  - The child is seated at the table and a doll is placed in different locations around the table.
  - At each location the child is asked to select the doll's view from a number of photos.
  - Piaget found that preschool children were unable to choose the correct photo and cited this as evidence of egocentrism.

- A key feature of the 'intuitive thinking' substage is the start of primitive reasoning. However, thinking is still limited by:
  - *centration*
  - lack of understanding of reversibility.

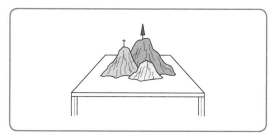

Figure 7.1 **Piaget's three mountains task**
Source: after Piaget & Inhelder (1969)

- Piaget demonstrated this through *conservation* and *class inclusion* tasks.
- Conservation measures awareness that altering an object's appearance does not change its quantitative properties.
    - In conservation of liquid (see Figure 7.2) the child is shown two identical beakers, each filled to the same level with liquid (a) and asked if these beakers contain the same amount of liquid (most children say yes).
    - The liquid from one beaker is then poured into a third beaker that is taller and thinner than the first two (b) and the child is asked if the amount of liquid in the new beaker is the same as in the original beaker, which has not been altered (c).
    - Children do not answer correctly until the concrete operational stage; in the pre-operational stage most say no, justifying their answers in terms of the differing height of the liquid.
- According to Piaget, children under the age of seven fail on conservation tasks because they:
    - attend to one characteristic of the task (the height of the liquid), to the exclusion of other features, such as the beaker's shape
    - do not engage in the logical reasoning that the liquid must still be the same because it has only been poured from one beaker to another and could easily be poured back.
- Class inclusion demonstrates the understanding of hierarchical classification.
    - Children are shown a picture of a set of objects such as horses and cows and asked 'Are there more cows or more animals?'
    - Despite knowing that cows are a type of animal and being able to count the number of cows and animals correctly, pre-operational children will say that there are more cows.
    - According to Piaget this is because they can only make one grouping at a time. Once they have assigned the cows to the class 'cows' they cannot mentally undo that to include the cows in the larger 'animal' class and

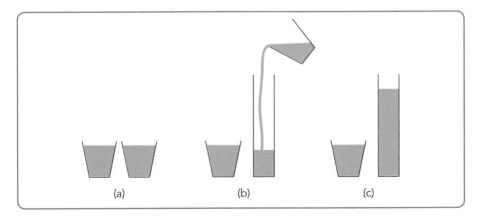

(a)   (b)   (c)

Figure 7.2 The beaker test (conservation of liquid)

so are unable to understand the relationship between cows and animals. Without reversible mental operations, the classes 'cow' and 'animal' cannot exist simultaneously in the child's mind.

- Piaget's experiments are reliable – if you replicated them exactly you would get the same results as Piaget – but is his interpretation of the findings valid?
- Piaget's tasks have been criticised for not allowing younger children to demonstrate their logical reasoning. One criticism is that the tasks do not make human sense.
  - Children fail the three mountains task because they do not understand the social context, not because they are egocentric. Given a more familiar task that is socially relevant, young children show they are able to take another's perspective. For example, Hughes (1975) showed children a board with two barriers and asked them to hide a model of a boy where he could not be seen by the toy policemen placed at the end of each barrier (see Figure 7.3). He found that 90 per cent of three- to five-year-olds could do this task.
  - Changing the tasks so that they make sense to the child – giving a reason for transferring liquid to a new beaker, for example – means that even four-year-olds are able to succeed in conservation and class inclusion tasks.

Figure 7.3 Hughes' test of egocentrism
Source: after Hughes (1975)

- Donaldson (1978) also criticised the procedural aspect of these tasks, arguing that the child has to work out the implicit social rules of the situation as well as the explicit problem that is being posed.
  - In the classic conservation tasks, the same question is asked before any changes are made and again after the transformation.
  - Children have learnt that adults usually only ask a question twice if a wrong answer has been given, so assume the adult wants a different response.
  - Since the only thing that has changed since the question was first asked is something to do with the materials, a plausible guess is that the tester wants the child to say the amounts are different.
  - If the children are only asked the question once (after the transformation) the social rules do not present the same problem and younger children are more likely to get the answer right.

Key terms

Animism: the attribution of consciousness to inanimate objects; this is often demonstrated by describing them as having human qualities and feelings. One example might be a child describing rain as 'the clouds crying'.

Egocentrism: According to Piaget, young children tend to perceive the world exclusively from their own point of view. They show no awareness that others have different perspectives. It must be remembered that this represents a cognitive rather than a moral limitation; the egocentric child is not deliberately ignoring everyone else's perspective – they simply do not realise others may not have access to the same information as themselves. Egocentric behaviour in Piagetian terms does not indicate selfishness, but, rather, limited cognitive functioning.

Centration: the tendency to focus on one feature of an object or situation at a time. In conservation of liquid tasks, for example, young children focus on the most salient aspect of the transformation – the height of the liquid in the beaker – to the exclusion of all other features of the task, such as the altered shape of the beaker. Conservation is only possible once children are able to decentre – that is, switch attention from one element of a task to another and take both into account at the same time. According to Piaget, egocentrism also demonstrates this inability to decentre – the egocentric child is unable to consider the perspectives of others as well as their own.

Concrete operational stage (7–11 years)

- Children understand reversible mental operations and can decentre, as demonstrated by their ability to conserve and answer class inclusion questions correctly. More importantly they can give a logical reason for their answers.
- Reasoning is still limited because, although the child can reason logically and understand causal relationships, they can only do so if that reasoning is tied to specific concrete examples; they cannot yet engage in hypothetical or abstract reasoning.

Formal operational stage (11 years onwards)

- Thinking is more logical at this stage: adolescents develop plans to solve problems and test possible solutions in a systematic and organised way as opposed to the trial and error fashion that typifies the approach of younger children.

- The ability to engage in abstract reasoning also increases; adolescent thinking is no longer tied to specific concrete examples as it was during late childhood, meaning that they can engage in *hypothetico-deductive reasoning*. This change in cognitive skills is reflected in the growing ability of adolescents to handle increasingly complex scientific and mathematical concepts.

- Evidence suggests that changing cognitive skills reflect underlying structural and functional neurological development during adolescence.

  - MRI studies demonstrate considerable structural changes in the prefrontal cortex, believed to represent the fine-tuning of neural circuitry, which in turn increases the efficiency of the cognitive systems they specifically serve.

  - There is also some suggestion that functioning in the frontal cortex increases with age (for example, Rubia et al., 2000).

Key term

Hypothetico-deductive reasoning: this typifies reasoning in the formal operational period and can be defined as using hypothesis and deduction to solve a problem. Hypothetical reasoning goes beyond the confines of everyday experience to include things about which we have no experience or direct knowledge. This represents a vast leap in thinking from the concrete operational stage, where reasoning is based in the physical (concrete) world of experiences. Children and adolescents with formal operations can reason about abstract (hypothetical) problems in their minds (symbolically) and reach logical conclusions without any physical experience.

Further reading Theories of cognitive development

Topic	Key reading
Object permanence	Smith, L. B., Thelen, E., Titzer, R., & McLin, D. (1999). Knowing in the context of acting: The task dynamics of the A-not-B error. *Psychological Review, 106*(2), 235–260. Available online at: www.indiana.edu/~cogdev/labwork/SmithThelen1999.pdf
Structure and function	Casey, B. J., Giedd, J. N., & Thomas, K. M. (2000). Structural and functional brain development and its relation to cognitive development. *Biological Psychology, 54*, 241–257. Available online at: www.medinfo.hacettepe.edu.tr/tebad/umut_docs/interests/fmr/aging/MAIN_structural_fonctional.pdf

Vygotsky's social constructivist theory

- Vygotsky also believed that children develop qualitatively different ways of thinking about the world based on active, motivated interaction with the environment.
- However, he believed that cognitive development was based in social interactions, not in individual exploration of the environment.
- As described in Chapter 1, cultural tools such as language are essential to this development.
- This belief is reflected in the zone of proximal development (ZPD), which refers to a child's developmental potential. For learning to take place, a teacher must work within this zone.
- Progression through the ZPD is described in terms of four stages.
  - *Stage 1:* performance is directly assisted by more capable others through scaffolding.
  - *Stage 2:* involves self-guidance as the learner takes over the role of the teacher in relation to their own learning. This may mean talking themselves through the task, remembering instructions previously given, etc.
  - *Stage 3:* performance becomes automatic.
  - *Stage 4:* stressors (for example, fatigue) or changes in the exact conditions of the task may unsettle us, setting us back to an early stage of the process. For example, when we are tired we may find a task much harder and have to rely on self-guidance to complete a task satisfactorily.
- During a learning interaction, the teacher uses techniques such as *scaffolding* (Wood, Wood, & Middleton, 1978):
  - the child is taken step by step through the task
  - the level of help is varied so that it is contingent on the child's needs
  - in the early stages of mastering a task, a child may need direct instruction and modelling
  - as they become more proficient at a task, guidance will become less direct as the child takes control.
- This model presents development as an apprenticeship in which the expert (adult or other more skilled individual) teaches the novice (the child) how to succeed.
- As children develop mastery of tasks, they move from being regulated by teachers and others to self-regulation.

Fawcett and Garton (2005). The effect of peer collaboration on children's problem-solving ability

This study investigated the impact of collaborative social interactions on children's problem-solving abilities. A total of 100 children aged between 6 and 7 years of age took part in the study. All the children completed a pre-test, comprising a block-sorting task, which identified them as either high or low on sorting ability. Children were then matched to a partner (or allocated to a control group) on the basis of their sorting ability, resulting in 10 pairs of high/high scorers, 10 pairs of low/low scorers and 20 pairs of high/low scorers. The remaining 20 children (10 high scorers and 10 low scorers) were allocated to the control group and so did not engage in the collaborative activity. Children in the intervention group completed a card-sorting activity, either individually or in same-gender pairs. The pairs consisted of same- or different-ability children who operated under either a 'talk' (encouraged to explain the sorting task) or 'no talk' (talking discouraged) condition. All children were then retested on the block-sorting task. It was found that children who collaborated improved their scores on the sorting task significantly more than children who worked individually. However, the greatest gains were for those children of lower sorting ability who had to talk to each other about the task during the collaboration. This highlights the importance of language as a cognitive tool for learning and development and the value of peer interactions for cognitive growth.

Fawcett, L. M., & Garton, A. F. (2005). The effect of peer collection on children's problem-solving ability. *British Journal of Educational Psychology* 75(2), 157–169

Zone of proximal development (ZPD): a central concept to social constructivism, the ZPD is a child's learning potential. It represents the distance between a child's actual and potential developmental levels. A child's actual developmental level is determined by their independent problem solving, while their potential developmental level is determined by the problem solving they can achieve with instruction from an adult or more knowledgeable peer. Children develop new ways of thinking and problem solving through working with more knowledgeable others on tasks that are within this zone – that is, tasks which are neither so easy they can be completed without help, nor so difficult success is beyond the child even with assistance.

Scaffolding: the process through which a teacher or more competent peer assists the learner on a task within the ZPD as necessary. The aim is to simplify a task to make it achievable and to encourage and motivate the learner to engage in and complete the task. To be effective, the assistance given must be contingent upon the needs of the learner and support should be removed as it becomes unnecessary – just as scaffolding is removed from a building during construction. During early stages of engagement with a new task the learner may benefit from being shown what to do (modelling or demonstration) or direct instruction. As they move through the zone, help may become more indirect and include features such as asking questions to help the learner to reach their own solutions.

> **?** *Sample question* **Essay**

Compare and contrast the theories of Piaget and Vygotsky.

Test your knowledge

7.1 What are the four stages of Piaget's theory?

7.2 What is the main achievement of the sensorimotor stage?

7.3 What are the characteristics of the concrete operational stage?

7.4 What is the ZPD?

Answers to these questions can be found on the companion website at:
www.pearsoned.co.uk/psychologyexpress

Further reading Theories of cognitive development

Topic   *Key reading*

Vygotsky   Wertsch, J. V., & Sohmer, R. (1995). Vygotsky on learning and development. *Human Development, 38*, 332–337.

Information-processing approach

This approach analyses how we manipulate information, monitor it and create strategies for handling it (Munakata, 1998), using a computer metaphor to explain development.

- Computer hardware determines the amount of data it can process (capacity) and speed of processing; human capacity and speed of information processing is limited by neurological development.

- Computer software limits the kind of data that can be input and how it can be manipulated (for example, word processing software cannot process statistics); the problem-solving strategies acquired limit human information processing.

- Biological changes in the brain (for example, in the frontal lobes), and the blooming and pruning of synaptic connections, affect functioning at a structural level.

- Myelination (see Chapter 3 for a definition of this process) increases the speed of processing by increasing the speed of electrical impulses in the brain.

- Practice leads to the ability to process information with little or no effort (*automaticity*), thereby reducing processing speed as once a task has become automatic there is no need to engage in conscious thought, so reducing the burden on working memory.

- An increase in capacity improves information processing (Mayer, 2008) – for example, the ability to hold several facts in mind at one time increases with age.

- Processing speed can affect competence in thinking (Bjorklund, 2005) and increases dramatically across the childhood years and into adolescence: 10-year-olds are almost twice as slow at information-processing tasks than young adults, 12-year-olds are 1½ times slower, but children aged 15 years perform as well as young adults (Hale, 1990).

- Encoding speed and the ability to ignore irrelevant information increases with age (Siegler, 1998).

- Information processing is also affected by *attention*: the focusing of mental resources. Attention improves processing. However, children, like adults, can only focus on a limited amount of information at one time.

- Memory is important for cognitive processing. In particular, working memory is a mental workbench where we manipulate and assemble information when making decisions, solving problems or understand written or spoken language.

- Most criticisms of Piaget's theory assume that Piaget is right when he states that human reasoning depends upon mental structures, but maintain that Piaget overestimates the age at which these structures develop. Information-processing models provide a different challenge, proposing that children cannot do these tasks because the demands are too much for developing processes such as memory and attention.

- In response, *neo-Piagetians* have taken some of these ideas and integrated them with Piaget's theory, arguing that development through the stages and changes in logical structures is enabled by increasing working memory capacity and processing efficiency (Demetriou et al., 2002).

Key term

Working memory: refers to the cognitive system that provides temporary storage and manipulation of the information necessary for complex tasks as language comprehension, learning, problem solving and decision making. It is like a mental 'workbench' where we assemble and manipulate information during such tasks. Working memory has been found to require the simultaneous storage and processing of information. It consists of the central executive and two slave systems. The central executive controls the cognitive processes such as attention and the manipulation of information within the slave systems. The slave systems are the visuospatial sketch pad, which manipulates visual images, and the phonological loop, which stores and rehearses speech-based information.

Further reading Theories of cognitive development

Topic	Key reading
Information processing	Kail, R., & Bisanz, V. (1982). Information processing and cognitive development. In W. H. Reese (Ed.), *Advances in child development* (p. 17). London: Academic Press.

School and cognitive development

The role of school

In Western societies school provides an important context for children's cognitive development. There is, however, a lot of debate about the best way for schools to help this development and the theories of Piaget and Vygotsky have influenced *progressive* teaching methods including:

- a child-centred approach
- active learning (for example, *discovery learning*)
- *readiness to learn*
- *co-operative* and *collaborative* learning.

One important distinction between Piagetian and Vygotskian approaches concerns what can be taught. Piaget believed children had to have the right mental structures in place for learning to occur (for example, reversibility is needed to learn about conservation). Vygotsky, however, believed that anything could be taught as long as it was within the child's ZPD. If Vygotsky is right, then would it be possible to teach a skill such as conservation to children who are not yet at the operational stage of development?

- Field (1981) found that three- and four-year-old preschoolers who are not yet able to conserve can be taught this skill.
- However, four-year-olds were better conservers than the three-year-olds and were more likely to retain this skill over time.
- The short-term nature of the conservation shown by the younger children suggests that they had not actually learnt a new thinking skill, but had simply rote learnt the 'correct' answers.

- This suggests that new ways of thinking can be taught, but a child has to be ready to learn those skills.
- But is school essential to the development of advanced cognitive skills such as hypothetical thinking? Cross-cultural studies of children who do not experience formal schooling suggest that cognitive skills develop at different rates and manifest themselves in different ways, depending on the context in which a child lives (Cole, 1990).
  - Nunes, Schliemann and Carraher (1993) showed that Brazilian child street traders who had not been exposed to formal schooling had difficulty finding the correct solution to maths problems presented in written form, but were successful when the same problem was presented in oral form. This demonstrates that children possess the ability to solve hypothetical problems, but, because of a lack of experience and training in written mathematical problems, they fail when these problems are presented as they would be in a formal school setting.
  - This suggests that development of logical thought is not influenced by schooling – it will develop anyway, but school influences *how* those skills develop and are manifest, by teaching the language and expectations of a specific cultural setting in relation to cognitive tasks (Cole, 1990).

Key terms

Discovery learning: this approach to teaching is based on the Piagetian principle that children learn about the world around them through active exploration of the environment. For younger children, discovery learning includes hands-on exploration and manipulation of objects and carrying out experiments. As cognitive skills become more sophisticated, it may also include finding out about topics and problem-based learning where learners address real-life and abstract questions and controversies.

Collaborative learning: in this approach, children work together to explore a problem, answer a question or create a project. Simply defined, it is a group of learners working on a shared assignment.

Co-operative learning: this is a specific kind of collaborative learning. In co-operative learning, students work together in small groups on a structured activity. They are individually accountable for their work and the work of the group as a whole is also assessed.

CRITICAL FOCUS

Atypical development and school experiences

As well as looking at the evidence from cross-cultural research, we can look at research that considers the school experiences of children who are developing atypically. In their paper 'School experiences after treatment for a brain tumour', Upton and Eiser (2006) describe how lengthy school absences can impact upon cognitive performance for school-age brain tumour survivors. They discuss how school absence interacts with a range of other factors, including the social context and the child's neurological functioning to influence the special educational needs of these children.

Upton and Eiser also note that long absences from school mean children fall behind their classmates and performance is most affected in subjects such as literacy and numeracy where prior knowledge and skills are vital. This is also true for children with chronic health problems that do not involve neurological difficulties.

What does this tell us about performance, ability and school? Does performance on a task necessarily demonstrate ability? Performance on tests is frequently used as a measure of cognitive ability, but what does this really tell us? You know from reading about cross-cultural studies that children may be able to think logically but cannot demonstrate that skill if the tasks do not make social sense. Is this the same for children who have long school absence due to illness or is a different mechanism at work? Is their cognitive development delayed, disrupted or is it simply that their knowledge of the language of performance testing is lacking? How might such studies help provide a critique of stage theories of cognitive development?

Learning to read and write

Reading and writing are perhaps two of the most significant skills that children learn at school. Vygotsky saw language as an essential cultural tool for learning and he included written language as a part of this. While humans have shared knowledge across generations for centuries through the spoken word, written language expands our ability to transmit information to others in different geographical and temporal locations. Modern technology – for example, the Internet and the World Wide Web – have created even more opportunities to share knowledge and information in this way.

Another advantage of writing is the way it enhances our cognitive functioning (Menary, 2007). For example, writing things down can be a great memory aid and working things out on paper expands our thinking power, allowing us to deal with a larger quantity and complexity of material.

Reading

Learning to read involves mastering and integrating a number of separate skills.

- English and other European languages use an alphabetic script where each symbol (letter) represents a phoneme. The child has to develop a conscious awareness of the sound/symbol association.
- Word recognition may mean segmenting a word into its underlying phonological elements before identifying it. For example, the word 'cat' can be decoded into its phonological form ('kuh, ah, tuh'). Alternatively, we may recognise a whole word by its overall visual appearance.
- Once the word is identified, higher-level cognitive functions, such as intelligence and vocabulary, are applied to understand the word's meaning

Factors affecting reading progression include:

- early exposure to books: understanding that books tell stories, they have a right and a wrong way up, the writing goes from left to right
- knowing the letters of the alphabet when they start school

- children with greater knowledge of nursery rhymes show better phonemic awareness (Maclean, Bryant, & Bradley, 1987)
- programmes encouraging parents and carers to enjoy books with their children from an early age have been found to improve children's scores in maths and English (Hines & Brooks, 2005; Wade & Moore, 1998), suggesting a general impact on symbolic functioning.

Writing

The cognitive and linguistic strategies children use to read are the same ones that they use to write. However, they also need fine motor skills, which can be developed by play activities involving the manipulation of objects, such as:

- art and crafts
- play dough
- jigsaw puzzles
- building blocks.

There is evidence that motor development has a much wider role to play in the development of cognitive skills. Studies of children with *specific learning difficulties* have highlighted the co-occurrence of motor and language difficulties (Viholainen et al., 2002), suggesting that motor and language problems share a common underlying neuro-cognitive mechanism. There is increasing evidence that structurally the interface for the integration of cognitive and motor functioning is the cerebellum (see Figure 7.4).

The cerebellum is responsible for:

- co-ordinating movement
- planning
- motor activities
- learning and remembering physical skills.

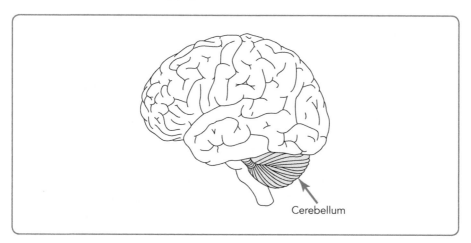

Cerebellum

Figure 7.4 A cross-section of the brain, demonstrating the position of the cerebellum

143

Evidence from neuroimaging studies suggests that the cerebellum also plays an important role in a range of high-level cognitive functions such as language, previously believed to be under the sole control of the cortex (Booth et al., 2007). For example, there is some evidence that dyslexia is associated with cerebellar impairment in about 80 per cent of cases (Nicolson, Fawcett & Dean, 2001). This suggests that cognitive functioning may rely on shared motor and cognitive neural systems (Diamond, 2000; Ojeman, 1984).

Key terms

Specific learning difficulties (SpLD): this is an umbrella term that covers a wide range of difficulties, including dyslexia (reading and writing difficulty), dysgraphia (writing difficulty), dyspraxia (motor difficulties), dyscalculia (difficulty with numbers and mathematical calculations), attention deficit hyperactivity disorder (ADHD, concentration difficulties and heightened impulsiveness) and autistic spectrum disorder (ASD, emotional, behavioural and social difficulties). All SpLDs typically affect a student's motor skills, information processing and memory.

Dyslexia: the most common form of SpLD, dyslexia, causes reading, writing and spelling problems. Difficulties persist despite appropriate learning opportunities. Dyslexia is due in part to processing difficulties, including visual and auditory perceptual skills. People with dyslexia may also show difficulties with short-term memory, concentration and organisation. Dyslexia varies between individuals and can occur in people of all abilities.

Test your knowledge

7.6 How have theories of cognitive development influenced teaching methods?

7.7 What is the relationship between school and cognitive development?

7.8 In what way is context important for cognitive functioining?

Answers to these questions can be found on the companion website at: **www.pearsoned.co.uk/psychologyexpress**

 ## Sample question   *Problem-based learning*

The couple who live next door had their first child, a girl called Alice, six months ago. The health visitor has told the parents about Bookstart and has suggested they start reading to baby Alice. Alice's dad thinks this is nonsense – how can a baby understand stories? Books, he insists, are for three- and four-year-olds. Alice's mum asks you what you think she should do. She doesn't want Alice to miss out on any learning opportunities, but also doesn't want to argue with her husband. What would you advise? Is there any evidence you could give to your neighbour to try and convince her mum that reading to Alice is time well spent?

? *Sample question*   *Essay*

Critically evaluate the importance of formal schooling for children's cognitive development.

Further reading **School and cognitive development**

Topic	Key reading
Culture and learning	National Research Council (1996). *Mathematics and science education around the world: What can we learn from the survey of mathematics and science opportunities (SMSO) and the third international mathematics and science study (TIMSS)?* Washington, D.C.: National Academy Press.
Social context and cognitive development	Nunes, T., Schliemann, A. D., & Carraher, D. W. (1993). *Street mathematics and school mathematics.* New York: Cambridge University Press.
Reading programmes	A number of studies assessing the effectiveness of Bookstart are available from the following website, including the study carried out in Sheffield by Hines, M., & Brooks, G. (2005). *Sheffield babies live books: An evaluation of the Sheffield Bookstart project.* Sheffield: University of Sheffield. Visit: www.booktrust. org.uk/show/feature/search/Bookstart-studies.
Dyslexia	Nicolson, R. I., Fawcett, A. J., & Dean, P. (2001). Developmental dyslexia: The cerebellar deficit hypothesis. *Trends in Neurosciences, 24*(9), 508–511.

Chapter summary – pulling it all together

→ Can you tick all the points from the revision checklist at the beginning of this chapter?

→ Attempt the sample question from the beginning of this chapter using the answer guidelines below.

→ Go to the companion website at www.pearsoned.co.uk/psychologyexpress to access more revision support online, including interactive quizzes, flashcards, You be the marker exercises as well as answer guidance for the Test your knowledge and Sample questions from this chapter.

Answer guidelines

 Sample question Essay

Critically evaluate the importance of the social context to the development of cognitive functioning in childhood.

Approaching the question

Your answer should aim to provide an analysis of how cognitive development occurs in childhood and the impact that social factors may have.

Important points to include

- Begin by outlining how this issue is relevant to cognitive development.
- Discuss the different theoretical approaches, including:
  - constructivist
  - social constructivist
  - information processing.
- For each you will need to:
  - highlight the relative importance given to social factors
  - give examples of how social context has been shown to influence the way cognitive development unfolds and how social context may influence whether or not children can demonstrate cognitive skills
  - evaluate the ability of each theory to explain development and identify any gaps in the theories by comparing and contrasting approaches.

Make your answer stand out

It is really easy to fall into the trap of simply comparing and contrasting Piaget and Vygotsky. A good answer will remember to take a critical stance, evaluating the importance of social context for each. Linking your evaluation to applied issues, such as the importance of school context, will demonstrate your ability to reach beyond theory into practice.

Explore the accompanying website at www.pearsoned.co.uk/psychologyexpress
→ Prepare more effectively for exams and assignments using the answer guidelines for questions from this chapter.
→ Test your knowledge using multiple choice questions and flashcards.
→ Improve your essay skills by exploring the You be the marker exercises.

8

Moral development

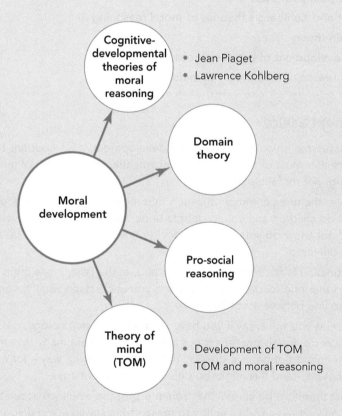

Cognitive-developmental theories of moral reasoning
- Jean Piaget
- Lawrence Kohlberg

Domain theory

Moral development

Pro-social reasoning

Theory of mind (TOM)
- Development of TOM
- TOM and moral reasoning

A printable version of this topic map is available from
www.pearsoned.co.uk/psychologyexpress

Introduction

Moral development refers to our understanding of right and wrong. Theories of moral development usually focus on our moral reasoning – how we make judgements about whether something is right or wrong. As children develop they become less dependent on external rewards and punishments and more reliant on a personal sense of right and wrong. This is thought to reflect their internalisation of society's moral code. This shift from external to internal moral code has been the main focus of a lot of the research and theory in this area.

→ *Revision checklist*

Essential points to revise are:

❏ Piaget and Kohlberg's theories of moral reasoning

❏ Domain theory

❏ The development of pro-social reasoning

❏ Moral reasoning and theory of mind

Assessment advice

- In any assessment you do about moral development, it is important to be aware that most of the literature concerns the development of moral reasoning, not moral behaviour.

- Therefore, the most common question that most of the literature addresses is 'What do children and young people understand about what is right and wrong?' not 'How do young people decide how to behave when faced with a moral dilemma?'

- This distinction is not always made clear and, in the past, it has often been assumed that one follows from the other: you understand what is right and wrong so you behave accordingly.

- However, as you will know if you have studied social psychology, our behaviours do not always reflect our attitudes. There are many reasons why someone might not behave the way they say is the 'right' way – for example, peer pressure – and this might be different at different ages.

- You must therefore be careful that you interpret the evidence accurately – if a study only shows a child's ability to reason then say so – and if you can link to evidence from social psychology about the differences between attitudes and behaviour, then you will be showing synthesis of your knowledge and understanding of psychology.

Sample question

Could you answer this question? Below is a typical essay question that could arise on this topic.

 Sample question   *Essay*

Critically evaluate the factors that influence the development of moral reasoning.

Guidelines on answering this question are included at the end of this chapter, whilst further guidance on tackling other exam questions can be found on the companion website at: **www.pearsoned.co.uk/psychologyexpress**

Cognitive-developmental theories of moral reasoning

Jean Piaget

According to Piaget (1932), an understanding of right and wrong reflects increasing sophistication in a child's thinking processes.

- Children under five years of age have no understanding of morality.
- Between the ages of five and seven years children believe rules and justice are unchangeable and beyond our control. They also judge whether an action is right or wrong by its consequences (heteronomous morality).
- From around seven to ten years of age children are in transition, showing some features of heteronomous morality and autonomous morality.
- At around the age of 10–12 years children's understanding shifts to autonomous morality, recognising that rules are created by people and intentions are as important as consequences.

Piaget believed that the shift from heteronomous to autonomous morality depended upon three things.

- Changes in cognitive skills as described in Chapter 7 (see Table 8.1).
- He believed that the decline in egocentrism and increase in operational thinking allowed children to view problems from different perspectives and so understand how their actions might affect others.
- Peer interactions – in particular, playing games.
  - Through the give and take of social interactions and playing games, children experience disagreements that have to be solved.

- They also learn to negotiate the rules of a game, thereby recognising that rules are man-made rather than handed down from a greater authority.
- In this way, children learn that social rules make co-operation with others possible.
- Piaget believed that games act as models of society.
  - Rule-based games stay the same as they are passed from one generation to the next; in the same way, social institutions provide rules about how to behave in certain social situations.
  - Rule-based games only exist if people agree to participate in them; social institutions only exist because people want to be members of those institutions.
- According to Piaget, children shift from judging right and wrong based on cause to judging it based on intention as they move into adolescence (Cushman, 2008).

Table 8.1 **Piaget's stages of cognitive and moral development**

Level of moral reasoning	Age	Stage of cognitive development
Pre-moral judgement	0–5 years	Sensorimotor stage and pre-operational stage (symbolic functioning)
Heteronomous morality	5–7+ years	Pre-operational stage (intuitive thinking) and concrete operational stage
Autonomous morality	10–12 years	Formal operational stage

? Sample question *Information provider*

According to Piaget, children learn about morality through games in the playground. Your local schools are thinking of cutting back playtime because of worries about supervision and bullying. As a developmental psychologist you are worried about the impact this might have on children's development. Design a poster to persuade teachers and parents about the importance of playtime for the development of moral reasoning.

Lawrence Kohlberg

Piaget's theory of moral development was developed further by Lawrence Kohlberg during the 1950s (Kohlberg, 1958). According to Kohlberg there are three universal levels of moral development, each divided into two stages (see Table 8.2).

- Initially children make judgements about right or wrong based solely on how actions will affect them.
- Over time they recognise that they may need to take others needs into account when determining what is right or wrong.
- Eventually it is recognised that morality concerns a set of standards and principles that account for human rights, not individual needs.
- Kohlberg suggested that most adolescents reach Level II and most of us stay at this level of reasoning during adulthood.
- Only a few individuals reach the post-conventional level of reasoning, Level III.
- Stage 6 is so rare that it has since been removed.

Evidence supports the view that children and adolescents progress through the stages Kohlberg suggested, even if they may not reach the level of post-conventional reasoning (Flavell, Miller, & Miller, 1993; Walker, 1989). Cross-cultural studies also provide some evidence for the universality of Kohlberg's first four stages (Snarey, 1985). However, this theory is not without criticism and Kohlberg's model has been accused of both cultural and gender biases.

- Kohlberg's theory is said to be culturally biased because it emphasises ideals such as individual rights and social justice found mainly in Western cultures (Shweder, 1994).
- Some cultures (for example, American) have been found to place greater value on a justice orientation (Stage 4); other cultures (for example, Indian) place a greater weight on interpersonal responsibilities, such as upholding obligations to others and being responsive to other people's needs (Stage 3) (Miller & Bersoff, 1992).
- It has also been observed that women are more likely to use Stage 3 than Stage 4 reasoning.
- According to Gilligan (1982; 1996) the ordering of the stages reflects a gender bias: placing abstract principles of justice (Stage 4) above relationships and concern for others (Stage 3) is based on a male norm and reflects the fact that most of Kohlberg's research used male participants.
- Gilligan argues that these orientations are different, but one is not necessarily better than the other.
- However, there is some debate about the extent of the evidence to support Gilligan's claims of gender differences in moral reasoning. Jaffee and Hyde (2000) found that gender differences in reasoning were small and usually better explained by the nature of the dilemma than by gender.
- The evidence now seems to suggest that care-based reasoning is used by both males and females to evaluate interpersonal dilemmas, while justice reasoning is applied to societal dilemmas.
- Kohlberg has also been criticised by proponents of domain theory for not differentiating reasoning about morality from reasoning about social conventions (Turiel, 1983).

Table 8.2 Kohlberg's stages of moral development

Level and stage		Description
Level I: Pre-conventional reasoning	Stage 1: Heteronomous morality	Moral behaviour is tied to punishment. Whatever is rewarded is good; whatever is punished is bad. Children obey because they fear punishment
	Stage 2: Individualism, instrumental purpose and exchange	Pursuit of individual interests is seen as the right thing to do. Behaviour is therefore judged good when it serves personal needs or interests. Reciprocity is viewed as a necessity; 'I'll do something good for you if you do something good for me.' Fairness means treating everyone the same
Level II: Conventional reasoning	Stage 3: Mutual interpersonal expectations, relationships and interpersonal conformity	Trust, caring and loyalty are valued and seen as the basis for moral judgements. Children and adolescents may adopt the moral standards of their parents in order to be seen as a 'good' boy or girl
	Stage 4: Social systems morality	Good is defined by the laws of society, by doing one's duty. A law should be obeyed, even if it's not fair. Rules and laws are obeyed because they are needed to maintain social order. Justice must be seen to be done
Level III: Post-conventional reasoning	Stage 5: Social contract and individual rights	Values, rights and principles transcend the law. Good is understood in terms of the values and principles that the society has agreed upon. The validity of laws is evaluated and it is believed that these should be changed if they do not preserve and protect fundamental human rights and values.
	Stage 6: Universal ethical principles	At this stage the individual has developed an internal moral code based on universal values and human rights that takes precedence over social rules and laws. When faced with a conflict between law and conscience, conscience will be followed even though this may involve personal risk.

Jaffee and Hyde (2000). Gender differences in moral orientation: A meta-analysis

This study was a meta-analysis of 113 studies of gender differences in moral reasoning. A *meta-analysis* is a statistical technique that combines the findings from a number of independent studies in order to give a more robust answer to a specific research question. Jaffee and Hyde were interested in finding out the extent to which the evidence supported Gilligan's (1982) critique of Kohlberg's theory of moral reasoning and her claim that justice and care orientations are strongly gender differentiated. They found that the effect size for gender differences in care reasoning was -.28, indicating a small difference favouring females. Likewise, the effect size for gender differences in justice reasoning was .19, indicating a small difference favouring males. Therefore they found no strong support for the claim that the care orientation is used predominantly by women and the justice orientation is used by men. Rather, they suggest that the type of moral reasoning an individual uses is highly sensitive to the context and content of the dilemma. In other words, individual differences and context are more important than gender for moral reasoning.

Jaffee, S. & Hyde, J. S. (2000). Gender differences in moral orientation: A meta-analysis. *Psychological Bulletin, 126*(5), 703–726

Kohlberg's moral dilemmas

Kohlberg used a range of moral dilemmas in his studies of moral reasoning. Perhaps the most famous is that of Heinz:

> A woman was near death from a special kind of cancer. There was one drug that the doctors thought might save her. It was a form of radium that a druggist in the same town had recently discovered. The drug was expensive to make, but the druggist was charging ten times what the drug cost him to produce. He paid $200 for the radium and charged $2000 for a small dose of the drug. The sick woman's husband, Heinz, went to everyone he knew to borrow the money, but he could only get together about $1000, which is half of what it cost. He told the druggist that his wife was dying and asked him to sell it cheaper or let him pay later. But the druggist said, 'No, I discovered the drug and I'm going to make money from it.' So Heinz got desperate and broke into the man's store to steal the drug for his wife.

Kohlberg then asked the children: Should Heinz have broken into the laboratory to steal the drug for his wife? Why or why not?

Kohlberg was less interested in whether the child felt Heinz should steal the drug or not and more interested in their justifications for Heinz' behaviour. For example, a child at Stage 1 would justify Heinz not stealing the drug by saying that he would be put in prison, meaning he is a bad person. Using the information provided in Table 8.2, can you work out what sort of justification a child in Stages 2–5 would provide to support Heinz not stealing the drug?

Further reading Cognitive-developmental theories

Topic	Key reading
Culture and morality	Shweder, R. A. (1994). Are moral intuitions self-evident truths? *Criminal Justice Ethics*, *13*(2), 24–31.
Cause and intention	Cushman, F. (2008). Crime and punishment: Distinguishing the roles of causal and intentional analyses in moral judgement. *Cognition*, *108*(2), 353–380.

Domain theory

- Turiel (1983) argues that the child's concepts of morality and social convention develop from the recognition that certain actions or behaviours are intrinsically harmful and these are therefore different from other actions having only social consequences.

- For example, hitting another person has intrinsic effects (the harm that is caused) on the well-being of the other person.

- Such intrinsic effects occur regardless of any social rules that may or may not be in place concerning hitting.

- The core features of moral cognition are therefore centred around considerations of the impact of actions on well-being and morality is structured by concepts of harm, welfare and fairness.

- In contrast, actions that are matters of social convention have no intrinsic interpersonal consequences.

  - For instance, in school, children usually address their teacher using their title and surname (for example, 'Mr Smith').

  - However, there is no intrinsic reason that this is any better than addressing the teacher by their first name (for example, 'Joe').

  - Only social convention – a socially agreed upon rule – makes the use of 'Mr Smith' more appropriate than 'Joe'.

- These conventions are arbitrary, in the sense that they have no intrinsic status, but they are important to the smooth functioning of the social group as they provide a way for members of society to co-ordinate their social exchanges.
- Understanding of convention is therefore linked to the child's understanding of social organisation.

- Recent research that has looked at children's beliefs about social exclusion suggests children are able to separate these two aspects of moral reasoning, but their ability to differentiate morality and social convention increases during adolescence (Killen, 2007; Killen & Stangor, 2001).

Test your knowledge

8.4 What is the difference between social convention and morality?

Answers to this question can be found on the companion website at:
www.pearsoned.co.uk/psychologyexpress

Further reading	Domain theory
Topic	Key reading
Social exclusion	Killen, M. (2007). Children's social and moral reasoning about exclusion. *Current Directions in Psychological Science, 16*, 32–36.

Pro-social reasoning

- This refers to the thinking involved in deciding whether or not to engage in pro-social behaviours – in other words to share or help others – when doing so may be costly to oneself.
- It has been suggested that this type of reasoning also goes through stage-like developmental changes (Eisenberg & Fabes, 2006).
- Eisenberg used stories that presented a dilemma contrasting self-interest and the interst of another child. For example, a child has to choose between going to a birthday party and stopping to help someone who has hurt themselves.
- Younger children focus on the gains to themselves by helping, whereas older children express more empathy for the injured person.
- A link has been found between more empathetic reasoning and higher pro-social behaviour: children with high levels of pro-social reasoning are less likely to cheat than those who score at lower levels (Eisenberg et al. 2003).
- It is possible that the changes seen in pro-social behaviour link to the development of another cognitive and social skill: theory of mind.

Theory of mind (TOM)

- This refers to the understanding that other people may have different mental states from us – that is, different thoughts, knowledge, desires, feelings and beliefs (Harris, 2006).
- TOM develops mainly over the first seven years of life, but is not fully complete until adolescence (see Table 8.3).
- TOM is important for social and emotional functioning: if you have TOM you are able to put yourself in somebody else's shoes, to imagine what it is they are feeling. It is therefore a part of empathy – our ability to understand and identify with another person's feelings.
- It has been noted that children with autism lack a TOM and this is thought to help explain the difficulty they have with social functioning (Baron Cohen, 2001).
- TOM is thought to be important for the development of moral reasoning because it allows us to think about other people's mental states and answer questions about wrongdoing, such as:
  - Did that person intentionally do wrong?
  - Was their behaviour premeditated?

These sorts of questions are key in a criminal case where questions of intention and premeditation are important.

Table 8.3 Development of theory of mind (TOM)

18 months–3 years	Recognise that other people see what is in front of their eyes, not what is in front of the child's eyes
	Can distinguish between positive and negative emotions and recognise those emotions in others
	Recognise that others have different desires
3–5 years	Realisation of false beliefs
5–7 years	Recognise that behaviours may not reflect thoughts and feelings
7+ years	Recognition of ambivalence occurs during adolescence

Development of TOM

- Although preschoolers try to attribute knowledge and mental states to others, it is not until around the age of four years that children demonstrate a coherent TOM (Gopnik, 1993).
- TOM is suggested to demonstrate a qualitative shift in children's thinking (for example, Wellman & Gelman, 1998).

- It is most commonly assessed by the 'false belief task' (Wimmer & Perner, 1983), such as the Sally Anne task shown in see Figure 8.1. TOM is demonstrated if the child answers that Sally will look in the basket for her ball as they recognise that Sally has a different mental representation of the situation from them – they possess knowledge Sally does not.

- Most typically, developing children do not answer correctly until they are four years old.

- However, it has been suggested that the TOM tasks underestimate children's abilities (Siegal & Peterson, 1994) for two reasons.

  - Younger children misinterpret the key false belief question – 'Where *will* Sally look?' – to mean 'Where *should* Sally look?' (Siegal & Peterson, 1994). Three-year-olds have been found to perform better when the question is reworded in a less ambiguous form – for example, 'Where should Sally look *first of all*' (Siegal & Beattie, 1991).

Figure 8.1 The Sally Anne task

- The burden on immature processing skills such as memory and reasoning are also too great (Flavell & Miller, 1998). This has been tested by the 'false photograph' task (Leslie & Thaiss, 1992), which has the same burden in terms of memory and inference, but does not require children to consider another's mind.
  - The child is shown a doll placed sitting on a box.
  - They are given an instant camera and asked to take a photo.
  - The doll is moved to a new position (for example, sitting on a mat).
  - The child is asked 'Where will the doll be in the developing photo?'
  - Four-year-olds are able to answer this question correctly – three-year-olds are not, suggesting that the three-year-olds' inability to answer the false belief task is related to poorer processing skills.

TOM and moral reasoning

- Sokol, Chandler and Jones (2004) explored the idea that TOM and moral reasoning were linked by showing children Punch and Judy shows. In one scenario Punch pushes a box off the stage because he thinks Judy is in there and he will be rid of her – she is not and no one is hurt. In the other scene Punch goes to help Judy, but accidentally knocks her off the stage.
- They found that children with more developed TOM were more likely to make judgements based on intention, suggesting a link between empathy and understanding of right and wrong

---

Test your knowledge

8.5 What are the developmental phases of theory of mind?

8.6 How are TOM and moral reasoning related?

Answers to these questions can be found on the companion website at: **www.pearsoned.co.uk/psychologyexpress**

? Sample question   Problem-based learning

John is studying GCSE history. He reads the chapters and, at the very end of the chapter, there is a URL for the book's website. On the website there is a practice quiz. He takes one of these before a class test. The test was exactly the same as the practice quiz and he got an A in the test. He now realises the teacher must take the questions from the online quiz to make the test. The other students do not know this, as they got Cs and Ds.

Should John feel guilty? Is this cheating and what should he do? How might a 7-year-old and a 12-year-old answer these questions?

? *Sample question*   **Essay**

To what extent does the evidence support cognitive developmental theories of moral reasoning?

Further reading Theory of mind

Topic	Key reading
Development of TOM	Leslie, A. (1987). Pretense and representation: The origins of 'theory of mind'. *Psychological Review, 94*(4), 412–426.
Moral reasoning and TOM	Sokol, B. W., Chandler, M. J., & Jones, C. (2004). From mechanical to autonomous agency: The relationship between children's moral judgments and their developing theories of mind. *New directions for child and adolescent development. Special Issue: Connections between theories of mind and sociomoral development, 103*, 19–36.

Chapter summary – pulling it all together

➜ Can you tick all the points from the revision checklist at the beginning of this chapter?

➜ Attempt the sample question from the beginning of this chapter using the answer guidelines below.

➜ Go to the companion website at www.pearsoned.co.uk/psychologyexpress to access more revision support online, including interactive quizzes, flashcards, You be the marker exercises as well as answer guidance for the Test your knowledge and Sample questions from this chapter.

Answer guidelines

Sample question   **Essay**

Critically evaluate the factors that influence the development of moral reasoning.

Approaching the question

Your answer should aim to provide an analysis of how different factors determine how children make decisions about what is right or wrong. You should aim to consider as many different factors as possible and draw upon your knowledge from other areas such as play and cognitive development, as well as the information in this chapter.

Important points to include

- Begin by defining the main issue that governs the debate about moral reasoning and whether or not it develops in a stage-like manner.
- Critically evaluate the evidence for a range of different factors thought to influence moral reasoning, including:
  - social factors such as peer relationships and play
  - cognitive factors such as Piagetian stage and TOM
  - gender differences
  - contextual factors, such as the nature of the dilemma.

> **Make your answer stand out**

It is really easy just to discuss Piaget and Kohlberg's theories. A good answer will take other theories into account and will debate the merits of differentiating between social convention and moral behaviour. It will also consider whether there are differences in reasoning and behaviour. Linking your evaluation to other areas of psychology (for example, social psychology), as well as to a range of topics within developmental psychology, will demonstrate your ability to synthesise the information you have learnt and make your answer stand out.

Explore the accompanying website at www.pearsoned.co.uk/psychologyexpress

→ Prepare more effectively for exams and assignments using the answer guidelines for questions from this chapter.
→ Test your knowledge using multiple choice questions and flashcards.
→ Improve your essay skills by exploring the You be the marker exercises.

Notes

9

The self, gender and identity development

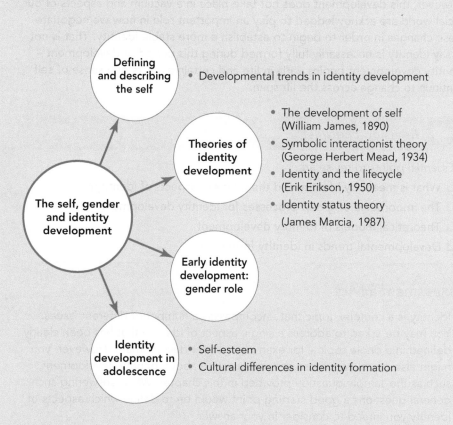

- Developmental trends in identity development

Defining and describing the self

Theories of identity development
- The development of self (William James, 1890)
- Symbolic interactionist theory (George Herbert Mead, 1934)
- Identity and the lifecycle (Erik Erikson, 1950)
- Identity status theory (James Marcia, 1987)

The self, gender and identity development

Early identity development: gender role

Identity development in adolescence
- Self-esteem
- Cultural differences in identity formation

A printable version of this topic map is available from
www.pearsoned.co.uk/psychologyexpress

Introduction

Our sense of who we are as individuals is an important part of psychological development. This sense of self is central to our social, emotional and personal development. It is our self-identity, our understanding of who we are as an individual and includes awareness of subjective experience and relationships with others. There are many aspects to identity and the importance of each may change as we age. Our gender identity, for example, is established quite early on during childhood, while other issues such as vocational or political identity do not develop until adolescence or later. Adolescence is an important time for identity formation and the physical and cognitive changes that happen in this phase of our lives can have an enormous impact on our developing sense of self. However, this development does not take place in a vacuum and aspects of our social world are acknowledged to play an important role in how we negotiate these changes in order to begin to establish a more stable identity. That is not to say identity is necessarily fully formed during this period of development – identity development begins early in life and certain aspects of a sense of self continue to change across the lifespan.

> ### ➜ *Revision checklist*
>
> *Essential points to revise are:*
> - ❏ What is meant by identity and the different aspects of identity?
> - ❏ The importance of group processes for identity development
> - ❏ Theoretical models of identity development
> - ❏ Developmental trends in identity formation

Assessment advice

- Identity is a complex topic that encompasses a number of different issues. You may be asked to address a single aspect of identity that has been clearly defined in a single topic – for example, gender development. However, you might also be asked a more general question about identity development, such as the sample question provided in this chapter. When answering such general questions a good starting point would be to define which aspects of identity you intend to consider in your answer.

- It is also worth remembering that, because identity concerns our own perceptions of who we are, it can be difficult to measure. Personal identity is subjective and therefore usually measured by self-report using either questionnaires or interviews. One problem with this is that measurement relies on the cognitive and language skills of the respondent. This raises issues of validity, especially when measuring identity in childhood.

- A related issue is the question of whether we can ever truly gain access to another person's beliefs about who they are. This is an area where psychological theory meets philosophical pondering and it is easy to get entangled in the debate about the nature of human consciousness. While this is a valid area of discussion, it is important to remind yourself that this is a topic where many of the great minds of the twenty-first century still cannot agree. It is better to focus your answer on the evidence that we have rather than the questions we cannot answer.

- Whatever kind of assessment you do, try to remember, much of the evidence that does exist about identity development has come from a Western perspective. Cultural contexts seem to play a central role in how we define identity and therefore which aspects of self are most valued: while Western society focuses on the development of a unique sense of self, more collectivist cultures may view the development of uniqueness and difference in a more negative light.

Sample question

Could you answer this question? Below is a typical essay question that could arise on this topic.

 Sample question **Essay**

Critically evaluate the theory that there is a developmental trend in identity development.

Guidelines on answering this question are included at the end of this chapter, whilst further guidance on tackling other exam questions can be found on the companion website at: **www.pearsoned.co.uk/psychologyexpress**

Defining and describing the self

Identity comprises a number of different aspects, some of which are shown in Table 9.1. The importance of these different areas of our personal identity may change across time and place. Intellectual identity may, for example, be felt more strongly during the school years; religion may be an important part of an individual's identity at home, but not at work.

Table 9.1 **Aspects of identity**

Aspect of identity	Components
Vocational identity	Career choice and aspirations; current or intended occupation
Intellectual identity	Academic aspirations and achievements
Political ideology	Political beliefs, values and ideals; may include membership of political groups
Spiritual/religious identity	Religious beliefs, attitudes to religion and spirituality; religious practices and behaviours; may relate to a specific moral and ethical code
Relationship identity	This may refer to intimate relationships and be defined by whether you are single, married, divorced, etc. or to social relationships such as friend, colleague, etc or to family relationships – mother, daughter, etc.
Sexual identity	Sexual orientation – heterosexual, homosexual, bisexual
Gender identity	The attributes and characteristics that our culture associates with belonging to one or the other of the sexes
Cultural identity	Where you were born and/or raised, and how intensely you identify with the cultural heritage/practices linked to this part of the world. May also include language preference
Ethnic identity	The extent to which you feel a sense of belonging to a particular ethnic group; membership. The ethnic group tends to be one to which you can claim heritage and the beliefs of the group may influence your thinking, perceptions, feelings and behaviour
Physical identity	Body image and beliefs about your appearance
Personality	Characteristics that define patterns of behaviour, such as being shy, friendly, gregarious, anxious, etc.

To develop our identity it is thought that we must first of all develop a sense of ourselves as separate, conscious individuals. Once we have recognised ourselves as separate from others, we can begin to establish our own identity. We usually do this by reference to other people.

Developmental trends in identity development

Our developing sense of identity has been suggested to follow a developmental sequence in which younger children define themselves in terms of concrete characteristics, while adolescents increasingly define themselves in terms of more abstract, internal characteristics. This idea is based primarily on research, which has shown that children's self-descriptions change with age, from observable and physical descriptors such as 'I am tall' to more psychological traits such as 'I am friendly' (Rosenberg, 1979). It has been suggested that this reflects children's increasing ability to distinguish themselves psychologically from others as they get older (Bannister & Agnew, 1977).

CRITICAL FOCUS

Rosenberg's study of self-descriptions

Rosenberg conducted open-ended interviews with individual children to find out about their self-perceptions. He interviewed a sample of 8–18-year-olds about various aspects of their sense of self. The children were selected at random from 25 schools in Baltimore, in the USA. Many of his questions explored aspects of their categorical selves that went beyond the simple self-description ('Who am I?') to include feelings of pride and shame in aspects of their selves ('What are my best things/weak points?'); their sense of distinctiveness as separate individuals ('In what ways am I the same as/different from other children?') and feelings about an ideal self ('What kind of person would I like to become?')

Rosenberg's first aim was to find a way of sorting the children's replies into meaningful categories. His second aim was to search for any patterns in the kinds of replies given by particular age groups that might suggest a developmental progression in children's sense of self. He was able to categorise the children's replies into a series of broad groups of self-descriptions, as follows.

Physical

Descriptions of self that could be observed or identified or potentially be described by others; they are mainly about physical features or physical activities such as:

- *objective facts* – for example, 'I am eight years old'; overt achievements – for example, 'I can swim 25 metres'
- *manifested preferences* – for example, 'I like milk'
- *possessions* – for example, 'I've got a blue bike'
- *physical attributes* – for example, 'I've got brown hair and blue eyes'
- *membership categories* – for example, 'I am a girl'.

Character

Descriptions of self that refer to personal characteristics or traits: personality, emotional characteristics and emotional control. These qualities could still be inferred by others from the behaviour of an individual, but only the individual can have direct access to them. For example:

- *qualities of character* – for example, 'I am a brave person and I think that I am honest';
- *emotional characteristics* – for example, 'I am generally happy and cheerful'
- *emotional control* – for example, 'I don't get into fights', 'I lose my temper easily'.

Relationships

Descriptions of self that refer to interpersonal traits or to relationships with others, such as:

- *interpersonal traits* – for example, 'I am friendly and sociable', 'I am shy and retiring'
- *relationship to others* – for example, 'I am well liked by other children', 'Other people find me difficult to get on with'.

Inner

Descriptions of self that refer to an individual's more private inner world of emotions, attitudes, wishes, beliefs and secrets, such as self-knowledge – for example, rather than simply describing a personal trait such as shyness, they would tend to qualify this with explanations of the circumstances in which they felt shy, why they thought they were shy, how it affected them and how they coped with being shy.

Rosenberg found that the majority of the descriptors used by younger children were about physical activity and physical characteristics. The older children were more likely to use character traits to define the self. Rosenberg also found increasing reference to relationships. For example, when questioned about points of pride and shame, only 9 per cent of the 8-year-olds' responses consisted of interpersonal traits (for example, 'friendly', 'shy'), as opposed to 17 per cent of the 14-year-olds' and 28 per cent of the 16-year-olds'. Likewise, when asked about what kind of person they would like to become, 36 per cent of the 8-year-olds' responses were to do with interpersonal traits, as opposed to 69 per cent of the 14- to 16-year-olds'.

The oldest children (that is, those up to 18 years) made far more use of inner qualities, knowledge of which was only available to the individual. Their descriptions were concerned with their emotions, attitudes, motivations, wishes and secrets. Rosenberg also found that older children are much more likely to refer to self-control when describing themselves – for example, 'I don't show my feelings'. When questioned about points of shame, only 14 per cent of the 8-year-olds' responses related to self-control, while 32 per cent of 14-year-olds' responses referred to the capacity to hide self and feelings from others.

> **? Sample question**   *Essay*
>
> Read the description of Rosenberg's study above and then answer the following questions.
>
> - How robust is the evidence presented by Rosenberg?
> - How reliable and valid do you think these findings are?
> - What developmental changes other than sense of self might Rosenberg's findings reflect?

Theories of identity development

The development of self (William James, 1890)

Although an early theory of identity development, James' ideas continue to underpin many of the contemporary beliefs about how identity develops. According to this view there are two aspects to sense of self: the 'I' – also referred to as 'self-as-subject' or 'existential self' – and the 'me' – also known as 'self-as-object' or 'categorical self' (Lewis, 1990).

- The first step on the road to self-understanding is the recognition that I exist as an individual, have agency (the power to act) and distinct and unique experiences.
- Awareness of agency first develops in infancy when the baby begins to show understanding that they can cause things to happen and have the ability to control objects (Cooley, 1902).
- Infants learn that when they let go of something, it drops; when they touch a toy it moves; when they cry or smile, someone responds to them.
- This sense of agency emerges at around four months of age and is gradually consolidated.
- By the time the infant moves into early childhood this sense of agency is more clearly developed: a two-year-old child is more assertive, demanding and picky than a four-month-old baby.
- Tantrums associated with the 'terrible twos' are suggested to reflect the frustration felt by toddlers when attempts to control the world around them fail.
- However, it is difficult to know to what extent this demonstrates true sense of self as we can only infer understanding from behaviour.
- Studying self-awareness is difficult at any age as it can be difficult to articulate the different aspects of the 'I' and so even more difficult to study them empirically.
- Empirical investigations of the existential self in infants and toddlers are therefore limited and studies tend to be speculative (Damon & Hart, 1988).
- Empirical support for the emergence of self in late infancy/early childhood is provided by a classic investigation carried out by Lewis and Brooks-Gunn (1979):
  - the *rouge test* was carried out with 9–24-month-old infants.
  - self-recognition emerged at around 18–24 months.
  - at 18 months 50 per cent of the group recognised the reflection in the mirror as their own.
  - by 20 to 24 months, self-recognition increased to 65 per cent.
- It is important to remember that this is only *behavioural* evidence for awareness; it does not tell us anything about the *subjective* experience associated with this consciousness.
- Children's understanding of themselves as active agents continues to develop in early childhood and can be seen in their attempts to co-operate with others in play.
- They use their knowledge of their own power to act on their world, when they offer to share a toy or join in pretend play with a friend (Dunn, 1988).
- Once children have gained a certain level of awareness of the existential self, they begin to form increasing awareness of their categorical self as they begin to place themselves – and be placed by others – in different categories (for example, gender, nationality).

- The categorical self is thought to emerge primarily through our interactions with others.
- The child builds up their sense of identity from the reactions of others to them and from the view they believe these others have of them.
- Cooley (1902) called this the 'looking-glass self'; it is as if other people provide a 'social mirror' and children come to see themselves as they are reflected in others.

Key term

Rouge test: in this test, an experimenter surreptitiously places a dot of rouge on the nose of the child, who is then placed in front of a mirror and their reactions monitored. Self-recognition is shown when the child touches their nose or attempts to wipe away the rouge.

Symbolic interactionist theory (George Herbert Mead, 1934)

George Herbert Mead provides another classic but enduring theory of how identity develops. This theory focuses on the development of what James referred to as the categorical self. According to Mead (1934), the self and the social world are inextricably bound together.

- The self is essentially a social structure that can arise only through social experiences.
- Children begin to learn about the perceptions that others have of them and this is shown in their use of language, games and their play.
- In this way they become capable of reflecting on themselves.
- The child therefore cannot develop a sense of self without the chance to interact with others, in order to understand how others view the world, including how they view the child.
- Evidence to support this view comes from cases of extreme social deprivation early in life – for example, *feral* children or children like Genie, a girl who was kept locked in a room for several years by her abusive father (Rymer, 1993).
- These children have been shown to have poor communication skills and only a limited understanding of self.
- Victor, the original and perhaps most famous feral child, showed few of the elements of the understanding of self when he was found at the age of 12 years:
  - he was unable to recognise himself in a mirror
  - had no sense of his own psychological characteristics
  - had no understanding of social roles.
- It is generally believed that Victor was unable to develop the capacity to reflect on himself, because he did not have others around him whose

behaviour he could observe or who could give him feedback about his own behaviour and characteristics.

- An alternative explanation is that Victor was abandoned by his family because he was unresponsive socially – nobody knows anything about Victor's development before he was found, so this is as good an explanation as any.

- Caution is therefore necessary in drawing too many conclusions from this and similar cases.

- Other evidence that identity development is linked to social experiences comes from observations of children's play during the preschool years.

- Awareness of different social groupings can be seen in the choices children make regarding their play partners. For example:
  - by the age of three children show a preference for playing with peers of the same ethnicity (Urberg & Kaplan, 1989)
  - and gender (Maccoby, 2002)
  - this suggests that the preschooler has realised there are different groups in society and has begun to identify with those groups.

- A good example of how this process might happen is provided by theories of *gender identity* development, though it seems likely that development follows a similar pattern for all group identities.

Identity and the lifecycle (Erik Erikson, 1950)

- The central feature of Erikson's psychosocial stage theory (see Chapter 1) is the development of ego identity.

- However, it is Erikson's beliefs about the development of identity during adolescence that has been most widely considered and even tested empirically.

- According to Erikson, during adolescence, young people are faced with an overwhelming number of choices about who they are and where they are going in life.

- For Erikson, this is the crisis that has to be resolved at this developmental stage; if adolescents are not able to answer these questions adequately they will suffer from identity confusion, which will delay their development in the later stages of life.

- The search for identity is supported by what Erikson calls a *psychosocial moratorium*, by which he means that adolescents are relatively free of responsibility, which enables them to have the space to try out (and discard) different identities.

- Adolescents are therefore able to experiment with different roles and personalities until they find the ones that best suit them.

Identity status theory (James Marcia, 1987)

- This theory extends Erikson's work on identity development in adolescence.
- Marcia suggests that identity development is a staged process and has identified four different identity statuses, as shown in Table 9.2.
- Identity development in adolescence is concerned with exploration, followed by commitment. The crisis referred to by Erikson comes about when adolescents are in the process of questioning their identity.
- According to Marcia, adolescents are usually described by one of the first three statuses.
- However, there is increasing evidence that identity development is not solely a task of adolescence: some aspects of identity are already well on the way to being established before adolescence (for example, gender).
- Likewise, some of the most important changes in identity occur during early adulthood (Waterman, 1992).
- It has even been argued that identity is not stable and the identity we achieve in adolescence is not necessarily the one we will keep for life (Marcia, 2002).
- Personal experiences and changes in society are likely to lead us to question our beliefs and who we are. Perhaps the healthiest identity is one that is flexible, adaptive and open to change.

9.2 Stages of identity status

Identity status	Characteristics
Diffusion	The individual has not yet experienced a crisis or made any commitments; they are undecided about future roles and have not shown any interests in such matters
Foreclosure	The individual has made a commitment without experiencing a crisis – for example, they have simply followed the ideologies and aspirations of their parents
Moratorium	The individual is experiencing a crisis; commitments have not yet been strongly defined
Achievement	The individual has undergone a crisis and made a commitment

Key terms

Ego identity: according to Erikson, this is the conscious sense of self that we develop through social interaction. Our ego identity is constantly changing owing to new experiences and the information we acquire in our daily interactions with others. Erikson also believed that behaviour is motivated by a sense of competence. Each stage in Erikson's theory is concerned with becoming competent in one particular area of life. If the stage is handled well, the person develops a sense of mastery or ego strength. If, however, the stage is managed poorly, a sense of inadequacy will develop.

CRITICAL FOCUS

Identity status

There is continuing debate about the value of the identity status approach. How well do you think this theory explains identity development?

In order to answer this question, think about your own exploration and commitment to different aspects of identity. Would you describe yourself as diffused, foreclosed, in moratorium or as having achieved identity following a crisis? Is this approach more useful for some aspects of identity than others? Do you agree that foreclosure is a limitation to identity development?

Completing the following chart will help you focus on some of the relevant issues.

Identity component	Identity status			
	Diffused	*Foreclosed*	*Moratorium*	*Achieved*
Vocational				
Political				
Religious				
Relationships				
Achievement				
Sexual				
Gender				
Ethnic/cultural				
Physical				
Personality				

Test your knowledge

9.1 Name three theories of identity development.

9.2 What are Marcia's four stages of identity status?

9.3 What does Erikson mean by 'ego identity'?

9.4 What factors influence the development of the categorical self?

Answers to these questions can be found on the companion website at:
www.pearsoned.co.uk/psychologyexpress

Further reading Theories of identity development

Topic	Key reading
Marcia	Marcia, J. (2001). Identity in childhood and adolescence. In N. J. Smelser & P. B. Baltes (Eds.), *International Encyclopedia of the social & behavioral sciences* Oxford: Elsevier (pp. 7159–7163).
Ethnic identity	French, S. E., Seidman, E., Allen, L., & Aber, J. L. (2006). The development of ethnic identity during adolescence. *Developmental Psychology, 42*(1), 1–10. Available online at: www.uic.edu/depts/oce/OCEweb/06SU/Week1-TheDevelopmentofEthnicIdentity.pdf

Early identity development: gender role

One of the main aspects of identity that develops early in childhood is that of gender. It is commonly agreed that this identity is influenced by the understanding of social roles.

- Once children realise that there are two genders and they belong to one of them, they begin to show a clear motivation to behave in the ways a member of the gender 'should'. They dress, choose friends, activities and toys to suit this label.

- Bem (1989) suggests that having labelled themselves as either male or female, the child begins to develop a *gender schema.*

- This mental model of what males and females 'do' – the *gender role* – is based upon observations of other members of the same group.

- Children pay more attention to the behaviour of same-gender peers in order to remember more about how their own group behaves and imitate that behaviour (Ruble & Martin, 2006).

- Understanding that gender is constant is thought to be an important motivator for sex-typed behaviours (Kohlberg, 1966).

- Behaviours are often highly stereotyped and children's attitudes at this age are frequently sexist – even about their own gender and in the face of contradictory evidence.

- Children may even show hostility to the other gender (Ruble & Martin, 2006).

- On the face of it, such extreme behaviour does not seem to provide any developmental advantage. If childhood is preparation for adulthood, then surely children need to learn to co-operate with each other, not segregate themselves by gender?

- One explanation seems to be, it is only by committing wholeheartedly to a particular social group that the child can develop conceptual coherence – and this includes subscribing to an extreme version of gender-typed behaviour.

An alternative explanation is that the differences we see in male and female behaviour are biologically, rather than socially, determined.

- There is evidence to suggest that hormones play a role in behaviours such as aggression, play patterns and attitudes to gender roles (Reiner & Gearhart, 2004).
- It has also been found that children display preferences for gender-appropriate toys by six months, well before they have knowledge of gender roles (Alexander, Wilcox, & Woods, 2009).
- This is believed to provide strong evidence for a biological basis to this preference.
- However, given that the evidence in favour of a role for the environment in the development of gender identity is so strong, it seems unlikely that such differences are based in biology alone.
- By six months of age, infants have already notched up a lot of experiences in the world – perhaps their preferences for particular toys reflect these experiences and the choices made by the adults and others who make up their world.
- There is, for example, evidence that carers' responses to their children depend in part on whether their child is male or female (Maccoby, 2003), with fathers showing greater differential treatment than mothers (Leaper, 2002).
- Parents reward gender-appropriate choices and may even make early toy choices for their children that are linked to their child's sex.
- Social responses to a biological distinction, along with hormonally based differences in behaviour, thus set the scene for later cognitive and emotional development.

Once again, biological, social and emotional features of the child's world are working together to determine a child's development.

Test your knowledge

9.5 How might a child learn about gender roles from social interactions?

9.6 What evidence is there that biological factors influence gender identity development?

Answers to these questions can be found on the companion website at: **www.pearsoned.co.uk/psychologyexpress**

Further reading Gender identity

Topic	Key reading
Biological influences	Jurgensen, M., Hiort, O., Holterhus, P., & Thyen, U. (2007). Gender role behavior in children with XY karyotype and disorders of sex development. *Hormones and Behavior, 51*, 443–453.
Cognitive influences	Ruble, D., Taylor, L., Cyphers, L., Greulich, F., Lurye, L. & Shrout, P. (2007). The role of gender constancy in early gender development. *Child Development, 78*, 1121–1136.

Identity development in adolescence

Erikson's belief that adolescence is a time of identity crisis has predominated twentieth-century theories of adolescent development.

- This view of adolescence, as a tumultuous period, full of chaos and confusion caused by hormonal changes and identity crises, echoes that of other psychodynamic theorists such as Anna Freud (1958).

- However, this image of the troubled or delinquent teenager has been challenged and it seems that very few developmental psychologists still subscribe to this view.

- The consensus is that most of us negotiate adolescence with few serious personal or social problems.

- Coleman (1978) proposed a focal theory of adolescence, which suggests the issues that have to be dealt with in adolescence come to the teenager's attention at different times so they are able to deal with issues of identity individually, thus making the task manageable.

- It is only when issues come to a head all at the same time that there will be a crisis in adolescence.

- There is evidence that for a minority of adolescents, adolescence can be very troubling. However, it is important to recognise that those children who do have an emotional time in adolescence usually have some pre-existing emotional problem (Graham & Rutter 1985; White & Edwards, 1990), while delinquent teenagers are likely to have had behaviour problems as children (Bates, 2003). All of which perhaps points to adolescence intensifying existing predispositions, not creating new ones.

It has been suggested that the hormones triggering growth and sexual development in adolescence also contribute to the psychological development taking place in this period, including identity formation.

- Identity development is strongly linked to social relationships and studies have shown links between testosterone levels and perceived social competence in boys (Nottlemann et al., 1987).

- Links have also been found between oestrodiol levels and the emotional responses of girls (Inoff-Germain et al., 1988).

- Identity is thought to be influenced by adolescent relationships, including involvement in cliques and crowds.

- According to Erikson, community membership is central to the achievement of identity as it requires solidarity with a group's ideals.

- Identification with cliques and crowds is argued to help the adolescent defend themselves against the loss of identity that may be provoked by the identity crisis.

- Thus adolescents deal with the difficulties they experience in committing to adult identities (the identity crisis) by making exaggerated commitments to certain style groups and by separating themselves from other style groups.

- They may use particular kinds of clothes and music to indicate their unique style and how it differentiates them from other groups.

- These cliques and crowds, clearly identified by their own sets of style, values and norms are what we often now refer to as 'youth culture'.

- According to Miles et al. (1998) identifying with youth culture gives adolescents some power over their identity in a rapidly changing world.

- Youth culture is a relatively modern phenomenon, thought to be precipitated by a specific historical and economic context.

- As the school-leaving age (for compulsory education) increased during the second half of the twentieth century, so the transition period between childhood and adulthood lengthened.

- At the same time, young people had increasingly larger financial resources available to them, which gave them consumer power.

- Studies of youth culture have suggested that such consumption is central to the construction of adolescent identities (Phoenix, 2005).

- Many such studies have focused on the links between consumption, style and identity and have concluded that style is a crucial means of sustaining and defining group boundaries (Croghan et al. 2006).

- Milner (2004) proposes that adolescents use their consumer power to gain a sense of acceptance and belonging with their peer group.

- However, the flip side of this is that failing to maintain such an identity can lead to problems such as teasing, social exclusion and loss of status (Blatchford, 1998; Croghan, et al., 2006).

- Given that such consumption is often linked to particular brands, an important issue to consider here is how economic disadvantage might impact upon adolescent popularity.

- Some evidence suggests that not having enough money to afford the 'right' brands leads to social exclusion, as branded items serve as markers of group inclusion that have to be genuine and cannot be faked (Croghan et al., 2006).

- Adolescents in this study regarded cheap versions of designer goods as a sign of style error, making group membership costly.

- Other studies (for example, Milner, 2004) suggest that, rather than engaging in conflicts around style, young people may express solidarity with these cliques by modelling themselves on the popular groups, but resisting the consumption of brand-name goods, thereby establishing a new, less high-status group.

Self-esteem

Self-esteem is another aspect of our identity that is important to adolescent development. Self-esteem is our feeling of self-worth, a value judgement we make about how 'good' we are.

- Self-esteem develops and changes as the child moves into adolescence, often in relation to bodily changes, with most adolescents showing some body dissatisfaction during puberty (Graber & Brooks-Gunn, 2001).

- How easily adolescents deal with physical changes depends partly on how closely their bodies match the well-defined stereotypes of the 'perfect' body for young women and young men promoted by the society in which they live.

- Girls tend to become increasingly dissatisfied as they move through puberty, while boys become increasingly satisfied.

- It is likely that this is linked to the natural increases that occur in body fat in girls and muscle mass in boys. When adolescents try to change their physique, girls are more likely to try to lose weight and boys to increase muscle tone (McCabe, Ricciardelli, & Finemore, 2002).

- Adolescents who do not match the stereotype may well need more social support from adults and peers to improve their feelings of self-worth regarding their physique.

- Late-maturing girls start to report greater satisfaction with their body shape than early-maturing girls (Simmons & Blyth, 1987), which may reflect differing body shapes at the end of puberty; early-maturing girls stop growing earlier and so tend to be shorter and stockier in comparison to their taller, thinner, late-maturing peers (Brooks-Gunn, Peterson, & Eichorn 1985).

- Early-maturing girls have also been found to be more vulnerable to emotional and behavioural problems, including depression, eating disorders and engaging in risky health behaviours, such as smoking, drinking, drug-taking and early sexual behaviours (Weisner & Ittel, 2002).

- However, there is evidence to suggest that the negative psychosocial consequences of early puberty may not last into later adolescence or adulthood (Blumstein Posner, 2006).

- In contrast, the evidence suggests that, for boys, the advantage lies in early maturity, with early-maturing boys having more successful peer relationships than their late-maturing counterparts (Simmons & Blyth, 1987).

- There is, however, some disagreement about whether or not this remains an advantage across the lifespan (Brooks-Gunn, Peterson, & Eichorn 1985).

- What is becoming more evident, however, is that the link between an adolescent's beliefs about their appearance and their sense of self-worth – an important aspect of an individual's identity – should not be underestimated (Frisen & Holmqvist, 2010).

Cultural differences in identity formation

Thus in many ways this developing sense of adolescent identity can be seen as an important step on the road to adult independence, since in Western society the goal of self-development is to establish our individuality or a sense of our own uniqueness and separateness from others. The extent to which this search for individuality is a universal goal of development has, however, been questioned (Guisinger & Blatt, 1994). Studies from anthropology have suggested that this Western view, with its emphasis on the distinctiveness of the individual from others, differs from that of other cultures. There is evidence non-Western cultures have a more sociocentric ideal of the person that minimises rather than accentuates self–other distinctions (Kim & Berry, 1993). This has led some psychologists to challenge the tradition of emphasising the importance of the development of the self as separate from others (Guisinger & Blatt, 1994). However, this has also been challenged by cross-cultural studies, which have shown that, while students from collectivist cultures do place more value on collectivist identity, they may also place a high value on individualism (Carpenter & Karakitapoglu-Aygün, 2005). It has been suggested that this might reflect cultural changes (Matsumoto, 1999).

Key term

Self-esteem: is our global assessment of self-worth. As such it often reflects perceptions that do not always match reality (Baumiester et al., 2003). We tend to make judgements about our abilities in different aspects of our lives based on our successes or failures. However, failure does not automatically lead to low self-esteem. The impact of any failures – or successes – on our global self-esteem depends to a great extent on the importance we place on that aspect of our lives. Thus for the adolescent who places little value on their athletic identity, but a great deal on their intellectual identity, coming last in the hurdles is unlikely to have much impact on self-esteem. By the same token, coming bottom of the class in a test may well have an important negative impact on their feelings of self-worth.

? Sample question   Problem-based learning

Emily is 17 years old. She recently gave birth to Jack, who is now three months old. This was an unplanned pregnancy and Emily and Jack are living in Emily's childhood home with her mother Anna and brother Michael who is 15 years old. Emily has recently split up with Jack's father, who felt he was too young to be a dad (he is also 17 years old). Emily has dropped out of school to look after her baby, giving up plans to go to university. She is having difficulty caring for Jack. She feels Anna is not supportive enough; she would like Anna to mind Jack so she can go back to school. However, Anna says she cannot give up her own job to look after Jack as she needs the money support herself and Michael. She has also made it very clear that she believes Emily has to look after her own child and take responsibility. Although she loves Jack very much, Emily is beginning to feel resentful that she has been left to look after a baby when all her friends – including Jack's father – are still having fun. She is lonely and feels she is missing out on her youth.

How might the unplanned changes in Emily's life affect her developing identity? How could Anna help her daughter negotiate this difficult time?

? Sample question   Essay

To what extent does the evidence support Erikson's view that identity development is a key task of adolescence?

? Sample question   Information provider

Design a workshop for secondary school teachers with the title 'Youth Culture'. What sort of information could you give that would help the teachers understand the importance of group allegiance for the teenagers they teach?

Further reading Adolescent identity

Topic	Key reading
Consumption and identity	Croghan, R., Griffin, C., Hunter, J., & Phoenix, A. (2006). Style failure: Consumption, identity and social exclusion. *Journal of Youth Studies, 9*, 463–478.
Self-esteem	Holmqvist, K. & Frisen, A. (2010). Body dissatisfaction across cultures: Findings and research problems. *European Eating Disorders Review, 18*(2), 133–146.
Identity and culture	Carpenter, S. & Karakitapoglu-Aygün, Z. (2005). Importance and descriptiveness of self-aspects: A cross-cultural comparison. *Cross-Cultural Research, 39*(3), 293–321.

Chapter summary – pulling it all together

→ Can you tick all the points from the revision checklist at the beginning of this chapter?

→ Attempt the sample question from the beginning of this chapter using the answer guidelines below.

→ Go to the companion website at www.pearsoned.co.uk/psychologyexpress to access more revision support online, including interactive quizzes, flashcards, You be the marker exercises as well as answer guidance for the Test your knowledge and Sample questions from this chapter.

Answer guidelines

 Sample question   *Essay*

Critically evaluate the theory that there is a developmental trend in identity development.

Approaching the question

This is a very general question on identity development. Your answer should therefore start by defining identity and making clear which aspects you will consider. You should then go on to discuss the theories that suggest a developmental trend and what that trend is thought to be. Remember to provide evidence for and against this idea in order to give a full evaluation.

Important points to include

● Begin by defining identity, showing how it is comprised of many facets. Describe briefly the way it has been suggested to develop over time, moving from existential to categorical self, and how categorical self, is also thought to develop as we age.

● Outline the problems with testing empirically something that is so subjective.

● Provide an overview of the theories that have suggested a developmental trend. You might want to include theories developed by:

  ● James
  ● Erikson
  ● Marcia.

● Provide evidence that supports the idea of a developmental trend such as that of Rosenberg, Marcia, Lewis and Brooks-Gunn. Remember to be critical in your analysis of the evidence. Consider other evidence as well that

179

suggests some aspects of identity development (for example, gender) are completed early in life, while other aspects develop more in adolescence and beyond.

Make your answer stand out

Identity is a complex topic. Because of its subjective nature it is very difficult to measure and test empirically. A good answer will make this difficulty very clear, without becoming too bound up with the philosophical debates about what consciousness and identity are. It is easy to focus on the social aspects of identity development and the importance of group membership. However, you need to remember that the ability to develop relationships with others and become members of a group depend on a range of other abilities and factors including social and communication skills, which in turn rely on cognitive and language abilities. Linking your evaluation to these other factors will demonstrate your ability to synthesise the information you have learnt.

Explore the accompanying website at www.pearsoned.co.uk/psychologyexpress

→ Prepare more effectively for exams and assignments using the answer guidelines for questions from this chapter.

→ Test your knowledge using multiple choice questions and flashcards.

→ Improve your essay skills by exploring the You be the marker exercises.

Notes

Adulthood

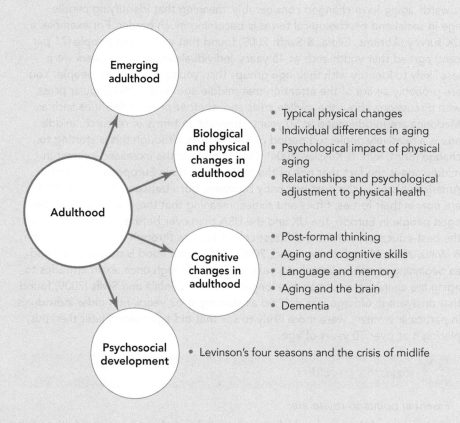

- Emerging adulthood

- Biological and physical changes in adulthood
  - Typical physical changes
  - Individual differences in aging
  - Psychological impact of physical aging
  - Relationships and psychological adjustment to physical health

- Adulthood

- Cognitive changes in adulthood
  - Post-formal thinking
  - Aging and cognitive skills
  - Language and memory
  - Aging and the brain
  - Dementia

- Psychosocial development
  - Levinson's four seasons and the crisis of midlife

A printable version of this topic map is available from
www.pearsoned.co.uk/psychologyexpress

Introduction

Developmental psychologists usually agree that in Western industrialised societies young people enter adulthood between the ages of 18 and 20 years. Unlike adolescence, which is usually heralded by the onset of puberty, adulthood has no obvious physical marker to announce its arrival. However, most people reach their final height at this age and our organs and body systems have also reached maturity (Wold, 2004). In addition, there are cultural, social and psychological markers that help determine the shift to adulthood and these may differ across cultures. For many years middle adulthood has been described in the literature as beginning at 40 years of age: current average life expectancy in the UK is 80 years (ONS, 2010), thus making 40 years the midpoint of life. However, life expectancy in the UK has almost doubled over the past century and attitudes towards aging have changed considerably, meaning that identifying middle age in social and psychological terms is becoming much harder. For example, a UK survey (Abrams, Eilola, & Swift, 2009) found that while most people (71 per cent) agreed that youth ends at 45 years, individuals aged 50–60 years were less likely to identify with their age groups than younger and older people. You are probably aware of the attention that middle age gets in the popular press, with discussions about the midlife crisis and whether or not celebrities such as Madonna are middle-aged at 50 years. However, in terms of research, middle age is a relatively neglected period of the lifespan, although this is starting to change (Brim, Ryff, & Kessler, 2004). One reason for the increased interest in middle age is the fact that one of the largest cohorts in European and North American history – the post-war baby boomers, born between 1946 and 1964, are now in their forties, fifties and sixties, meaning that there are more middle-aged people in Europe, the UK and the USA than ever before. In addition, this is the best-educated, richest and fittest cohort to pass through middle age (Martin & Willis, 2005; Metz & Underwood, 2005). Older adulthood is usually described as beginning at approximately 65 years of age, although once again attitudes to aging are changing as people live longer. Abrams, Eilolala and Swift (2009) found that on average old age was defined as starting at 63 years, but, older individuals, in particular women, were more likely to say that old age started later than this, placing it at over 70 years of age.

> **➔** *Revision checklist*
>
> *Essential points to revise are:*
> - ❏ Understand the way in which cognitive abilities change across adulthood
> - ❏ Be able to evaluate the idea that a midlife crisis is inevitable
> - ❏ Be able to discuss critically the relationship between physical aging and psychological well-being in adulthood
> - ❏ Critically understand the impact of social and cultural beliefs on adult experiences

Assessment advice

- It is easy to assume that aging is all about decline. However, it is important to remember that a lifespan approach to development proposes that development is multidirectional. Thus, as some aspects of functioning decline, other aspects improve.

- A good example of this is cognitive functioning, where processing speed usually declines with age, but increases in knowledge and experience can improve decision making.

- The extent to which decline takes place seems to be related to a number of factors, including biology, our socio-cultural environment and individual experiences. The relationship between these different factors is complex and should be explored carefully. As with other areas you have studied, remember to take a critical approach to aging and to take all aspects of development into consideration from cognitive through to social. Good assessment answers will try to take account of many factors and make links between the different areas of psychology.

Sample question

Could you answer this question? Below is a typical essay question that could arise on this topic.

| ✱ *Sample question* | *Essay* |

The negative effects of aging are inevitable: you cannot fight nature. Discuss the accuracy of this statement for psychological aspects of aging.

Guidelines on answering this question are included at the end of this chapter, whilst further guidance on tackling other exam questions can be found on the companion website at: **www.pearsoned.co.uk/psychologyexpress**

Emerging adulthood

- It is increasingly recognised that the transition into adulthood is a critical point in the lifespan (Arnett, 2000; 2006).

- Entering adulthood is about much more than physical maturity or reaching a specific chronological age.

- It usually means being independent in psychological and economic terms.

- The point at which a young person enters adulthood will therefore be determined by choices about whether or not to go on to college or university, as well as individual differences in psychological development.

- Cultural expectations and beliefs about adulthood are also going to be important. In developing countries, marriage is often a marker of entry into adulthood and this often occurs much earlier than in Western societies (Arnett, 2000).

- The growing trend for young people delaying their entry into the adult world in Western society has led to the introduction of the term 'emerging adulthood' to describe the period between adolescence and adulthood (Arnett, 2000; 2006).

- This period is usually described as ranging from 18 to 25 years of age and is characterised by exploration and experimentation with identity, lifestyle and career (Arnett, 2006).

- Arnett also describes emerging adults as able to be self-focused because they have few duties or commitments to others (for example, no children or aging parents to look after).

- Emerging adulthood is an age of possibilities, with many young people optimistic about their plans for the future (Arnett, 2006).

- The move from adolescence to adulthood is marked by continuity for most individuals: well-adjusted adolescents continue to be well-adjusted as adults, and troubled adolescents become troubled adults (Schulenberg et al., 2006).

- However, for some people the move to adulthood is less straightforward and the increased responsibility and independence of adulthood proves to be a difficult one to cope with; for others, this shift is a positive one that provides them with the opportunity to turn their lives around and follow a more positive course (Schulenberg & Zarrett, 2006).

- Most young people of this age do not see themselves as fully fledged adults; however, they do not feel like adolescents either (Arnett, 2000).

- Young people see adulthood as a psychological state in which an individual feels able to assume responsibility for their actions and capable of interacting with other adults (especially parents) as equals (Sassler, Ciambrone, & Benway, 2008) and making independent decisions (Shulman & Ben-Artzi, 2003).

- The idea that adolescence can bridge the gap between childhood and adulthood no longer works in modern society, where the timing and sequencing of traditional experiences that represent the process of becoming an adult, such as leaving home, finishing school, starting work and getting married and having children, are more flexible than they used to be (Furstenberg, Kefalas, & Napolitano, 2005).

  - Social norms and expectations in relation to all these processes have changed dramatically since the post-war years. In the UK, for example, there is an expectation that more young people will stay in education for longer and this is encouraged by government policy, which aims to promote post-16 education (DfES, 2007).

- This social change, made in response to economic changes in the nature of available employment, has been influenced by changes in the labour market; increasing technologies have, for example, changed the emphasis in skills needed for jobs in the UK in the twenty-first century (Friedberg, 2008).

- This need for longer education has meant that many young people delay their entry into the economic market, which in turn leads to financial independence being delayed until the early or mid-twenties for many young people today (Cohen & Cashon, 2003).

- This often means that young people are still living in the family home in their early twenties (Heath, 2008) and increased economic dependency on parents is a well-recognised feature of emerging adulthood.

- However, the reason for this dependency is not just financial. A number of demographic factors influence this dependency, including gender and social class.

  - Males are much more likely to be still living at home in their early twenties than females: in the UK in 2006, for example, 58 per cent of young men aged 20–24 years and 39 per cent of young women of the same age were still living with their parents (Heath, 2008).

  - Young people from middle-class families also tend to leave home at a younger age than their peers from working-class families, usually because they are more likely to go to university at the age of 18 years, although many return once they have completed their studies (Ford, Rugg, & Burrows, 2002).

  - Even if they do go to university, students from working-class backgrounds are more likely than their middle-class peers to remain living at home with their parents (Patiniotis & Holdsworth, 2005).

Test your knowledge

10.1 What factors influence when we negotiate the move to adulthood?

10.2 What psychological factors are seen as important for 'being an adult'?

10.3 How do demographic factors affect progression in this period of development?

Answers to these questions can be found on the companion website at: **www.pearsoned.co.uk/psychologyexpress**

Further reading Emerging adulthood

Topic	Key reading
Conceptions of adulthood	Sassler, S., Ciambrone, D., & Benway, G. (2008). Adulthood upon returning to the parental home. *Sociological Forum*, *23*, 670–698.

Biological and physical changes in adulthood

It is easy to imagine that physical changes in adulthood are all about decline rather than development. However, this is not inevitable and when and if deterioration of physical abilities takes place depends on a number of factors other than biological age. These include lifestyle choices and demographic factors such as socio-economic status, job type and gender.

Typical physical changes

- Young adults are generally at the peak of physical fitness.
- However, the aging process has already begun: the body has been aging since birth, but it is not until middle age that we begin to see the effects of this aging.
- Only minor physical changes are seen in the twenties and thirties, but many people begin to notice physical changes in their forties.
- One of the most noticeable effects is a loss of elasticity in the skin, especially in the face. This results in the lines and wrinkles that are seen as one of the first signs of aging.
- Both genders may experience greying of the hair or the hair may thin.
- Weight changes typically seen across the lifespan include weight gain in middle age, followed by weight loss when people reach their sixties (Whitbourne, 2005).
- Aging involves a decline in efficiency in most bodily systems from the twenties onwards.
- Strength and flexibility begin to wane in both genders in middle age (Samson et al., 2000); motor performance slows (Newell, Vaillancourt, & Sosnoff, 2006) and reaction times decrease.
- However, it seems that avoiding a sedentary lifestyle will make such deterioration less marked (Earles, & Salthouse, 1995).
- Both moderate exercise and a healthy diet have been found to protect against stroke, heart disease and late onset diabetes (Yung et al., 2009).
- Women experience the menopause in middle age, with the hormonal changes that result in the loss of the ability to reproduce in middle to late adulthood.
- An increase in the incidence of chronic disease, such as oesteoarthritis, hypertension and heart disease, is also seen in older adults.

Individual differences in aging

- Individual differences in physical functioning increase with age (Harris et al., 1992).
- Measurements such as aerobic capacity, strength and reaction times vary more widely among 70-year-olds than 20-year-olds.

- This is in part due to lifestyle choices noted earlier – for example, physically active older adults are more likely to retain strength (Amara et al., 2003).

- This is perhaps not so surprising, given that muscles atrophy if not used and the heart functions less well if the individual leads a sedentary lifestyle (Rosenbloom & Bahns, 2006).

- Health problems may also contribute to differences in decline. A classic study in the 1960s showed how deterioration in physical and psychological functioning in men aged 65–91 was linked to subclinical disease (Birren et al., 1963).

- Socio-economic status is reported to make a difference to health and disability. Studies using self-reported measures of health demonstrate greater problems among older people in disadvantaged socio-economic groups (Marmot et al., 2001). This probably demonstrates the advantages of having greater material resources and opportunities to promote health and lifestyle.

Key term

Subclinical disease: when a person has an illness that demonstrates no recognisable clinical signs or symptoms, they are said to have subclinical disease. This may be because the disease is in a very mild form or because it is at an early stage of development.

Psychological impact of physical aging

- There are many negative stereotypes associated with aging in our society. 'Old' is often associated with unattractive, meaning that adults of retirement age may see themselves as 'past it' or a drain on society.

- There is an increasing drive to maintain physical looks through interventions such as cosmetic surgery (Rohrich, 2000), although as Grossbart and Sarwer (2003) note, it is likely that cosmetic surgery patients are looking for more than changes in their physical appearance, such as improvements in body satisfaction, self-esteem or quality of life.

- There is evidence that cultural attitudes towards the physical changes of aging can influence the way in which these are experienced. For example, menopause is experienced by women in all societies, but there are differences in how this is experienced.

  - Hot flushes are more likely to be reported and viewed as a negative experience in Western cultures, where the menopause is viewed as a loss, than in cultures where menopause represents a healthy, positive life stage (Flint, 1982; Gold et al., 2000; McMaster, Pitts, & Poyah, 1997).

  - Attitudes towards the menopause help to explain individual differences in the experience of menopause in Western society. While some view this as a medical condition to be treated by medication, others see it as a normal transition (Alder & Ross, 2000).

- The majority of people have some type of chronic physical health problem by the time they reach 65, but, there is enormous variability in terms of the impact that such health problems have on individual functioning. This is thought to be affected by:
  - how long the individual has had a health problem
  - illness severity and experience of pain
  - psychological factors such as personality and attitude, which may mediate the impact of these illnesses on feelings of well-being
  - optimistic individuals (those with a positive outlook on life) have been found to live longer (Snowdon, 2002).

Relationships and psychological adjustment to physical health

- In early adulthood, an individual is concerned with developing the ability to share intimacy, seeking to form relationships and find intimate love.
- The trend towards greater intimacy with the opposite sex that began in adolescence continues in early adulthood (Reis et al., 1993).
- Long-term relationships are formed and often marriage (or cohabitation) and children result.
- Young adults tend to have more friends than middle-aged or older adults and a number of reasons for this have been suggested.
  - As adults marry, have children and take on increasing responsibilities in other areas of life, so their social networks shrink (Fischer et al., 1989).
  - According to socio-emotional selectivity theory, the realisation that life is decreasing prompts adults to narrow their choice of social partners to those who bring most emotional pleasure, usually family and close friends (Carstensten, 1992).
- However, friendships do remain important across the lifespan, even if greater selectivity is shown and the quality of friendships is closely related to well-being in adulthood (Pinquart & Sorensen, 2000).
- The importance of a supportive social network for physical as well as psychological health has been noted (Charles & Mavandadi, 2004).
- Evidence suggests having a small, harmonious group of friends is related to better cardiovascular, endocrine and immune systems.
  - Having good friends and happy family relationships keeps blood pressure in the normal range and improves the body's ability to deal with stress (Uchino, Cacioppo, & Kiecolt-Glaser, 1996).
  - This is thought to be because emotional and social functioning are closely linked even in infancy and the two are co-dependent (Charles & Mavandadi, 2004).

- Social relationships affect health and well-being through the effects they have on emotional regulation.
  - Negative features, such as separation from caregivers, abuse and emotional deprivation, raise stress levels in infants, which disrupts neural development, making these individuals more susceptible to stress in later life (Gunnar & Quevedo, 2007).
  - Warm, responsive parenting helps infants cope with stressful events and, similarly, close relations in later life help people keep their emotions in check and avoid stress-related illness (Charles & Mavandadi, 2004).

Test your knowledge

10.4 How might psychological and social factors affect physical aging?

10.5 What impact do the physical changes associated with aging have on our psychological well-being?

Answers to these questions can be found on the companion website at:
www.pearsoned.co.uk/psychologyexpress

Further reading Biological and physical changes in adulthood

Topic	Key reading
Psychological impact of physical aging	Netz, Y. Wu, M., Becker, B. J., & Tenenbaum, G. (2005). Physical activity and psychological well-being in advanced age: A meta-analysis of intervention studies. *Psychology and Aging, 20*, 272–284.

Cognitive changes in adulthood

Post-formal thinking

- Piaget's theory of cognitive development focused very clearly on the years of childhood and adolescence. However, we now recognise that cognitive development goes beyond this and a fourth stage of cognitive development called *post-formal thought* has been suggested by a number of theorists (for example, Commons, Richards & Armon, 1984; Sinnott, 1994; Yan & Arlin, 1995).
- This stage has been suggested to be typified by relativistic thinking.
  - Perry (1970) studied cognitive growth in college students and found there was a shift from the initial assumption when entering college that there was an absolute truth to be found to a gradual recognition that questions might have many answers.
  - This led to the confusion of not knowing which was the 'right answer'.

- Eventually, however, many understood that some opinions are better supported than others and were able to commit one position by choosing between the relative perspectives.
- This move from absolutist to relativist thinking is thought to result in the use of a greater variety of thinking styles (Zhang, 2002).
- It is suggested that advanced thinkers relish the challenge of finding paradoxes and inconsistencies in ideas in order to attempt to reconcile them (Basseches, 1984).
- However, the extent to which this is a developmental sequence is subject to debate as this type of thinking has only been demonstrated in a minority of adults, particularly those who have experienced higher education, suggesting an important role for experience in developing adult thinking skills (Sinnott, 1996).
- Alternatively, it may be that these studies are only demonstrating one type of advanced thinking, linked to a particular set of experiences.
  - Adults have been shown to function cognitively at their highest in areas in which they have developed some expertise (Byrnes, 1996).
  - The 'expert' not only knows and remembers more about their specialist area but is also a more effective and efficient thinker (Proffitt, Coley, & Medin, 2000).
  - It may therefore be that a university education simply trains graduates to be experts in relativistic thinking.

Key term

Relativistic thinking: in this way of thinking, it is recognised that knowledge depends upon the subjective perspective of each individual and there is therefore no absolute truth: problems can be viewed in different ways and there may be more than one solution to a problem. Knowledge is relative and situational. Learners at this stage therefore critically reflect on multiple perspectives and determine the most suitable answer depending on the situation.

CRITICAL FOCUS

Post-formal thought

Read the paper by Kitchener, Lynch, Fischer, and Wood, (1993)

(available online at: https://gseweb.harvard.edu/~ddl/articlesCopy/Kitchener-etal1993DevRangeReflectJudgem.pdf).

Kitchener and colleagues, like many other theorists working in this area, suggest that an age-related trend can be seen in the development of reflective judgement, a skill thought to be linked to relativistic thinking. However, as Kitchener notes, in this study, age may in fact be confounded by experience. Thus, while this paper provides some evidence for a developmental progression in reflective judgement and relativistic thinking, it cannot say definitively what causes these developmental trends. So, although these cognitive changes may be purely age related, there are other factors that Kitchener and colleagues suggest may influence this change in thinking. They note specifically that education may account for the differences they found as the older participants were at college and the younger ones were not.

✳ Sample question   *Information provider*

Design a study to investigate the idea of post-formal operational thinking. What are the key issues you will test? State the research design and methods you will use, providing a justification for the approach chosen. Explain where you will get participants from and how they will be chosen, giving the reason for your choice.

Aging and cognitive skills

- There is some evidence to support the suggestion that mental abilities decline with age. Elderly adults have been found to perform worse than younger adults on Piagetian cognitive tasks, for example (Blackburn & Papalia, 1992).

- However, these studies have been cross-sectional in design and it is therefore suggested that this difference is actually caused by a cohort effect, brought about because the older adults who participated in these studies generally had less formal schooling than most younger adults today.

- Other studies that have taken a longitudinal approach have found cognitive skills either stay stable or improve over time (Salthouse, 2009).

- This is also supported by studies that have shown older adults in college perform as well as their younger classmates on cognitive tests (Blackburn, 1985).

- However, it has been argued that longitudinal studies also suffer from a methodological problem: practice effects (Salthouse, 2009).

- This would mean that the age trends seen in longitudinal comparisons are misleading: we do not actually get better at cognitive tasks as we age, but because of learning and experience (Salthouse, 2009).

- An alternative interpretation of this idea is that this practice might provide a protective role for cognitive functioning. Cognitive training studies, for example, have shown that in many cases cognitive decline in older people can be reversed (Blaskewicz Boron, et al., 2007).

- Bielak (2010) calls this the 'use it or lose it' hypothesis of cognitive aging.

- Evidence also suggests that different factors affect age-related changes in functioning.

  - Functioning based on accumulated knowledge, such as performance on tests of vocabulary or general information (known as crystallised abilities) are consistently found to increase until at least age 60 (Salthouse, 2009).

  - Decline is less likely in the absence of cardiovascular and other chronic diseases (Wendell et al., 2009).

  - Higher socio-economic status is linked to slower decline (Fotenos et al., 2008).

  - Involvement in a complex and intellectually stimulating environment promotes good functioning (Valenzuela, Breakspear, & Sachdev, 2007).

- Evidence from the British cohort study has shown that maintaining an active lifestyle can help to slow the process of cognitive decline linked to aging (Richards, Hardy, & Wadsworth, 2003).

Language and memory

- Research on language development tends to focus on the changes that take place in infancy and childhood, with the belief that in adulthood language skills are maintained (Thornton & Light, 2006).

- However, there is evidence that language development continues even into late adulthood: vocabulary increases (Willis & Schaie, 2005) and older adults often maintain or even improve their knowledge of words and what they mean (Burke & Shafto, 2004).

- However, in late adulthood some decline in language abilities may appear that could link to physiological changes which take place in old age, such as hearing difficulties leading to problems in distinguishing speech sounds (Gordon-Salant et al., 2006).

- Loss of memory skills may also result in problems of word retrieval – for example, the tip-of-the-tongue phenomenon that is typified by feeling confident a word is known but just out of reach (Thornton & Light, 2006).

- This decline is often compensated for by using very familiar words and much shorter sentences (Burke & Shafto, 2006).

- It may also explain the greater reliance on filled pauses, which is often seen in older adults (for example, saying 'um' or 'er'), and may provide a means of 'buying time' to retrieve the correct word.

- The factors responsible for declining language skills in older people are likely to be general cognitive-processing skills rather than language-specific ones (Obler, 2005).

- These include the decrease in information-processing speed and the decline in working memory, which is often seen as people age (Waters & Caplan, 2005).

CRITICAL FOCUS

Practice effects

Practice effects occur when a participant in a study is able to perform a task and then perform it again at some later time. This can mean that they become better at performing the task. According to Salthouse, the very fact that an individual has already been tested on a cognitive task could change their performance the next time they are tested – they have learnt how to do the task and so will find it easier and perform better. According to Salthouse this makes cross-sectional comparisons better measures of age-related change than longitudinal studies, because they do not involve testing

▶

the same individuals again. This demonstrates the way in which the method chosen by a researcher can influence the outcomes of a study. You may remember from Chapter 1 that there is often more than one way of designing a study and there is rarely a 'right' way. Usually a researcher has to decide which method will give the best answer to a question by considering what variables are most important to control for and the margin of error they are prepared to accept. Which approach do you think is best in this case? Is it better to risk the influence of practice by carrying out a longitudinal study in which the same people repeat the same measures over time? The advantage of this, of course, is that participants act as their own control and any between-subject external factors such as differences in gender, socio-economic and educational experience are eliminated. Alternatively, is it more important to ensure that the effects of practice are controlled by using a cross-sectional design that holds the possibility of cohort effects?

Aging and the brain

- Between the ages of 20 and 90 years of age the brain shrinks, losing between 5 and 10 per cent of its weight (Enzinger et al., 2005).
- A decrease in volume has also been observed.
  - The volume of the brains of older adults is around 15 per cent less than that of younger adults (Shan et al., 2005).
  - Brain volume reduces by 0.22 per cent every year between the ages of 20 and 65 years, then by 0.40 per cent per year from 65 to 80 years of age (Fotenos et al., 2008).
  - This is thought to be because of a combination of loss of dendrites, damage to myelin and the death of brain cells.
- Some areas of the brain shrink more than others as we age. The prefrontal cortex is one area that reduces in size and this has been linked to a decrease in cognitive function such as working memory (Grady et al., 2006).
- Recent evidence has supported the idea that it is the structural changes in the brain which cause the loss of functioning (Fan et al., 2008).
- However, we do not really know whether brain shrinkage leads to cognitive decline or vice versa and it is possible this cause and effect model is too simplistic as it fails to consider a number of environmental factors that may influence the impact of any biologically based changes in brain structure.
  - Fotenos et al., (2008) found a complex relationship between socio-economic status, structural changes in the brain and cognitive decline.
  - They carried out a large-scale neuroimaging study in which adults aged between 20 and 80 years of age underwent MRI scans and cognitive testing at the start of the study, then were retested and scanned 3 years later.
  - They found that in older adults with no cognitive decline, those of higher socio-economic status showed more loss of brain volume when compared to individuals of lower socio-economic status.

- This does not mean that high socio-economic status is related to greater loss of brain volume, but, rather, older adults from higher socio-economic groups respond differently to the same loss of brain volume than individuals from lower socio-economic backgrounds.
- Normally it is expected that high levels of loss of volume are linked to serious functional problems, such as those associated with dementia, which is the relationship seen in individuals of low to moderate socio-econiomic status.
- However, in individuals of higher socio-economic status, the same structural decline seems to be better tolerated – that is, it does not affect functioning.
- It has therefore been concluded that higher socio-economic status protects against cognitive decline. It is thought that one of the protective factors is a higher level of education.

Dementia

- The most common form of dementia, accounting for between 50 and 70 per cent of all dementia, is Alzheimer's disease.
- Alzheimer's is progressive, meaning that it involves a gradual decline in skills. It is also irreversible.
- The disease is characterised by gradual deterioration in memory, reasoning, language and, eventually, physical functioning.
- Most people with Alzheimer's are 65 and older, making it predominantly a disease of old age.
- However, up to 5 per cent of people with the disease have what is known as early onset Alzheimer's. This form of the disease often appears when someone is in their forties or fifties.
- Many of the risk factors for Alzheimer's are ones we cannot change, such as age and genetics.
- However, it is now commonly believed that Alzheimer's disease occurs as a result of complex interactions between genes and other risk factors such as diet and lifestyle choices.
- This is an example of the diathesis-stress model (see Chapter 2).
- This means that in individuals with the genetic potential for Alzheimer's disease, certain environmental factors such as lifestyle choices may trigger Alzheimer's.
- Without those triggers the individual might not develop dementia.
- For example, it has been found that there is a link between obesity and Alzheimer's disease. Kivipelto et al. (2005) found obesity in middle age to be associated with an increased risk of dementia and Alzheimer's disease later in life.
- Other studies have suggested that health problems in middle age, such as high blood pressure and Type 2 diabetes, also increase the risk for dementia, including Alzheimer's disease.

- Obesity, high blood pressure and diabetes are all health problems that can affect the heart and blood vessels and it is thought that if the vessels in the brain are affected, this can result in dementia.

- It has also been found that older adults with Alzheimer's disease are more likely to have heart disease than individuals without Alzheimer's (Hayden et al., 2006).

- It therefore makes sense that avoiding the risk factors associated with heart disease, such as smoking, obesity and a sedentary lifestyle, might also protect against dementia.

Key term

Dementia: this is an umbrella term used to refer to any brain disorder in which the main symptoms include deterioration of mental functioning. Individuals with dementia often lose the ability to look after themselves. They may also no longer recognise familiar places or people – including close family members such as their children or a spouse (Clark, 2006).

Test your knowledge

10.6 How might physical health influence cognitive decline?

10.7 Why might socio-economic status be a protective factor in cognitive aging?

10.8 What are the problems associated with cross-sectional and longitudinal studies of aging?

Answers to these questions can be found on the companion website at:
www.pearsoned.co.uk/psychologyexpress

Further reading Cognitive skills and aging

Topic	Key reading
Post-formal thought	Kitchener, K. S., Lynch, C. L., Fischer, K. W., & Wood, P. K. (1993). Developmental range of reflective judgement: The effect of contextual support and practice on developmental stage. *Developmental Psychology, 29*(5), 893–906. Available online at: https://gseweb.harvard.edu/ddl/articlesCopy/Kitchener-etal1993DevRangeReflectJudgem.pdf
'Use it or lose it' hypothesis	Bielak, A. M. (2010). How can we not 'lose it' if we still don't understand how to 'use it'? Unanswered questions about the influence of activity participation on cognitive performance in older age: A mini-review. *Gerontology, 56*(6), 507–519.
Study design	Salthouse, T. A. (2009). When does age-related cognitive decline begin? *Neurobiology of Aging, 30*, 507–514.

Psychosocial development

Levinson's four seasons and the crisis of midlife

According to Levinson (1986; 1996), the lifespan can be divided into four seasons: pre-adulthood, early adulthood, middle adulthood and late adulthood (see Table 10.1).

- Each season or era lasts 20–25 years and has a distinct character.
- The transition between eras requires a basic change in the character of a person's life, which may take between three and six years to complete.
- Within the broad eras are periods of development, each of which is characterised by a set of tasks – for example, in the early adult transition period, the two primary tasks are to move out of the pre-adult world and to make a preliminary step into the adult world.
- A major theme throughout the various periods is the existence of 'the dream' – a vision of life's goals.
- Levinson proposed that adults go through a repeated process of building a life structure and assessing and altering it during transition periods.
- For Levinson, the transition from age 40 to 45 is an especially significant time of life – a time of midlife crisis when men and women question their entire life structure, raising unsettling questions about where they have been and where they are heading.
- Levinson based his theory on a series of in-depth interviews and characterised 80 per cent of the men he studied as experiencing intense inner struggles and disturbing realisations in their early forties; women, however, experience significant crisis during the transition at age 30, as well as in the transition to middle age.
- This theory is important because of the clear focus on adult development. Along with Erikson, Levinson is perhaps the major theorist of this time period. To what extent, however, is his image of midlife crisis supported by the evidence?

There is support for Levinson's idea that early adulthood is the time we explore vocational possibilities.

- The evidence supports a process of making tentative commitments and revising them as necessary before establishing yourself in what you hope will be a suitable occupation (Super, Savickas, & Super, 1996).
- More than twice as many tentative and exploratory vocational decisions are seen at age 21 than at age 36, and this is true for both men (Philips, 1982) and women (Jenkins, 1989).
- Careers tend to peak during the forties (Simonton, 1990), when there is a tendency for adults to define themselves in terms of their work.

Table 10.1 Levinson's stages of development

Stage	Age	Season	Characteristics
Pre-adulthood	0–17	Spring	Childhood and adolescence. During this time one usually lives with the family, which provides protection, socialisation and support of growth
Early adult transition	17–21		Period of questioning. Young people make the transition from adolescence to early adulthood and explore the possibilities for an adult identity. They form 'the dream' – a vision of their life goals
Entering the adult world	22–28	Summer	Adults build their first life structure, often by making and testing a career choice and by getting married/ forming a stable relationship. They work to succeed, find a supportive partner and/or mentor and do not question their lives much
Age 30 transition	28–33		Period of questioning. Adults ask whether their life choices and relationships are what they want. If not they may make small adjustments in their life structures or plan major changes such as a career change, divorce or return to education
Settling down	33–40		This is time for building and living a new and often different life and for 'making it' or realising 'the dream'. An adult may outgrow their need for a mentor and become their own person. Adults at this stage tend to be ambitious, task-orientated and unreflective
Midlife transition	40–45	Autumn	This is a major period of questioning. Successful adults ask whether the dreams they formulated as young adults were worth achieving. If they have not achieved their dreams they face the reality that they may never achieve them and may again make major changes in their life structure. They terminate early adulthood and initiate middle adulthood
Entering middle adulthood	45–50		Although adults' physical and mental powers are somewhat diminished after 40, they are normally still ample for 'an active, full life' throughout middle adulthood. If conditions for development are reasonably favourable, middle adulthood can be an era of personal fulfilment and social contribution. This means, that adults have to come to terms with the three major developmental tasks of the midlife transition: (1) reviewing their lives in early adulthood and reappraising what they have done with it; (2) modifying the negative elements of the present structure and testing new choices; (3) dealing with the polarities in their lives.
Age 50 transition	50–55		A period of questioning. A crisis is possible, especially if none occurred during the midlife transition

Table 10.1 Continued

Stage	Age	Season	Characteristics
Culmination of middle adulthood	55–60	Autumn	A satisfying era (similar to the earlier settling down stage) if adults have adjusted to role changes
Late adult transition	60–65	Winter	Time to prepare for retirement and coming physical decline, making this a major turning point
Late adulthood	65–?		Adults now create a new life structure for retirement and aging

- However, factors such as personality and gender seem to mediate career success. Conscientiousness, extraversion and emotional stability are associated with job performance (Ozer & Benet-Martinez, 2006) and, even at the start of the twenty-first century, many women still subordinate career goals to family goals (Kirchmeyer, 2006).

There is much less evidence to support Levinson's suggestion of a midlife crisis.

- Many studies support the idea that midlife is a time of self-reflection and even a time when goals may change (Hermans & Oles, 1999).

- However, the image of the adult experiencing a crisis during midlife remains largely unsubstantiated (Hedlund & Ebersole, 1983).

- As they age, many people show increased satisfaction with their jobs, are more involved in their work and less interested in seeking out new jobs (Rhodes, 1983).

- The evidence suggests that middle life may well be challenging, but only a vulnerable few will experience this as a crisis (Freund & Ritter, 2009).

KEY STUDY

Levinson with Darrow, Klein, Levinson and Mckee (1978). *The season's of a man's Life* and Levinson with Levinson (1996). *The seasons of a woman's life*

Levinson based his theory of adult development on a series of in-depth interviews with 40 adult males between 35 and 45 years of age at the time the interviews were carried out during the late 1960s (Levinson, et al., 1978). He was motivated to carry out this study because he wanted to try and make sense of his own midlife transition. A clinical psychologist trained in psychoanalysis, Levinson called the interviews 'biographical', explaining to participants that the primary task was to construct the story of a man's life. The aim was to cover the entire life sequence from childhood to the present time in each person's life. Through his study Levinson claims to have discovered that the lifecycle evolves through a sequence that may be expressed in terms of age, eras and seasons of life, as described earlier in this chapter. The men that Levinson interviewed worked as either as biology professors, novelists, business executives or industrial labourers. The biographical interviews lasted one or two hours and from six to ten interviews were carried out with each participant. The questions asked focused on the individual's accounts of their own experiences in their post-adolescent years, focusing on topics such as the men's background (education, income, etc.) and beliefs about issues such as religion and politics. The men were also asked about major events or turning points in their lives. Over half the men Levinson spoke to described midlife as the last chance to reach their personal goals. These goals were linked to key events such as reaching a particular level of income or career point such as supervisor or full professor. These men described their lives as stressful but manageable. The remaining men felt negatively about their lives because they were in a dead end or pointless job. Some of them felt this way despite a good income. A very small number of these men had decided to do something about this 'flawed life structure' and had started to rebuild their lives/careers.

In the 1980s Levinson interviewed 45 women of the same age (Levinson with Levinson with Levinson, 1996). The sample comprised equal numbers of women who were either homemakers, college instructors or businesswomen. He found that in general women go through the same type of lifecycles that men do. However, they were less likely to enter adulthood with specific goals and, as a result, were less likely to define success in terms of key career events. Rather than focusing on external events, women usually sought changes in personal identity in midlife. For example, they might become more independent or self-reliant in middle age. Often such changes were closely linked to the family lifecycle. It is notable that the homemakers found traditional patterns difficult to sustain and often paid a big price in restrictions on self-development; career women experienced considerable stress and difficulty in breaking down barriers in formerly 'male' occupations and in pushing for a more equitable division of housework.

Thus, according to Levinson, an individual's life structure is shaped by the social and physical environment. Many individuals' life structures primarily involve family and work, although other variables such as religion, race and economic status may also be important.

Levinson, D. J., with Darrow C. N., Klein, E. B., Levinson, M. H., & Mckee, B. (1978). *The seasons of a man's life*. New York: Ballantine Books and Levinson, D. J., with Levinson, D. J. (1996). *The seasons of a woman's life*. New York: Knopf

Test your knowledge

10.9 What are the main tasks of Levison's four seasons of aging?

10.10 What are the pros and cons of the evidence on which Levinson based his idea of a midlife crisis?

Answers to these questions can be found on the companion website at:
www.pearsoned.co.uk/psychologyexpress

? Sample question   Problem-based learning

Read the following scenario.

Annabel, a close friend, is teetering on the verge of a midlife crisis. There are only six months left until her fortieth birthday and she's not happy at waving goodbye to her thirties. Your friend turns uncharacteristically quiet when the subject turns to her milestone birthday. She has told you that she is really dreading this birthday and her fear is getting worse as the big day ▶

draws closer. On deeper probing you find out that she feels she has not really achieved anything worthwhile in her life and is starting to feel resentful about her own situation. A mother of three children, she has devoted the past ten years to bringing up her family and supporting her husband as he climbs the career ladder. Annabel once had her own promising career in marketing, but didn't feel she could balance the demands of full-time work and having a young family. While she loves her children dearly and doesn't regret the time spent with them, she feels that her own life has been on hold and as she reaches her fortieth birthday she is starting to wonder if she has left it too late to make her mark on the commercial world. She is confused and uncertain about what to do next. Is it too late for her to go back to marketing, given her time out of the workplace? Should she try to develop a new career or should she just accept her status as 'homemaker' – after all, her husband has a secure, well-paid job so she has no financial reason to work. Annabel admits that in many ways she is very lucky: the family live in a five-bedroom house in a pleasant part of town, the children are in good schools, everyone is healthy and happy and she has a good relationship with her husband. Yet she can't quite get rid of the nagging feeling that there should be more to life.

Can you help this friend improve her well-being? What advice might you give and what practical solutions can you devise?

? *Sample question*   *Essay*

To what extent does the evidence support the idea that the midlife crisis is an inevitable stage of adulthood?

Further reading **Psychosocial development**

Topic	*Key reading*
Midlife crisis	Freund, A. M. & Ritter, J. O. (2009). Midlife crisis: A debate. *Gerontology*, *55*(5), 582–591.

Chapter summary – pulling it all together

→ Can you tick all the points from the revision checklist at the beginning of this chapter?

→ Attempt the sample question from the beginning of this chapter using the answer guidelines, opposite.

→ Go to the companion website at www.pearsoned.co.uk/psychologyexpress to access more revision support online, including interactive quizzes, flashcards, You be the marker exercises as well as answer guidance for the Test your knowledge and Sample questions from this chapter.

Answer guidelines

 Sample question **Essay**

The negative effects of aging are inevitable: you cannot fight nature. Discuss the accuracy of this statement for psychological aspects of aging.

Approaching the question

Your answer should aim to provide a detailed evaluation of the possible effects of biological aging on cognitive and psychosocial functioning. You will need to consider the impact of the environment and individual experiences as well as biological factors.

Important points to include

- This is essentially a question about the roles of nature and nurture and how they affect development. You should therefore start by outlining this age-old controversy, showing how it is relevant to the topic of aging. You might want to explain that it is generally accepted today both nature and nurture play a part in development; the question is now about the relative contributions of each.
- You now need to consider the evidence surrounding a range of cognitive and psychosocial functions in adulthood such as:
  - post-formal thinking
  - crystallised abilities
  - language
  - dementia
  - relationships.
- For each topic you choose, remember to consider both biological and environmental explanations.

Make your answer stand out

While this can easily be answered by taking a 'compare and contrast' approach to the question, a good answer will go beyond this. You should remember to take a critical stance, evaluating the methodological approaches of any research studies cited. Try to link the different aspects of development, including physical, cognitive, social and emotional, to show how each influences the other. Try to use what you have learnt about other periods of development to inform your thinking here. For example, it is generally accepted that cognitive skills are socially situated and experience helps determine a child's ability to perform certain tasks. Why, therefore, should development progress any differently in adulthood? Making these links and applying the principles learnt elsewhere shows synthesis of knowledge and will make your answer stand out.

Explore the accompanying website at www.pearsoned.co.uk/psychologyexpress

→ Prepare more effectively for exams and assignments using the answer guidelines for questions from this chapter.

→ Test your knowledge using multiple choice questions and flashcards.

→ Improve your essay skills by exploring the You be the marker exercises.

Notes

11

Death, dying and bereavement

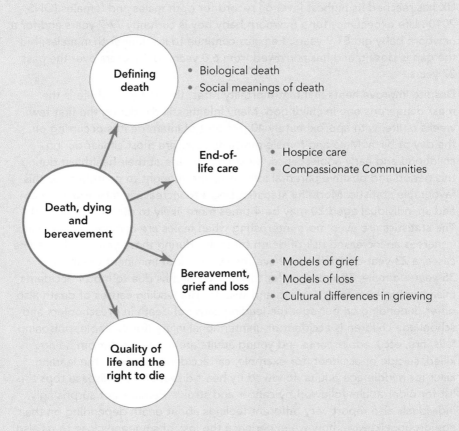

- Defining death
  - Biological death
  - Social meanings of death

- End-of-life care
  - Hospice care
  - Compassionate Communities

- Death, dying and bereavement

- Bereavement, grief and loss
  - Models of grief
  - Models of loss
  - Cultural differences in grieving

- Quality of life and the right to die

A printable version of this topic map is available from
www.pearsoned.co.uk/psychologyexpress

Introduction

The final stage of the lifespan is death. As famously noted by Benjamin Franklin, death is one of life's certainties. However, there is much confusion in our society about when life begins and when it ends: on the one hand proponents and opponents of abortion argue about when life actually begins; on the other there are arguments about whether a person in an irreversible coma is truly alive or whether a terminally ill patient in agonising pain should be kept alive or allowed to die naturally.

Death can come at any time in the lifecycle, although we tend to believe that death in old age is the most natural. While life expectancy has increased over time, the greatest increase is in survival at birth. Life expectancy at birth in the UK has reached its highest level on record for both males and females (ONS, 2010). Life expectancy for a newborn baby boy is currently 77.7 years and for a newborn baby girl 81.9 years. Females continue to live longer than males, but the gap is closing and has narrowed from 6.0 years to 4.2 years over the past 27 years.

Despite improvements in infant mortality rates, the first year of life is the most dangerous one in childhood. Many infants still die during the first few weeks of life, with approximately 40 per cent of infant deaths occurring on the day of birth. Male and female mortality rates are most similar during childhood and early adolescence. Most children are at their healthiest during this period and positive parental influences are thought to contribute to this favourable statistic. Mortality statistics begin to increase in late adolescence and an individual aged 20 may be 4 times more likely to die than at age 10. The statistics are even more interesting when males are compared to females – there is an increased risk of death for males during these years and, in some cases, a 23-year-old male may have the same risk of imminent death as a 35-year-old male. The reasons for this include deaths due to motor accidents, misadventure due to risk-taking and suicide. The leading causes of death also differ depending on our age: the leading cause of death in preschoolers and school-age children is accident or unintentional injury (for example, poisoning, falls, fire, etc.); adolescents and young adults are more at risk from being killed, suicide or accident (for example, car accident); cancer is the leading killer for middle-age adults, followed by heart disease; heart disease tops the list for older adults followed by cancer and stroke. Perhaps not surprisingly, individuals also report very different feelings about death depending on their age group. Likewise, how we experience the loss of someone close to us also differs depending on our age and developmental stage.

> ### → *Revision checklist*
>
> *Essential points to revise are:*
> - ❑ Biological and social definitions of death
> - ❑ Factors that impact on feelings of grief and loss
> - ❑ Models of end-of-life care
> - ❑ Ethical issues concerning quality of life and the right to die

Assessment advice

- As with prenatal development and birth, it is easy to see death and dying as very biological processes. However, you are studying psychology, not medicine, and it is therefore important to focus your answer on the wider issues related to bereavement and loss.

- As psychologists we are interested in the biological definition of death, but primarily because of the social impact that such definitions will have. It is important to remember that the social meaning people attach to death is more important to psychologists than biological definitions since these emotional beliefs will impact on how people negotiate bereavement and loss.

- Whatever kind of assessment you do, try to remember there will many factors that affect how someone copes with death and dying. The obvious one from a developmental perspective is age and developmental level. Thus our understanding of death is affected by cognitive abilities. However, as a good student you will know by now, nothing is that simple. How might experiences, social contexts and cultural norms also affect how death impacts on us? As with other areas you have studied, remember to take a critical approach and to take all aspects of development into consideration from cognitive through to social.

- Finally, remember that although death is the end of the lifespan for each and every one of us, death affects not only the dying but also those left behind. What are the impacts on development for individuals who experience death of a loved one? Is there a critical age at which loss might impact on developmental processes or are individual factors such as social support more important? Good assessment answers will try to take account of many factors and make links between the different areas of psychology.

Sample question

Could you answer this question? Overleaf is a typical essay question that could arise on this topic.

Sample question   *Essay*

Evaluate the importance of social, cultural and developmental influences on our beliefs about death, dying and bereavement.

Guidelines on answering this question are included at the end of this chapter, whilst further guidance on tackling other exam questions can be found on the companion website at: **www.pearsoned.co.uk/psychologyexpress**

Defining death

Biological death

- Death is hard to define as it is not a single event but a process.
- Different body systems die at different rates.
- Death was once defined as having no heartbeat/pulse or no longer breathing.
- However, some individuals who lack a pulse or are not breathing can now be revived before their brains cease to function and kept alive by artificial life support systems.
- The UK, unlike many other countries, does not have a legal definition of death. Guidelines for the diagnosis and confirmation of death are purely medical and are provided by the Academy of Medical Royal Colleges (AMRC).
- Medical guidelines are mainly concerned with confirmation of death in hospital and in circumstances where the diagnosis of death may be more difficult (patients on ventilators, for example).
- Medical guidelines rely on a diagnosis of brain death.
- However, this is not based on whether or not the heart is still beating and, while in most cases this function will cease once withdrawal of life support systems occurs, many people still see a beating heart as indicative of life.
- It has therefore been argued that these decisions should include a more social element in order to ease the burden on the family of the dying (Kellehear & O'Connor, 2008).

Social meanings of death

- As Kellehear has noted, death is a psychological and social as well as a biological process.
- The social meaning attached to death has changed across the course of history (Aries, 1981). In contrast to the middle ages, when individuals were

encouraged to recognise their own mortality and prepare for death with dignity, Western society today engages in a denial of death.

- Death has been removed from the home in the UK and familiarity with death has decreased considerably since the 1900s, when most people died in their own homes (Thorpe, 1993).

- Some 200 years ago, the death rate was such that half of all children died before the age of 10 years and one parent usually died before a child grew up. Nowadays, many people do not experience the death of someone close to them until they are well into midlife (Department of Health, 2008).

- It is perhaps not so surprising, therefore, that, as a society, death and dying are subjects not openly discussed (Kellehear, 2005).

- Surveys have shown that, given the opportunity and support, most people would prefer to die at home, yet in practice only a minority are able to do so (Department of Health, 2008): many people (58 per cent) die in acute hospital settings, which are often not their preferred place of care.

- Much of the responsibility for end-of-life care is given over to hospice and palliative care services (Kellehear, 2005).

- According to Kellehear (2005), this type of care emphasises the person as an individual and therefore the focus is placed on providing services to them as patients within these institutions or as patients at home.

Key term

Brain death: this medical definition of death focuses primarily on irreversible brain stem damage and notes that in the absence of neurological functioning 'the patient is dead even though respiration and circulation can be artificially maintained successfully for a limited period of time' (AMRC, 2008: 13). A diagnosis of brain death is made using factors such as fixed and dilated pupils, lack of eye movement and the absence of respiratory reflexes. This definition is important because it has been argued that the current emphasis on brain death is at least in part driven by the need to harvest (healthy) organs for transplant. Because it is clinically based, this definition takes no account of the emotional and social aspects of death, treating it as a purely biological phenomenon. From a psychological perspective this has implications for the bereaved family.

Test your knowledge

11.1 What is the medical definition of death in the UK?

11.2 How does this differ from how most of us perceive death?

11.3 How have the experiences of death and dying changed over time?

Answers to these questions can be found on the companion website at:
www.pearsoned.co.uk/psychologyexpress

Further reading End-of-life care	
Topic	Key reading
Medical definitions of death	Seale, C. (2009). End-of-life decisions in the UK involving medical practitioners. *Palliative Medicine, 23*(6), 198–204. Available online at: www.eutanasia.ws/hemeroteca/t301.pdf

End-of-life care

Hospice care

The term 'hospice' is rooted in the idea of offering 'hospitality', such as shelter and a place to rest, to sick and weary travellers. The term was originally applied to specialised care for dying patients in 1967 by Dame Cicely Saunders at St Christopher's Hospice in London. There are many positive aspects to the hospice movement. The philosophy is one of caring rather than curing and the aim of this care is to help people find meaning in death (Clarke, 2002). This is just one difference between hospice and hospital care. Other features of hospice care include:

- treating the patient, not the disease
- focusing on quality, rather than quantity, of life
- however, this does not mean that there is ever any intention to shorten life; euthanasia is not promoted by the hospice movement
- pain control emphasis on, ensuring prevention and relief of symptoms
- hospice staff providing direct care to the patient or teaching the family to care for the patient between visits if care is provided in the patient's home
- social issues, such as ensuring that the patient designates a surrogate decision-maker and makes advance plans, plus hospice staff preparing patient and family for the time near death (Lynn, 2001)
- the individual and their family, not the experts, deciding what support they need
- care being kept as 'normal' as possible (preferably in the patient's own home)
- support being provided for family members as they go through the grieving process
- bereavement counselling being provided before as well as after death.

Research suggests that the benefits of hospice care include less pain at the end of life, fewer medical interventions and care more aligned to individual emotional needs (Seale, 1991). There also appear to be benefits for the family, including better well-being and fewer symptoms of grief (Ragow-O'Brien et al., 2000).

Compassionate Communities

Kellehear (2005) argues that a person must be seen not just as an individual but also as a social being, intricately connected to a community of friends, family and co-workers. This philosophy underpins the health promoting palliative care movement, which emphasises community-based care for people with life-threatening illnesses (Mitchell, 2008). This movement has already had some success in Australia where it originated and the approach is currently being explored in some regions of the UK under the name 'Compassionate Communities'.

- Compassionate Communities is a movement within the UK that believes the special needs of those living with life-threatening illness and those living with loss should be met through a supportive community rather than through the provision of centralised services.
- Individuals within a community are provided with an opportunity to work together alongside healthcare professionals.
- According to Kellehear (2005), the aim is to:
  - create more unity within the community
  - empower the community to support themselves using the resources available to them
  - increase social capacity and resilience towards experiences of dying, death and loss
  - promote quality of care in end-of-life care.

Test your knowledge

11.4 What are the main benefits of hospice care?

11.5 How do Compassionate Communities aim to improve end-of-life care?

Answers to these questions can be found on the companion website at:
www.pearsoned.co.uk/psychologyexpress

Further reading End-of-life care

Topic	Key reading
End-of-life care in the UK	Riley, J. (2008). A strategy for end of life care in the UK. *British Medical Journal, 337*, a943.
Compassionate Communities	Kellehear, A. (2000). Spirituality and palliative care: A model of needs. *Palliative Medicine, 14*(2), 149–155.

Bereavement, grief and loss

- *Bereavement* – that is, the loss, through death, of loved ones – can occur at any stage of life.
- *Grief* is the emotional response to loss.
- The observable expression of grief is called *mourning*.
- We have to recognise that grief can begin before the actual death and those dying can also grieve their own loss.
- The grieving process is dependent upon the relationship with the person, factors surrounding the loss (for example, sudden or impending), as well as unresolved issues with the deceased.
- Bereavement is a normal part of life, but carries high risk when no support is available.
- Severe reactions to loss may carry over into familial relations and cause trauma for children and spouses. For example, there is an increased risk of marital break-up following the death of a child.
- Loss of a child is often described as one of the most difficult deaths to adjust to: parents do not get 'over' the loss but instead learn to assimilate and live with death (Davies, 2005). It is thought that the dependent nature of the relationship, coupled with normal experiences of grief, can be overwhelming.
- Such factors influence whether a person will go through a 'normal' or 'abnormal' grieving process. For example:
  - death resulting from an accident, rather than from a long terminal illness where individuals have been told that their family member or friend will die, increases the likelihood of there being an abnormal grieving pattern.
  - death in old age is often negotiated more easily by families, as it is seen as more 'natural' than when a child, teenager or young adult dies, even if they were terminally ill.

Models of grief

According to Archer (1999), a widely held assumption is that grief proceeds through an orderly series of stages or phases with distinct features. Traditional models have one main commonality: the need for grief work, which is described as, 'an effortful process that we must go through entailing confrontation of the reality of loss and gradual acceptance of the world without the loved one' (Stroebe, 1998).

- Models of grief and loss emphasise that all individuals will experience particular emotional and physical states, but will vary as to the amount of time that is spent at each stage.

- All models emphasise the need to experience these stages in order to reach acceptance.
- Grief work models can be applied to the grief process that both adults and children will go through before reaching acceptance, although as the next section shows age will impact on how grief is displayed.
- Parkes' (1972; 1986) four-stage model describes the phases of bereavement and, in turn, grief work that an individual faces (see Table 11.1). According to this model, an individual has to work through the stages of grief in order to reach acceptance and move forward in life.
- More recent empirical work provides some support for these different aspects of grief (Maciejewski et al., 2007).

Table 11.1 **Parkes' four-stage model of grief work**

Name of phase	Reactions, emotions in each phase
Phase One	Initial reaction: shock, numbness or disbelief
Phase Two	Pangs of grief, searching, anger, guilt, sadness and fear
Phase Three	Despair
Phase Four	Acceptance/adjustment. Gaining a new identity

Source: based on Parkes (1986)

According to the World Health Organization, the need to offer family and significant others support, not only during the patient's terminal illness but also in bereavement, is significant and provides the contemporary philosophy of palliative care (WHO, 1990). Research (for example, Herkert, 2000) suggests that bereaved individuals are most helped by those who:

- say they are sorry for their loss
- make themselves available to serve as confidants
- let the bereaved express the painful feelings freely when they are ready.

It is less helpful when individuals:

- tell people how they should feel and cope, rather than simply asking how they are and how they are coping
- try to emphasise the positives, with comments such as 'At least he had a good innings' or 'At least he is no longer suffering', as such remarks may be well-intentioned, but are often not well received by those dealing with loss.

Grief responses across the lifespan

There are enormous differences in children's understanding of loss and how they cope with bereavement. This has often been understood in terms of the children's cognitive development. Table 11.2 indicates the different grief reactions a child may exhibit dependent on their age.

Table 11. 2 **Grief and developmental stages**

Age	Understanding of death	Behaviour/expression of grief
Infants	• Do not recognise death • Feelings of loss and separation are part of developing an awareness of death	• Separated from mother – sluggish, quiet, and unresponsive to a smile or a coo • Physical changes – weight loss, less active, sleep less
2–6 years	• Confuse death with sleep • Begin to experience anxiety by age 3	• Ask many questions • Problems in eating, sleeping and bladder and bowel control • Fear of abandonment • Tantrums
3–6 years	• Still confuse death with sleep, i.e., is alive but only in a limited way • Death is temporary, not final • Dead person can come back to life	• Even though saw deceased buried, still ask questions • Magical thinking based on lack of knowledge – his or her thoughts may cause someone to die • Under 5 – trouble eating, sleeping and controlling balder and bowel functions • Afraid of the dark
6–9	• Curious about death • Death is thought of as a person or spirit (skeleton, ghost, bogeyman) • Death is final and frightening • Death happens to others; it won't happen to me	• Ask specific questions • May have exaggerated fears • May have aggressive behaviours (especially boys) • Some concerns about imaginary illnesses. • May feel abandoned
9 yrs +	Everyone will die Death is final and cannot be changed Even I will die	• Heightened emotions, guilt, anger, shame • Increased anxiety over own death • Mood swings • Fear of rejection, not wanting to be different from peers • Changes in eating habits • Sleeping problems • Regressive behaviours (loss of interest in outside activities) • Impulsive behaviours • Feels guilty about being alive (especially related to death of a parent, sibling or peer)

Source: based on National Cancer Institute, U.S. National institutes of health http://www.cancer.gov/cancertopics/pdq/supportivecare/bereavement/Patient/allpages/

- Adolescents have a much clearer understanding of death and are more likely than younger children to recognise death as an inevitable biological process.
- However, despite this knowledge, there is evidence that many adults and adolescents share the belief of children that psychological functions such as knowing and thinking continue even when biological functions have stopped (Bering & Björklund, 2004), demonstrating a belief in an afterlife.

- Adolescents tend to grieve in much the same way that adults do, but may be reluctant to express their grief for fear of seeming abnormal or lacking in control.

- They may therefore express their anguish through delinquent behaviour and somatic ailments (Clark, Pynoos, & Goebel, 1994).

CRITICAL FOCUS

How can we help the grief process?

Read the scenario provided below and answer the question that follows.

Jim, his wife Rose and their three children were overjoyed at the news that Rose was expecting a baby. A couple of months into the pregnancy, Rose was unexpectedly taken into hospital with severe abdominal pains and bleeding. A few hours later, the couple had their worst nightmare confirmed: Rose had had a miscarriage. Both were shocked by the news. The senior staff nurse noticed that both Rose and Jim were finding it difficult to come to terms with the miscarriage and decided to help the couple with their grief, so that coming to terms with the miscarriage would be easier for both of them. The senior staff nurse introduced herself and said how sorry she was for the couple's loss. Rose looked at the nurse with a blank expression, while Jim replied that they would be fine and they could do nothing about it now. Rose was kept in hospital for a couple of days until her health became more stable. During her stay, the senior staff nurse and others encouraged Rose to talk about her feelings, but Rose did not reveal any of her emotions or feelings. Three days later Rose's physical health had improved and she was prepared for discharge. Knowing that Rose would be discharged, the nurse decided to talk to Jim and explain her concerns that Rose had shown no emotion. She gave Jim a leaflet listing organisations offering further support for Rose. When Jim became tearful, the nurse reassured him that the grieving process would become easier over time. She further emphasised the positive things in life that they needed to focus on, such as their three children, comparing their situation to those of others who have miscarried and have no children. Jim began to feel guilty about being upset and thanked the nurse for her help and concern.

Does the staff nurse help or hinder grief work?

Models of loss

Elizabeth Kübler-Ross was one of the first researchers to study patients and their families from the time of the diagnosis of a terminal illness up until death. This research resulted in more emphasis being given to palliative care and quality of life, even if a patient will die. Kübler-Ross suggested a five-stage model for the experience of dying, which has provided a framework for those working with individuals experiencing personal loss (see Table 11.3).

It is often assumed that terminally ill young children are unaware that they will die and are better off remaining that way. However, evidence shows that even preschool children with life-threatening illnesses such as leukaemia come to understand that they will die and death is irreversible (Bluebond-Langner, 1977).

Table 11.3 Kübler-Ross' five-stage model (1969)

Stage	Example	Explanation
Denial and isolation	'No, not me' or 'It can't be me – you must have the results mixed up'	During this stage there is constant denial of the new status a patient or family are prescribed. Denial acts as a buffer system, allowing the patient to develop other coping mechanisms. It can also bring isolation and the patient may fear rejection and abandonment in suffering and feel that nobody understands what the suffering is like
Anger	'It's not fair – why me?'	This is a stage when anger is taken out on practitioners such as nurses (and also on doctors, relatives or other healthy people). Typical reactions are, 'Because of you (the nurse), I can't go home and pick my children up from school' or 'Because of you (the nurse) I have to take time out so you administer pain to me' or 'It's OK for you; you can go home at the end of the day.' There is a shift from the first stage from 'No it can't be me it must be a mistake' to 'Oh yes it is me; it was not a mistake'
Bargaining	'Please God let me…'	This is an attempt to postpone death by doing a deal with God/fate/hospital. At this stage, people who are enduring a terminal illness and looking for a cure or 'a bit more time' will pay any price and will usually be manipulated at this stage. It is not uncommon for patients who have never been religious now to turn to religion – almost bargaining again – 'If I pray you will grant me another extra couple of days'. The problem is that even when a couple of extra days are granted, these are never enough; the patient wants more
Depression	'How can I leave all of this behind?'	This time is very much a quiet, dark and reflective time. It is very similar to someone actually experiencing depression. During this stage, the dying patient does not want reassurance from a nurse, but at the same time does not want to be ignored. During this time family members of the dying patient begin the five-stage model and so are very much attempting to be proactive – that is, in denial that the family member is going to die. They may even become angry at the patient for 'giving up'. The dying patient during this stage would like people around them to be quiet and this is where nurses can make a difference. All they want is for someone to be present, who does not question and is not angry. There will be questions the patient will ask and they need to be answered honestly (especially because they don't have to pretend to be strong away from the family). In addition to this, the patient during this stage would also like the nurse to anticipate questions

Table 11.3 Continued

Stage	Example	Explanation
Acceptance	'Leave me be, I am ready to die'	This stage is where the individual is neither depressed nor angry. He or she has worked through feelings of loss and has found some peace. During this stage the patient has accepted his or her situation and is ready to go. Also within this stage, family members are very angry or questioning why the patient is at peace when they still want to change the status of the patient. The patient, however, has begun the process of letting go during the depression stage and has now finished this process and accepts the inevitable. He or she is ready to move on

- Over time, terminally ill children stop thinking about the future and focus on the here and now.
- Children experience the same emotions in death as adults – fear, anger, sadness and, finally, acceptance.
- Preschool children may not talk about dying, but they can reveal their fears through temper tantrums.
- School-age children are better able to talk about their fears and there is evidence that talking to a child about their death can be beneficial, both for the child and the parents, if the child shows the desire to do so (Faulkner, 1997).
- School-age children often show a desire to continue with everyday activities, such as going to school for as long as possible, so as to feel 'normal'.
- The response of the adolescent to becoming terminally ill clearly reflects the developmental tasks of this period (Stevens & Dunsmore, 1996).
- The focus is often on body image, meaning that body changes such as weight gain or loss of hair will provoke feelings of distress.
- In the same way, a loss of identity can be felt when new-found independence is taken away on account of the reliance on parents and healthcare professionals that illness may bring.

Cultural differences in grieving

Sometimes a distinction is made between *grief* and *mourning*. Grief is seen as a subjective state, a set of feelings that arise spontaneously after a significant death, whereas mourning describes the way in which grief is displayed, which is often constrained by the rituals or behaviours prescribed by a culture.

- The Western approach to bereavement is not universal. Displays of grief and mourning take different forms across the world and are often heavily influenced by religion (Chachkes & Jennings, 1994).
- Funerals may be an occasion for avoiding people or for holding a party (Metcalf & Huntington, 1991).

- Most societies have some concept of spiritual immortality, yet even here there are cultural differences, ranging from the idea of reincarnation to the concept of ancestral ghosts who meddle in the lives of the living (Rosenblatt, 1993).

- Some cultures, especially those in Latin America, believe that mourning involves the display of intense, hysterical emotions that should be shared with the community (Cook & Dworkin, 1992), while others, such as the British, restrain their grief so as not to burden others.

Key terms

The terms grief, bereavement and mourning are often used as synonyms, but they all have different meanings.

Grief: is the normal process of reacting to any form of loss. Grief may be a reaction to physical loss, such as death, or in response to a social loss, such as divorce or loss of a job. Grief can be displayed physically, emotionally, cognitively and socially.

- Physical reactions may include eating and sleeping problems.
- Mental reactions may include anxiety, sadness and despair.
- Social reactions include readjusting to life without the deceased or readjusting to life after the diagnosis of a terminal illness.

Grief processes depend on the relationship with the person who died, the situation surrounding the death and the person's attachment to the person who died.

Bereavement: the period after a loss during which grief is experienced and mourning occurs. The time spent in a period of bereavement depends on how attached the person was to the person who died and how much time was spent anticipating the loss.

Mourning: the process by which people adapt to a loss. Mourning is also influenced by cultural customs, rituals and society's rules for coping with loss.

Test your knowledge

11.6 What are the differences between bereavement, grief and mourning?

11.7 What are the four phases of Parkes' model of grief?

11.8 Discuss how age affects displays of grief and feelings of loss.

11.9 How might an adolescent use behaviour to express their grief?

Answers to these questions can be found on the companion website at: **www.pearsoned.co.uk/psychologyexpress**

? Sample question   Essay

How might the Kübler-Ross model of dying be applied in a hospice with terminally ill adults?

> **?** *Sample question*   *Information provider*
>
> Design a resource for parents and other carers with information about the impact of bereavement on children of different ages. What are the key issues they need to know? How can you help parents identify feelings of loss in their child?

Further reading Bereavement, grief and loss

Topic	Key reading
Models of grief	Maciejewski, P. K., Zhong, B., Block, S. D., & Prigerson, H. G. (2007). An empirical examination of the stage theory of grief. *Journal of the American Medical Association, 297*(7), 716–723.
Grief therapy	Neimeyer, R. A., & Currier, J. M. (2009). Grief therapy: Evidence of efficacy and emerging directions. *Current Directions in Psychological Science, 18*, 352–356.
Loss of a child	Davies, R. (2005). Mothers' stories of loss: Their need to be with their dying child and their child's body after death. *Journal of Child Health Care 9*(4), 288–300.

Quality of life and the right to die

The letters 'DNR' written on a patient's file indicate that a doctor is not required to resuscitate a patient if their heart stops. Standing for 'do not resuscitate' these three letters are designed to prevent unnecessary suffering.

- For terminally ill patients, the letters DNR may be the difference between dying immediately or being kept alive through extreme, possibly painful, medical procedures, for days, weeks or even months.

- DNRs are therefore sometimes seen as a form of *euthanasia*, the practice of assisting someone to die more quickly.

- Sometimes called 'mercy killing', euthanasia takes one of two forms:
  - *passive euthanasia* – death is hastened because of the withdrawal of care (for example, switching off a life-support machine) or non-intervention (for example, following a DNR order)
  - *active euthanasia* – involves deliberately acting to end a person's life by, for example, administering a fatal dose of pain medication.

- Euthanasia is an emotive subject and people often have firm views on whether such a practice is right or wrong.

- Some people make a moral distinction between active and passive euthanasia, arguing that it is acceptable to withhold treatment and allow a terminally ill patient to die, but not to kill someone by a deliberate act.

- Others argue that this distinction is unfounded, since both letting someone die and actively killing someone result from a deliberate act, the intended outcome of which is someone's death.

- Active euthanasia is illegal in most countries, including the UK, but one study suggests that almost half of NHS doctors have been asked by a patient to take active steps to hasten death and a third of those asked complied with the patient's request (Ward & Tate, 1994).

- In the UK, the British Medical Association (BMA) and the Royal College of Nursing (RCN) and the Resuscitation Council (UK) have provided guidelines on the use of DNR orders and are clear that these should only be issued after discussion with patients or their families.

- The most difficult cases are those involving patients who know they are terminally ill, are suffering a lot of pain, but who could live for several months.

- The BMA guidelines state that circumstances in which a DNR may be issued include:
  - when a patient's condition is such that resuscitation is unlikely to succeed
  - when a mentally competent patient has consistently stated that he or she does not want to be resuscitated
  - if there is a *living will*, which says the patient does not want to be resuscitated
  - if successful resuscitation would not be in the patient's best interest because it would lead to a poor quality of life (QoL).

The final point raises an important issue: at what point does life cease to have 'quality' and who decides that an individual's life is no longer worth living? Two main issues have been found to be important in determining terminal patient's QoL (Shahidi, Bernier & Cohen, 2010):

- the patient's physical and mental state
- the relationships and support provided by others.

Normally QoL is judged by the individual themself, as QoL is defined by our subjective experiences, states and perceptions (Burckhardt and Anderson, 2003).

- However, some have questioned whether a terminally ill patient is always capable of judging the quality of their life.

- This raises a new question: if the patient is found incapable of judging their life quality, then who should – a family member, a medic or other healthcare professional?

- Consideration of QoL is closely linked to decisions about what is in an individual's best interests.

- The challenge is to define what a person's best interests are and how they can best be met: can someone's best interests ever be met by withdrawing or administering a particular treatment?
- Advocates of euthanasia argue that it is not in the best interests of a terminally ill patient to suffer pain needlessly when their life is close to the end.
- The failure to end that suffering, even if the only way of doing so is to intentionally end the patient's life, is seen as going against the duty of the health professional to do what is best for the patient's well-being.

Key terms

Quality of life (QoL): is a complex concept, which concerns an individual's satisfaction with all aspects of their life from the physical to the social and psychological. Many things can affect QoL, including income, social and physical environment, interpersonal relationships and health. QoL is subjective and so can be known only to the individual concerned. It is now widely accepted that it is important to understand and improve the QoL at the end of life. One concern in medicine today is that we can improve the length of people's lives, but we do not always know at what cost. However, trends in QoL at the end of life are poorly understood because of the difficulty in finding out such information.

Test your knowledge

11.10 What does DNR stand for?

11.11 Is there a difference between active and passive euthanasia?

11.12 How is quality of life (QoL) usually defined?

11.13 What are the main issues surrounding QoL in terminally ill patients?

Answers to these questions can be found on the companion website at: **www.pearsoned.co.uk/psychologyexpress**

? Sample question   Problem-based learning

Rachel was diagnosed with a brain tumour at the age of eight years. Now aged 12, she has spent the past 4 years in and out of hospital undergoing a range of treatments, including chemotherapy and radiation, but the tumour shows no signs of going away. The location of the tumour makes it inoperable and the family has all but given up hope of a cure. However, a new chemotherapy treatment has recently become available in England and is being trialled at the children's hospital where she is treated and her consultant has asked if Rachel would like to be included in the trial. Rachel and her family have been told that the treatment has a 50 per cent chance of success, but this is the only treatment left open to Rachel. Rachel herself has refused this treatment. She explained to the consultant that she has had enough of hospitals, needles and being poked and prodded. She does not want to be a guinea pig for some new treatment that might not even work. All she wants is to be able to spend time at home with her family. She accepts that refusing this treatment means she will probably die within a few months, but thinks the chances of success are not a good enough reason for spending more time in hospital undergoing painful treatment. She has stated that if she is going to die anyway she would rather do so at home. Her mother is upset by this turn of events, but says she understands Rachel's reasoning and will support her decision.

Should Rachel be allowed to decide that she no longer wants any treatment?

Based on your knowledge of cognitive development, at what age should someone be deemed able to make their own decisions?

Is Rachel's mother right to support Rachel's decision or should she force her child to be treated?

Further reading Quality of life and the right to die

Topic	Key reading
Attitudes to euthanasia	Ward, B. J., & Tate, P. A. (1994). Attitudes among NHS doctors towards requests for euthanasia. *British Medical Journal*, *308*, 1332–1334. Available online at: www.bmj.com/content/308/6940/1332.full
QoL	Diehr, P., Lafferty, W. E., Patrick, D. L., Downey, L., Devlin, S. M., & Standish, L. J. (2007). Quality of life at the end of Life. *Health and Quality of Life Outcomes*, 5, 51. Available online at: www.hqlo.com/content/5/1/51

CRITICAL FOCUS

Interpreting statistics: changing mortality rates in the UK 1971–2006

Figure 11.1 shows mortality rates for the UK in 2006. What does this data tell you about:

• differences in male and female death rates in 2006?

• age-related trends in mortality rates in 2006?

At what ages are male and female mortality rates similar? Why do you think we see this pattern?

The patterns shown in Figure 11.1 reflect those described at the start of this chapter: females show lower mortality rates throughout most of the lifespan when compared to males; mortality rates drop after infancy, then do not start to increase until middle adulthood (35–54); the highest increase in mortality is seen in old age. .

Figures 11.2 and 11.3 show the mortality rates for males and females over 30 years.

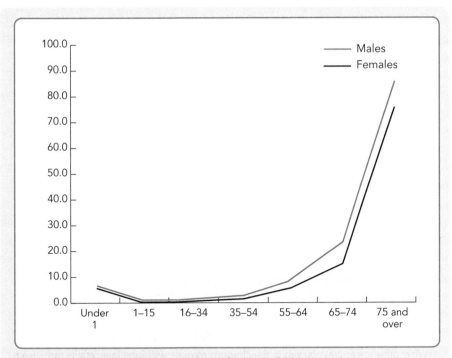

Figure 11.1 Mortality rates per 1000 in the UK in 2006
Source: adapted from data from the Office for National Statistics licensed under the Open
Government Licence v.1.0

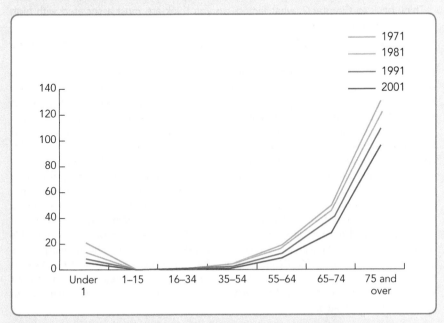

Figure 11.2 Male mortality rates per 1000 in the UK, 1971–2001
Source: adapted from data from the Office for National Statistics licensed under the Open
Government Licence v.1.0

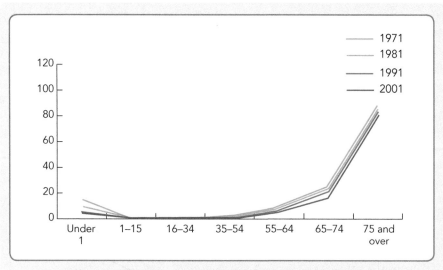

Figure 11.3 Female mortality rates per 1000 in the UK, 1971–2001
Source: adapted from data from the Office for National Statistics licensed under the Open
Government Licence v.1.0

Compare these graphs in order to answer the following questions.

● What differences can you see in the changes to male and female mortality rates from
1971 to 2001? Why do such differences exist?

● When was the biggest change to infant mortality rates for both males and females?
Think back to Chapter 2: what factors do you think are most associated with high
infant mortality?

The data spanning 1971–2001 demonstrates another issue raised at the start of the
chapter – the reduction in the gap between male and female mortality rates. While
life expectancy continues to increase for both males and females, a greater increase is
seen in male life expectancy. This is thought to relate to improvements in prevention
and treatment of life-limiting diseases experienced mainly by males, such as heart
disease. Infant mortality rates appear to have reduced the most between 1971 and
1981, although a gradual decline is still seen from 1981 to 2001. A range of social and
biological factors are associated with high infant mortality, including low birth weight,
which often links to maternal behaviours such as smoking and drinking. Other factors
include multiple births, marital status, age of mother, country of birth of mother and
father's social class. Social class differences in infant mortality rates are wider in the
post-neonatal period (deaths between 28 days and a year) than the neonatal period
(deaths under 28 days). According to Norman et al. (2008), health inequalities in infant
mortality remain between different social groups. The initial rapid decline seen in this
data set is therefore thought to be related to a general reduction in health inequalities
in the early 1970s and 1980s (Norman et al., 2008). Further reduction in 1981–1991 is
thought to be related to the 'Back to Sleep' campaign that encouraged parents to put
their baby to sleep on their backs, which reduced the number of sudden infant death
syndrome (SIDS) deaths.

Chapter summary – pulling it all together

→ Can you tick all the points from the revision checklist at the beginning of this chapter?

→ Attempt the sample question from the beginning of this chapter using the answer guidelines below.

→ Go to the companion website at www.pearsoned.co.uk/psychologyexpress to access more revision support online, including interactive quizzes, flashcards, You be the marker exercises as well as answer guidance for the Test your knowledge and Sample questions from this chapter.

Answer guidelines

 Sample question *Essay*

Evaluate the importance of social, cultural and developmental influences on our beliefs about death, dying and bereavement.

Approaching the question

Your answer should aim to provide an analysis of how personal experiences, the wider social context and developmental level help determine how individuals will respond to loss. You should aim to consider how individuals respond to knowledge of their own death as well as loss of a significant other. Remember that even though death has a clear biological component, this is not the only factor to influence what we believe – there are also social and emotional definitions.

Important points to include

● Begin by defining the main issue, which is that while there are medical definitions of death based on biological processes, this is not how most people define death.

● Compare and contrast medical and social definitions of death, remembering to discuss the way the social context has impacted on definitions of death. You might want to look at factors that change what we believe about death, such as:

  ● historical context
  ● cultural norms
  ● religious beliefs.

- You should then look at the way in which, even in a specific social context, individual differences are important to our beliefs about death and bereavement. You will need to consider:
  - developmental stage/age
  - nature of the loss, for example:
    - own life or that of another person
    - sudden or expected loss
    - age of/relationship to the deceased
  - personal experiences of death and illness.
- Remember to link these ideas to other areas of developmental psychology you have studied, such as how aging affects readiness for death and children's cognitive development. This will demonstrate your ability to provide a synthesis of the many aspects of developmental psychology.

Make your answer stand out

It is really easy just to take a descriptive approach in which you outline the differences between social and medical definitions of death, age-related responses to bereavement, etc. A good answer will remember to take a critical stance, evaluating the links between contextual and individual factors. At a societal level, for example, beliefs about death are changing because of increases in medical knowledge. How might this also affect beliefs at an individual level? You might expect that someone educated in medicine, for example, because of their specialist knowledge, will respond differently to knowing that their loved one is brain dead, compared to someone without that training. However, we also know that interpersonal relationships affect how we interpret information – might a social and emotional response outweigh an intellectual one? Will that response be different depending on the age of the loved one or the nature of the relationship? Acknowledging complexities such as this and carefully analysing them, rather than presenting grief responses simplistically, will really make your answer stand out.

Explore the accompanying website at www.pearsoned.co.uk/psychologyexpress
- → Prepare more effectively for exams and assignments using the answer guidelines for questions from this chapter.
- → Test your knowledge using multiple choice questions and flashcards.
- → Improve your essay skills by exploring the You be the marker exercises.

Notes

Notes

And finally, before the exam . . .

How to approach revision from here

You should be now at a reasonable stage in your revision process – you should have developed your skills and knowledge base over your course and used this text judiciously over that period. Now, however, you have used the book to reflect, remind and reinforce that material you have researched over the year/ seminar. You will, of course, need to do additional reading and research to that included here (and appropriate directions are provided) but you will be well on your way with the material presented here.

It is important that in answering any question in psychology you take a research- and evidence-based approach to your response. For example, do not make generalised or sweeping statements that cannot be substantiated or supported by evidence from the literature. Remember as well that the evidence should not be anecdotal – it is of no use citing your mum, dad, best friend or the latest news from a celebrity website. After all, you are not writing an opinion piece – you are crafting an argument which is based on current scientific knowledge and understanding. You need to be careful about the evidence you present: do review the material and from where it was sourced.

Furthermore, whatever type of assessment you have to undertake, it is important to take an evaluative approach to the evidence. Whether you are writing an essay, sitting an exam or designing a webpage, the key advice is to avoid simply presenting a descriptive answer. Rather it is necessary to think about the strength of the evidence in each area. One of the key skills for psychology students is critical thinking and for this reason the tasks featured in this series focus upon developing this way of thinking. Thus you are not expected to simply learn a set of facts and figures, but to think about the implications of what we know and how this might be applied in everyday life. The best assessment answers are the ones that take this critical approach.

It is also important to note that psychology is a theoretical subject: when answering any question about psychology, not only refer to the prevailing theories of the field, but also outline the development of them as well. It is also important to evaluate these theories and models either through comparison with other models and theories or through the use of studies that have assessed them and highlighted their strengths and weaknesses. It is essential to read widely – within each section of this book there are directions to interesting and pertinent papers or books relating to the specific topic area. Find these papers, read these papers, and make notes from these papers. But don't stop there. Let them lead you to other sources that may be important to the field. One thing

227

that an examiner hates to see is the same old sources being cited all of the time: be innovative, and as well as reading the seminal works, find the more obscure and interesting sources as well – just make sure they're relevant to your answer!

How not to revise

- **Don't avoid revision**. This is the best tip ever. There is something on the TV, the pub is having a two-for-one offer, the fridge needs cleaning, your budgie looks lonely . . . You have all of these activities to do and they need doing now! Really . . . ? Do some revision!
- **Don't spend too long at each revision session**. Working all day and night is not the answer to revision. You do need to take breaks, so schedule your revision so you are not working from dawn until dusk. A break gives time for the information you have been revising to consolidate.
- **Don't worry**. Worrying will cause you to lose sleep, lose concentration and lose revision time by leaving it late and then later. When the exam comes, you will have no revision completed and will be tired and confused.
- **Don't cram**. This is the worst revision technique in the universe! You will not remember the majority of the information that you try to stuff into your skull, so why bother?
- **Don't read over old notes with no plan**. Your brain will take nothing in. If you wrote your lecture notes in September and the exam is in May is there any point in trying to decipher your scrawly handwriting now?
- **Don't write model answers and learn by rote**. When it comes to the exam you will simply regurgitate the model answer irrespective of the question – not a brilliant way to impress the examiner!

Tips for exam success

What you should do when it comes to revision

Exams are one form of assessment that students often worry about the most. The key to exam success, as with many other types of assessment, lies in good preparation and self-organisation. One of the most important things is knowing what to expect – this does not necessarily mean knowing what the questions will be on the exam paper, but rather what the structure of the paper is, how many questions you are expected to answer, how long the exam will last and so on.

To pass an exam you need a good grasp of the course material and obvious, as it may seem, to turn up for the exam itself. It is important to remember that you aren't expected to know or remember everything in the course, but you should be able to show your understanding of what you have studied. Remember as well that examiners are interested in what you know, not what you don't know. They try to write exam questions that give you a good chance of passing – not ones to catch you out or trick you in any way. You may want to consider some of these top exam tips:

- Start your revision in plenty of time.
- Make a revision timetable and stick to it.
- Practise jotting down answers and making essay plans.
- Practise writing against the clock using past exam papers.
- Check that you have really answered the question and have not strayed off the point.
- Review a recent past paper and check the marking structure.
- Carefully select the topics you are going to revise.
- Use your lecture/study notes and refine them further, if possible, into lists or diagrams and transfer them onto index cards/post-it notes. Mind maps are a good way of making links between topics and ideas.
- Practise your handwriting – make sure it's neat and legible.

One to two days before the exam
- Recheck times, dates and venue.
- Actively review your notes and key facts.
- Exercise, eat sensibly, and get a few good nights' sleep.

On the day
- Get a good night's sleep.
- Have a good meal, two to three hours before the start time.
- Arrive in good time.
- Spend a few minutes calming and focusing.

In the exam room
- Keep calm.
- Take a few minutes to read each question carefully. Don't jump to conclusions – think calmly about what each question means and the area it is focused on.
- Start with the question you feel most confident about. This helps your morale.
- By the same token, don't expend all your efforts on that one question – if you are expected to answer three questions then don't just answer two.
- Keep to time and spread your effort evenly on all opportunities to score marks.
- Once you have chosen a question, jot down any salient facts or key points. Then take five minutes to plan your answer – a spider diagram or a few notes may be enough to focus your ideas. Try and think in terms of 'why and how' not just 'facts'.

And finally, before the exam . . .

- You might find it useful to create a visual plan or map before writing your answer to help you to remember to cover everything you need to address.
- Keep reminding yourself of the question and try not to wander off the point.
- Remember that quality of argument is more important than quantity of facts.
- Take 30-60 second breaks whenever you find your focus slipping (typically every 20 minutes).
- Make sure you reference properly – according to your university requirements.
- Watch your spelling and grammar – you could lose marks if you make too many errors.

→ *Revision checklist*

❑ Have you revised the topics highlighted in the revision checklists?

❑ Have you attended revision classes and taken note of and/or followed up on your lecturers' advice about the exams or assessment process at your university?

❑ Can you answer the questions posed in this text satisfactorily? Don't forget to check sample answers on the website too.

❑ Have you read the additional material to make your answer stand out?

❑ Remember to criticise appropriately – based on evidence.

Test your knowledge by using the material presented in this text or on the website: **www.pearsoned.co.uk/psychologyexpress**

Glossary

accommodation According to Piaget, this is one of the processes through which the construction of knowledge takes place. In accommodation children modify/adapt their existing schemas to fit new information – for example, separating cars from other vehicles.

AIDS (acquired immune deficiency syndrome) A condition caused by a virus that causes the body to lose immunity to infection.

animism A term used in developmental psychology to explain young children's patterns of thought and speech in which feelings, beliefs and desires are invested in the non-human or non-living.

anoxia A decreased supply of oxygen to the body tissues.

anthropology The discipline that studies humankind.

applied behavioural analysis (ABA) A behaviourist intervention, based on the principles of Dr Lovaas, in which rewards/tokens are used to manipulate children's behaviour. ABA is used with children with learning difficulties, such as autistic spectrum disorder (ASD).

assimilation According to Piaget, this is one of the processes through which the construction of knowledge takes place. In assimilation, children evaluate and try to understand new information based on their existing schemas – for example, all four-wheeled vehicles are cars.

attention deficit hyperactivity disorder (ADHD) A hyperactivity disorder characterised by an inability to focus on one task at a time and a pervasive impulsivity, often resulting in behavioural or developmental delay problems.

autonomous morality Also known as moral independence (stage). According to the Piagetian theory of moral development, the later stage is characterised by a child's determination of what is right is adapted to fit within the given circumstance.

behavioural The term used to characterise the theoretical or empirical analysis of an objective behaviour.

bereavement An emotional reaction felt after the death of a loved one.

blastocyst The inner layer of cells that develops during the germinal period. These cells later develop into the embryo.

brain death A medical definition of death, focusing primarily on irreversible brain stem damage.

case study An in-depth look at an individual person or group. Often uses a combination of qualitative and quantative data to collect detailed information on one person or group.

causal relationship The suggestion that one condition/event causes another condition/event.

centration The centring of one's attention on an aspect of a situation to the exclusion of others. This concept is very important in Piagetian theory of cognitive development.

cerebral palsy The term cerebral palsy is an umbrella term that encompasses non-progressive motor conditions that cause physical difficulties. 'Cerebral' refers to the cerebrum, which is the part of the brain affected, and 'palsy' refers to difficulties with motor abilities.

chickenpox A contagious disease that causes a rash of red spots on the body.

cliques and crowds A gathering of people with a common interest or focus, such as music or fashion. A small, exclusive group of friends.

chromosones Threadlike structures composed of bundles of genes. Chromosones come in 23 pairs, a member of each pair coming from each parent.

collaborative learning A group of learners working on a shared assignment.

Compassionate Communities A public health end-of-life care model, pioneered by Professor Allan Kellehear. In this model of end-of-life care, the community has a primary role in supporting the health and social well-being of people as they approach the end of their lives.

confounding variable A variable the researcher cannot systematically control that may affect the outcomes of the research.

conservation A Piagetian term to explain when a child (or adult) understands that a quantitative aspect or set of materials/stimulus displayed does not change or is not affected by the transformation of the display. This can be tested by the task in which water in a jar is poured into different-shaped containers and children have to state whether or not there is a change in the amount of water.

co-operative learning Students working together in small groups on a structured activity. They are individually accountable for their work and the work of the group as a whole is also assessed.

cranium The part of the skull that encloses the brain.

cross-sectional research A research method predominantly used in developmental, clinical and social psychology, in which a large group of participants from different backgrounds and ages are studied at one time point.

crystallised abilities Refers to the information and skills that are acquired through experience in a cultural environment.

dementia An umbrella term used to refer to any brain disorder in which the main symptoms include deterioration of mental functioning.

DES stands for diethylstilbestrol, a synthetic form of oestrogen, a female hormone. It was prescribed between 1938 and 1971 to help women with certain complications of pregnancy. The use of DES declined following studies in the 1950s that showed it was not effective in preventing pregnancy complications. However, when given during the first five months of a pregnancy, DES can interfere with the development of the reproductive system in a foetus. For this reason, although DES and other estrogens may be prescribed for some medical problems, they are no longer used during pregnancy.

diathesis-stress model A model that hypothesises abnormal behaviour patterns are owing to a combination of genetic susceptibility and a stressful environment.

discovery learning An education method based on Piagetian theory. In discovery learning, active participation by the student takes place through problem-solving situations where the learner draws on his or her own past experience and existing knowledge to discover facts and relationships and new truths to be learned. Students interact with the world by exploring and manipulating objects, wrestling with questions and controversies or performing experiments. It is believed that, as a result, students may be more likely to remember concepts and knowledge discovered on their own because they are better able to make sense of them.

domain theory The theory that knowledge is structured in domains.

Down's syndrome (DS) A condition present at birth, due to a chromosomal abnormality caused by faulty cell division soon after fertilisation. DS approximately occurs 16/17 times in every 10,000 births and the occurrence increases with the rise of the mother's age.

dyslexia A specific learning difficulty causing reading, writing and spelling difficulties.

ecological validity The extent to which research findings can be generalised outside of the research context. Do they reflect real life?

ectoderm Is the outer layer of the embryonic cellular structure, which develops into the outer skin, nervous system, pineal gland and a part of the pituitary.

egocentric/egocentrism In Piagetian theory, egocentric behaviour is displayed by young children who are unable to distinguish between their own perception of the world and that of others.

ego identity The conscious sense of self we develop through social interaction.

Electra complex A psychoanalytic term used to describe a girl's romantic feelings towards her father and anger towards her mother. It is comparable to the Oedipus complex, said to be experienced by boys.

embryo An organism in the early stages of prenatal development, where there are no physical similarities to its mature form.

empiricism A tradition developed by John Locke that proposes children are blank slates on which experiences are imprinted. It is only later on in life through a long learning process that children's perceptual and other abilities develop.

endoderm The inner layer of the embryonic cellular structure, which develops into the digestive tract and viscera.

ethnocentric The perspective in which one's own ethnic group and social practices are used as the basis to evaluate the practices of other ethnic groups, with the implication that one's own ethic group is superior.

euthanasia A means of producing an easy and painless death advocated by patients who are suffering from intractable pain that accompanies the terminal stages of incurable diseases.

experiment A method of investigating causal relationships between variables or to test a hypothesis.

experimental A research design where the independent variable is manipulated.

fear of strangers An emotive situation of apprehension towards someone a child/adult does not know.

feral child A child reared in social isolation by either animals or with indirect contact with humans.

foetal distress A term used with reference to signs in a pregnant woman, either before or during childbirth, that suggest the foetus may not be well.

foetus A term used from the third month of pregnancy to refer to an organism in the late stages of prenatal development.

folic acid Given to pregnant women to aid the development of a healthy foetus, as it can reduce the risk of neural tube defects (NTDs), such as spina bifida. It is also known as vitamin B_9.

Fragile X A genetic disorder identified by a weak arm on the X chromosome.

gender identity The child's awareness of their gender – that is, whether they are a boy or girl. Gender identity usually develops by the age of three years.

gender role The public expression of behaviours and attitudes that indicates to others the affiliation to maleness or femaleness.

gender schema A cognitive structure used by children to organise their gender knowledge into a set of expectations for their gender and what it is appropriate to imitate.

genes Units of hereditary information composed of DNA, the complex molecule that contains our genetic information.

gene mutation A permanent change in the DNA sequence that makes up a gene, which can range from a single DNA building block to a large part of a chromosome.

genetic epistemology The approach that focuses on the development of knowledge. The approach is underpinned by the ideas that (1) knowledge develops through organising and adapting one's surroundings;

(2) knowledge is not based on innate, given ideas but on active construction by individuals; (3) that this construction of knowledge occurs through the need to update knowledge due to contradictions in a changing environment.

genotype The set of genes, which carry hereditary factors that influence the development of an individual.

grasp reflex A neonatal reflex that occurs when something touches the palm of an infant. The infant responds by grasping tightly.

grief The intense emotional feeling associated with the loss of someone with whom a deep emotional bond existed. The emotions experienced include numbness, disbelief, separation anxiety, despair, sadness and loneliness.

heteronomous morality Also known as moral realism (stage). According to the Piagetian theory of moral development, this is the first stage of moral development. This stage is characterised by a child accepting what's right by the rules of authority. This is also the name given to Kohlberg's first stage of moral reasoning, in which moral thinking is tied to punishment.

holophrases The utterance of a single word that forms part of a whole phrase or perhaps a sentence.

hospice A specialised nursing home for terminally ill patients, so that they can live out their final days in dignity. The hospice movement is committed to making the end of life as free from pain, anxiety and depression as possible. The goals of hospices contrast with those of a hospital, which are to cure disease and prolong life.

hypothetico-deductive reasoning Piaget's formal operational concept that adolescents have the cognitive ability to develop hypotheses; it best guesses ways to solve problems.

hypothetico-deductive A method that records observations to develop explanatory theories. The predictions of those theories are then tested.

id A Freudian term to explain the instinctive, innate pre-birth nature of a person's personality. The id is the presocialised, infantile part of a person's personality.

innate Refers to characteristics believed to exist at birth as a result of genetic factors; something that is instinctive, not learnt.

insecure–avoidant A type of attachment behaviour in which a child who is deemed insecure–avoidant treats their parent and a stranger in a similar way and appears to show little distress when left with the stranger.

insecure–disorganised A type of attachment behaviour in which a child shows a lack of attachment behaviour. In their actions and responses to their parent/caregiver the child is either confused or apprehensive, showing avoidance or resistance.

insecure–resistant A type of attachment behaviour in which a child who is deemed insecure–resistant becomes very distressed upon separation from their parent, but, because of their over-activation with their parent and with little interest in the environment, the child finds it difficult to be comforted by their parent upon reunion.

internal working model (IWM) A model that suggests children have an internal representation of their relationship with their mother or other attachment figures. It is suggested that these cognitive structures embody the child's memories of the day-to-day interactions with their attachment figure. These schemas/structures are then used as a guide to the child's actions with the attachment figure.

interviews A qualitative approach where data is collected in a conversation-like style with a participant. Interviews can be formatted to be structured, with pre-prepared questions for each participant, or unstructured, where there is no set list of questions.

joint attention This is the process by which one person alerts another to a stimulus via non-verbal means, such as gazing or pointing. For example, the infant may first look at an object, then the mother quickly follows, to then focus on the object. This joint attention provides opportunities to learn how to do things.

joint-action formats A term coined by Jerome Bruner to refer to the joint attention episodes that characterise parent–child interactions. According to Bruner, these episodes are essential for learning new skills, including language.

language acquisition device (LAD) An innate mechanism hypothesised by Noam Chomsky, in which children are pre-programmed with the underlying rules of universal grammar. Based on the language the child is exposed to, they will select the appropriate rules for the one language spoken.

LAD *Language acquisition device.*

language acquisition support system (LASS) Bruner's term to describe the range of interactive precursors, such as joint picture book reading, that help to support language development in children. These social interactions provide a scaffolding environment to structure the child's early language utterances.

LASS *Language acquisition support system.*

larynx The top part of the windpipe, containing the vocal cords.

leukaemia A life-threatening disease, characterised by abnormally low levels of white blood cells in the blood and body tissue.

libido A Freudian psychoanalytical term to explain mental or physical sexual desire or pleasure.

lifespan approach The understanding of a person's development through life from birth to death.

living will A form of advanced medical directive that defines treatment preference, if the patient cannot make medical decisions on their own behalf.

longitudinal study A study of an individual, or group of individuals, over a long time period.

maternal responsiveness A key aspect of mothering described by John Bowlby, in which the mother is sensitive to the child's needs, meaning that her response to the child is contingent on their needs.

maturation The biological process that underpins growth and development. The genetic instructions facilitating the development of instinctive behavioural patterns when a certain growth point or time period as been reached.

menopause The gradual but permanent cessation of a woman's menstrual activity.

mental operations The set of mental abilities and skills that allow a child to process and manipulate information to be able to solve problems.

meshing Describes the way in which a mother and child will interact.

mesoderm The middle layer of the embryonic cellular structure that develops into the muscles and bones.

meta-analysis The statistical procedure that combines the findings from a number of studies to determine whether or not there is a significant trend.

microencephaly A neurodevelopmental disorder, in which the circumference of the head is smaller than a person of the same sex and age.

mitosis A cell division process in which a somatic cell divides into two identical daughter cells, each with a complete set of chromosomes.

models An informal theory that illustrates relationships observed in data or nature.

motherese Sometimes also called parentese or baby talk, referring to the way in which carers alter their speech patterns to fit the developmental level of the child. Characteristics of motherese include short sentences, a high pitch and sing-song intonation. Babies appear to prefer to listen to motherese and this is thought to focus their attention and so aid language learning.

mourning The actions or expressions of a person who is bereaved.

multidirectional In relation to human development, this means that as some capacities/behaviours decrease, others will expand.

multidisciplinary As a person's development is multidimensional and multidirectional, it should therefore be seen that different disciplines such as psychologists, sociologists, neuroscientists and medical researchers all have different but complementary perspectives on age-related changes.

myelinated/myelination This is the process in which myelin (the fatty sheath that covers the *axon* of a *neuron*) is formed around the neurons. Myelination occurs in the sixth month of a foetus' life, and continues through childhood. Myelin increases the speed with which chemical messages can be passed from cell to cell in the nervous system.

nativist/nativism A contrasting approach to that of empiricism, nativism suggests that children's skills and abilities are present when they are born, so children are not blank slates at birth.

neonate A newborn child.

neo-Piagetians Developmental theorists who have elaborated on Piaget's theory, giving more emphasis to information processing, strategies and precise cognitive steps.

neural tube The development of the central nervous system, formed by the fusion of the neural folds.

neurogenesis The process by which neurons are generated.

neuron Nerve cell that handles information processing at the cellular level.

non-nutritive sucking preference procedure Asseses an infant's attention and perceptual processes by recording the rate of an infant's sucking on a pacifier nipple. Sucking on the nipple produces stimuli, such as a voice recording or a set of images, rather than nutrients/food. If an infant sucks more at a specific set of stimuli or sucks in order to produce that stimuli, it is inferred that they are showing a preference for that stimuli.

norms A value that is used in statistical analyses to compare individual/group conditions – it is usually used to refer to a typical or usual value or behaviour.

object permanence A child's ability to understand that an object exists even if the object is no longer visible to the eye.

observation A qualitative method that watches and records participants' behaviour.

Oedipal complex In Freudian terms, this is a subconscious sexual desire in a male child for the parent of the opposite sex, usually accompanied by hostility to the parent of the same sex.

oestrodiol The predominant sex hormone in females. This hormone is the one responsible for the growth of the female uterus, Fallopian tubes and vagina. It promotes breast development and the growth of the outer genitals. It also plays a role in the distribution of body fat in women and stops the process of growing taller.

ontogeny The development of an individual organism.

operant conditioning The association made between a behaviour and the consequence of the behaviour, controlled by a discriminative stimulus. Operant conditioning can either reinforce behaviour or, if aversive, discourage the behaviour from reoccurring.

over-extension The term used to explain young children's extension of a word to cover events/objects beyond that which the word is normally used for, such as calling a cat a 'doggie'.

perinatal Refers to the period immediately before and after birth.

pharynx The part of the throat situated immediately behind the mouth and nasal cavity. The pharynx is part of the digestive system and also the respiratory system; it is also important in vocalisation.

phenotype The observable, physical structure and function of an organism.

phoneme The smallest unit of speech that constitutes a change in meaning, such as 'rate' and 'late'. The two words mean completely different things, but only differ by one phoneme. A phoneme is therefore a set of sounds that are not visually identical but which are treated as equivalent sounds.

phylogeny The evolution of behaviour.

pincer grasp The grasping of an object between the thumb and forefinger. The ability to perform this task is a milestone of fine motor development in infants, usually occurring from 9 to 12 months of age.

placenta The 'life support system' for a foetus. It is an organ consisting of embryonic and maternal tissue that the foetus is attached to via the umbilical cord.

plasticity Refers to the extent to which the direction of development is guided by environmental factors as well as initiated by genetic factors. According to this idea, all organisms, including humans with the same genotype, vary in developmental pattern, in phenotype or in behavior according to varying environmental conditions. This term is also sometimes used to refer specifically to the flexibility of the brain tissue to assume the functions normally carried out by other tissue.

popularity In developmental research, usually defined by the number of children who name a target child as 'liked', 'disliked', 'friend' or 'best friend' (Newcomb, Bukowski, & Pattee, 1993).

positivist approach An approach that suggests human experiences and social behaviours can be reduced to observable, measureable and categorised facts.

prenatal Prior to birth.

proximity-seeking behaviours In attachment theory, this describes the child's efforts to gain (or regain) contact with their mother or other carer. This includes behaviours such as clambering on to the adult, creeping, crawling or walking and actually making contact, through their own efforts.

puberty The part of an individual's development where the sex organs become reproductively functional.

qualitative approach A research method that emphasises collecting data on the meaning of the behaviour or experiences of the individual/group concerned. Data is collected through various approaches, such as interviews or participant observations. Data collected is then normally transcribed and analysed, using theoretical approaches such as grounded theory and discourse analysis. Qualitative research is therefore a method of collecting data through words.

quality of life (QoL) Relates to an individual's satisfaction with all aspects of their life, from the physical to the social and psychological.

quantitative A research method that collects data through numbers. Data is collected through experiments and statistical tests are then used to analyse the data to find out relationships or correlations in data sets.

quasi-experiment A study where the researcher does not have control over all variables. Often used to refer to the use of naturally occurring phenomenon that cannot be manipulated by the researcher for ethical reasons. For example, if testing the contribution of fathers to child development, it would not be ethical to assign some children to families with fathers and others to fatherless families. Instead, comparisons are made between families where fathers are or are not present by choice.

questionnaire survey A study where a prepared set of questions is sent out to a large number of people to complete individually.

reinforcement The strengthening of learning through a bond between a response and a tangible reward or environment.

relativistic thinking The assumption that knowledge is constructed by each individual through a unique personal framework.

resilience The ability of people to cope with stress and adversity.

reversibility In a series of operations, if their order is reversed, it will restore the original state. In part of Piaget's conservation theory, understanding that this is possible results in the establishment of conservation.

rouge test Used to measure young children's self-concept. In the test, a dot of red rouge or lipstick/face paint is put on the child's face before they are put in front of a mirror to see if the child touches the red dot. If they do, it is determined the child has acquired a self-concept.

rubella Also known as German measles. It is a mild disease, but can have serious complications for women who are in the early stages pregnancy, as the foetus could potentially develop mental retardation, heart disease or deafness.

scaffolding An interactive process in which an adult/older peer structures a task for the child to respond to. As the child's ability to complete the task is increased, the peer or adult decreases/modifies the structural support until the child can learn independently.

schema A basic cognitive structure that individuals use to make sense of the world.

schizophrenia An umbrella term for a number of psychotic disorders with various cognitive, emotional and behavioural manifestations.

secure base A concept related to attachment theory that states the carer provides a secure and dependable base for the child to explore the world.

self-esteem The degree to which an individual values their self. Thus an individual might have high self-esteem, equating to high value of oneself.

self-concept domain-specific evaluations of the self.

separation anxiety A psychoanalytical term that hypothesises the anxiety a child would experience though the loss of their mother.

social competence Usually refers to an individual's ability to get on with others, read social situations and interact with peers.

social learning A process based on the works of Bandura and Walters that suggests someone will imitate observed behaviour in another person if it appears the behaviour will have reinforcing consequences, but will inhibit the behaviour if the observed consequence is punishment.

socio-cultural context An approach that attempts to understand the impact of an individual's environment on their development.

socio-dramatic play Involves an element of make-believe or pretence.

specific learning difficulties A condition/ disorder that significantly affects a child's learning in comparison to the majority of children of their age.

spina bifida A developmental birth defect, caused by the incomplete closure of the embryonic *neural tube*.

status hierarchy Refers to levels of social dominance commonly seen within adolescent social networks.

strange situation An experimental method developed by Mary Ainsworth, in which a young child is placed in increasingly strange situations to observe their emotional reactions.

subclinical disease This is the period prior to the appearance of the symptoms of a disease. The disease is developing, but no signs have yet been noticed by the individual or others around them.

sudden infant death syndrome (SIDS) A term used to explain the sudden or inexplicable death of an infant or very young child.

symbolic interactionist theory This is an important perspective in the social sciences that places emphasis on micro-scale social interaction. This approach is derived from American pragmatism, especially the work of George Herbert Mead and Charles Cooley. According to Mead, people interact with each other by interpreting or defining others' actions instead of merely reacting to others' actions.

symbolic play Imaginative play, where a child may pretend to be other people or act out 'real-life situations', such as nurses/doctors, or pretend an object is another object, such as a banana for a mobile/telephone.

syphilis An infectious venereal disease that enters the nervous system through a break in the skin or a mucous membrane, most commonly during sexual intercourse.

tabula rasa From the Latin, meaning 'blank slate'. This is the phrase that John Locke used to refer to a child's mind at birth, which he believed was unformed and featureless.

telegraphic speech A term developed by Roger Brown to explain the observation in children's early stages of language of a highly reduced form of speech, in which unessential words are dropped out like a telegram.

teratogen A Greek word, meaning 'creating a monster'– a reference to environmental hazards/abnormalities that can occur in prenatal development through, for example, drugs or harmful substances.

testosterone This is the primary testicular hormone in a man, which stimulates the maturation of the male genitals and the development of hair growth, production of sperm and voice changes.

thalidomide A drug that is no longer prescribed but which was given to pregnant women in the 1950s to prevent morning sickness. This led to babies being born with severe limb deformities if taken during first two months of pregnancy.

theory An interconnecting set of statements that structure how we observe and categorise facts about the world.

theory of mind (TOM) The understanding that people have different emotions, thoughts and feelings from oneself.

transactional model This approach describes the way in which innate skills and abilities interact with the environment. In this model the child's behaviour can change the social context of development by influencing the responses of others to them. In the same way, the pre-existing beliefs, etc., of the individual in the child's environment will influence how they respond to the child. In this way the child and context shape each other.

trophoblasts Are cells that develop at the first stage of pregnancy, formed on the outer layer of a *blastocyst*, that provide nutrients to the embryo and develop into a large part of the placenta.

ulnar grasp An early manipulatory skill used by infants, in which objects are grasped by pressing the fingers against the palm.

umbilical cord The vascular tube that connects the foetus with the placenta, which passes it oxygen and nutrients.

under-extension The extension of a word meaning to too few instances by a young child – for example, when a child restricts a word such as 'dog' to situations in which the child is playing with a toy, but then fails to refer to the animal in the park as 'dog'.

visual cliff A piece of equipment developed by Gibson and Walk to investigate depth perception in human infants and animals.

visual cortex The part of the brain that specialises in processing information and pattern recognition.

working memory Refers to the cognitive system that provides temporary storage and manipulation of the information necessary for complex tasks such as language comprehension, learning, problem-solving and decision-making.

zone of proximal development (ZPD) The conceptual zone/space between a child completing a task on their own and where the task can be completed with assistance from an adult or older peer. This defines the way in which an adult/older peer through conversational interaction can scaffold a child's learning.

ZPD *Zone of proximal development.*

References

Abrams, D., Eilola, T., & Swift, H. (2009). Attitudes to age in Britain 2004–2008. *Department for Work and Pensions.* Research report no. 599. Available online at: http://research.dwp.gov.uk/asd/asd5/rports2009-2010/rrep599.pdf

Acredolo, L., & Goodwyn, S. (1998). *Baby signs.* Chicago, IL: Contemporary Books.

Adolph, K. E. (2002a). Learning to keep balance. In R. V. Kali (Ed.) *Advances in child development and behaviour.* Burlington, MA: Academic Press.

Adolph, K. E. (2002b). Babies' steps make giant stride towards a science of development. *Infant Behaviour and Development, 25,* 86–90.

Aguiar, A., & Baillargeon, R. (2002). Developments in young infants' reasoning about occluded objects. *Cognitive Psychology, 45*(2), 267–336.

Ainsworth, M., & Bell, S. (1970). Attachment, exploration and separation: Illustrated by the behaviour of one-year-olds in a strange situation. *Child Development, 41,* 49–65.

Alder, E. M., & Ross, L. A. (2000). Menopausal symptoms and the domino effect. *Journal of Reproductive and Infant Psychology, 18,* 75–78.

Aldred, C., Green J., & Adams C. (2004). A new social communication intervention for children with autism: Pilot randomised controlled treatment study suggesting effectiveness. *Journal of Child Psychology and Psychiatry, 45,* 1420–1430.

Alexander, G. M., Wilcox, T., & Woods, R. (2009). Sex differences in infants' visual interest in toys. *Archives of Sexual Behavior, 38*(3), 427–433.

Amara, C. E., Rice, C. L., Koval, J. J., Paterson, D. H., Winter, E. M., & Cunningham, D.A. (2003). Allometric scaling of strength in an independently living population age 55–86 years. *American Journal of Human Biology, 15,* 48–60.

AMRC (2008). A code of practice for the diagnosis and confirmation of death. London: AMRC. Available online at: www.aomrc.org.uk/reports-guidance.html

Archer, J. (1999). *The nature of grief: The evolution and psychology of reactions to loss.* New York: Routledge.

Aries, P. (1981). *The hour of our death.* New York: Oxford University Press.

Arnett, J. J. (2000). Emerging adulthood: A theory of development from the late teens through the twenties. *American Psychologist, 55*(5), 469–480.

Arnett, J. J. (2006). Emerging adulthood: Understanding the new way of coming of age. In J. J. Arnett & J. L. Tanner (Eds.), *Emerging adults in America: Coming of age in the 21st century.* Washington, D.C.: American Psychological Association.

Avigil, M., & Ornoy, A. (2006). Herpes simplex virus and Epstein-Barr virus infections in pregnancy: Consequences of neonatal or intrauterine infection. *Reproductive Toxicology, 21,* 436–445.

Axline, V. M. (1971). *Play therapy.* New York: Ballantine Books.

Azmitia, M., Kamprath, N., & Linnet, J. (1998). Intimacy and conflict: On the dynamics of boys' and girls' friendships during middle childhood and adolescence. In L. Meyer, M. Grenot-Scheyer, B. Harry, H. Park & I. Schwartz (Eds.). *Understanding the social lives of children and youth.* Baltimore, MD: P.H. Brookes.

Bahrick, L. E. (2001). Increasing specificity in perceptual development: Infants' detection of nested levels of multimodal stimulation. *Journal of Experimental Child Psychology, 79,* 253–270.

Baillargeon, E., Baillargeon, R., Spelke, E., & Wasserman, S. (1985). Object permanence in five-month-old infants. *Cognition, 20,* 191–208.

Bakermans-Kranenburg, M. J., Van IJzendoorn, M. H., & Juffer, F. (2003) Less is more: Meta-analyses of sensitivity and attachment interventions in early childhood. *Psychological Bulletin, 129,* 195–215.

Baltes, P. B. (2003). On the incomplete architecture of human ontogeny: Selection, optimization and compensation as foundation of developmental theory. In U. M. Staudinger and U. Lindenberger (Eds.), *Understanding human development: Dialogues with lifespan psychology.* Boston, MA: Kluwer.

Bannister, D., & Agnew, J. (1977). The child's construing of self. In J. K. Cole (Ed.), *Nebraska symposium on motivation, 1976.* (pp. 99–125) Lincoln, NE: University of Nebraska.

BAPT (2008). An ethical basis for good practice in play therapy. Available online at: www.bapt.info/downloads/Ethical%20Booklet%208095-2.pdf

Baron Cohen, S. (2001). Theory of mind in normal development and autism. *Prisme, 34,* 174–183.

Basseches M. (1984). *Dialectical thinking and adult development.* Norwood, NJ: Ablex.

Bates, J. E. (2003). Temperamental unadaptability and later internalising problems as moderated by mothers' restrictive control. Paper presented at the meeting for the Society for Research in Child Development, Tampa, FL.

Baumeister, R. F., Campbell, J. D., Krueger, J. I., & Vohs, K. D. (2003). Does high self-esteem cause better performance, interpersonal success, happiness or healthier lifestyles? *Psychological Science in the Public Interest, 4*(1), 1–44.

Bayley, N. (1993). *Bayley scales of infant development: Birth to two years.* San Antonio, TX: Psychological Corporation.

Bem, S. L. (1989). Genital knowledge and gender constancy in preschool children. *Child Development, 60,* 649–662.

Bergen, D. (1988). Stages of play development. In D. Bergen (Ed.), *Play as a medium for learning and development.* Portsmouth: Heinemann.

References

Bering, J. M., & Bjorklund, D. F. (2004) The natural emergence of afterlife reasoning as a developmental regularity. *Developmental Psychology, 40*, 217–233.

Berko Gleason, J. (1973). Code switching in children's language. In T. E. Moore (Ed.), *Cognitive development and the acquisition of language.* New York: Academic Press.

Bielak, A. M. (2010). How can we not 'lose it' if we still don't understand how to 'use it'? Unanswered questions about the influence of activity participation on cognitive performance in older age: A mini-review. *Gerontology 56*(6), 507–519.

Birren, J. E., Butler, R. N., Greenhouse, S. W, Sokoloff, L., & Yarrow, M. R. (Eds.) (1963). *Human aging: A biological and behavioral study.* Washington, DC: US Government Printing Office.

Bjorklund, D. F. (2005). *Children's thinking: Cognitive development and individual differences* (4th ed.). Belmont, CA: Wadsworth.

Blackburn, R. T. (1985) Faculty career development: theory and practice. In S. M. Clark & D. R. Lewis (Eds.), *Faculty vitality and institutional productivity.* New York: Teachers College Press.

Blackburn, J. A., & Papalia, D. E. (1992). The study of adult cognition from a Piagetian perspective. In R. J. Sternberg & C. A. Berg (Eds.), *Intellectual development.* New York: Cambridge University Press.

Blaskewicz Boron, J., Turiano, N. A., Willis, S. L., & Schaie, K. W. (2007). Effects of cognitive training on change in accuracy in inductive reasoning ability. *Journal of Gerontology, 62*(3), 179–186.

Blatchford, P. (1998). *Social life in school.* London: Falmer.

Blatchford, P., Creeser, R., & Mooney, A. (1990). Playground games and playtime: The children's view. *Educational Research, 32*(3), 163–174.

Blatchford, P., Pellegrini, T., Baines, E., & Kentaro, K. (2002). Playground games: Their social context in elementary/junior school. Final Report to the Spencer Foundation. Available online at: www.breaktime.org.uk/SpencerFinalReport02.pdf

Bloom, L. (1998). *Language acquisition in its developmental context.* Oxford: Oxford University Press.

Bloom, L., Lifter, K. & Broughton, J. (1985). The convergence of early cognition and language in the second year of life: Problems in conceptualisation and measurement. In M. Barrett (ed.), *Children's single-word speech.* London: Wiley.

Bluebond-Langner, M. (1977). Meanings of death to children. In H. Feifel (Ed.), *New meanings of death.* New York: McGraw-Hill.

Blumstein Posner, R. (2006). Early menarche: A review of research on trends in timing, racial differences, etiology and psychosocial consequences. *Sex Roles, 54* (5–6), 315–322.

Bonvillian, J. D., Orlansky, M. D., & Novack, L. L. (1983). Developmental milestones: Sign language acquisition and motor development. *Child Development, 54*, 1435–1445.

Booth, J. R., Wood, L., Lu, D., Honk, J. C., & Bitan, T. (2007). The role of the basal ganglia and cerebellum in language processing. Brain Research, *1133*, 136–144.

Bowlby J. (1969). *Attachment and loss: Attachment* (Vol. 1). New York: Basic Books.

Bowlby, J. (1944). Forty-four juvenile thieves: Their characters and home-life. *International Journal of Psycho-Analysis, 25*, 19–53.

Boyatzis, C. J., & Watson, M. W. (1993). Preschool children's symbolic representation of objects through gestures. *Child Development, 64*(3), 729–735.

Boysson-Bardies, B. (1999). *How language comes to children: From birth to two years* (trans. M. DeBoise). Cambridge, MA: MIT Press.

Bratton, S. C., Ray, D., Rhine, T., & Jones, L. (2005). The efficacy of play therapy with children: A meta-analytic review of treatment outcomes. *Professional Psychology: Research and Practice, 36*, 376–390.

Bretherton, I. & Mulholland, K. A. (1999). Internal working models in attachment relations: A construct revisited. In J. Cassidy & P. R. Shaver (Eds.), *Handbook of attachment: Theory, research and clinical applications* (pp. 89–111). New York: Guilford Press.

Bril, B. (1999). Dires sur l'enfant selon les cultures: Etat des lieux et perspectives. In B. Bril, P. R. Dansen, C. Sabatier & B. Krewer (Eds.), *Propos sur l'enfant et l'adolescent. Quel enfants pour quelles cultures*? Paris: L'Harmattan.

Brim, O. G, Ryff, C. D., & Kessler, R. C. (2004). *How healthy are we? A national study of of well-being at midlife.* London: University of Chicago Press.

Bristow, D., Dehaene-Lambertz, G., & Mattout, J. (2008). Hearing faces: How the infant brain matches the face it sees with the speech it hears. *Journal of Cognitive Neuroscience 21*(5), 905–921.

Brooks-Gunn, J., Petersen, A. C., Eichorn, D. (1985). The study of maturational timing effects in adolescence. *Journal of Youth and Adolescence, 14*, 149–161.

Brown, R. (1973). *A first language: The early stages.* Cambridge MA: Harvard University Press.

Brown, R., & Hanlon, C. (1970). Derivational complexity and order of acquisition in child speech. In J. Hayes (Ed.), *Cognition and the development of language.* New York: Wiley.

Bruner, J. S. (1993). Explaining and interpreting: Two ways of using mind. In G. Harman (Ed.), *Conceptions of the human mind: Essays in honor of George A. Miller,* (pp. 123–37). Hillsdale, NJ: Lawrence Erlbaum.

Bruner, J. S. (1983). *Child talk.* New York: W. W. Norton.

Bruner, J. S. (1975). The ontogenesis of speech acts. *Journal of Child Language, 2*, 1–19.

Buhrmester, D. (1990). Intimacy of friendship, interpersonal competence, and adjustment during preadolescence and adolescence. *Child Development, 61*, 1101–1111.

Buhrmester, D. (1996). Need fulfillment, interpersonal competence, and the developmental contexts of early adolescent friendship. In W. Bukowski, A. Newcomb, & W. Hartup, (Eds.) *The company they keep* (pp. 158–185). New York: Cambridge University Press.

Burckhardt, C. S., & Anderson, K. L. (2003). The quality of life scale (QOLS): Reliability, validity, and utilization. *Health and Quality of Life Outcomes, 1*(60)

Burke, D. M., & Shafto, M. A. (2004). Aging and language production. Current *Directions in Psychological Science, 13*, 21–24.

Bushnell, I. W. R. (2003). Newborn face recognition. In O. Pascalis & A. Slater (Eds.), *The development of face processing in infancy and early childhood* (pp. 41–53). New York: NOVA Science.

Byrnes, J. P. (1996). *Cognitive development and learning in instructional contexts.* Boston, MA: Allyn & Bacon.

Campos, J. J., Anderson, D. I., Barbu-Roth, M. A., Hubbard, E. M., hertenstein, M. J., & Witherington, D. (2000). Travel broadens the mind. *Infancy, 1*(2), 149–219.

Campos, J. J., Bertenthal, B. I., & Kermoian, R. (1992). Early experience and emotional development: The emergence of wariness of heights. *Psychological Science, 3,* 61–64.

Carpenter, S., & Karakitapoglu-Aygün, Z. (2005). Importance and descriptiveness of self-aspects: A cross-cultural comparison. *Cross-Cultural Research, 39*(3), 293–321.

Carson, V., Spence, J. C., Cutumisu, N., & Lindsey Cargill, L. (2010). Association between neighborhood socioeconomic status and screen time among pre-school children: A cross-sectional study. *BMC Public Health, 10,* 367. Available online at: **www.biomedcentral.com/1471-2458/10/367**

Carstensten, L. L. (1992). Motivation for social contact across the lifespan: A theory of socio-emotional selectivity. In Janis E. Jacobs (Ed.), *Nebraska symposium on motivation: Developmental perspectives on motivation (current theory and research in motivation).* Nebraska, NE: University of Nebraska Press.

Case-Smith, J. (2008). Play preferences of typically developing children and children With developmental delays between ages 3 and 7 Years. *OTJR: Occupation, Participation and Health, 28*(1), 19–29.

Chachkes, E., & Jennings, R. (1994). Latino communities: Coping with death. In B. Dane & C. Levine (Eds.), *AIDS and the new orphans: Coping with death,* (pp. 77–100). Westport, CT: Greenwood Press.

Charles, S. T., & Mavandadi, S. (2004). Social support and physical health across the life span: Sociomotional influences. In F. R. Lang & K. L. Fingerman (Eds.), *Growing together: Personal relationships across the life span,* (pp. 240–67). New York: Cambridge University Press.

Cintas, H. M. (1989). Cross-cultural variation in infant motor development. *Physical & Occupational Therapy in Pediatrics, 8,* 1–20.

Clark, D. C., Pynoos, M. D., & Goebel, A. E. (1994). Mechanisms and processes of adolescent bereavement. In R. J. Haggerty, L. R. Sherrod, N. Garmezy, & M. Rutter (Eds.), *Stress, risk and resilience in children and adolescence.* Cambridge: Cambridge University Press.

Clark, R., Hyde, J. S., Essex, M. J., & Klein, M. H. (2006). Lenghth of maternity leave and quality of mother–infant interactions. *Child Development, 68*(2), 364–383.

Cohen, L. B., & Cashon, C. H. (2003). Infant perception and cognition. In R. Lerner, A. Easterbrooks, & J. Mistry (Eds.), *Comprehensive handbook of Psychology: Volume 6: Developmental psychology: II: Infancy* (pp. 65–89). New York: Wiley.

Cole, M. (1990). Cognitive development and formal schooling: The evidence from cross-cultural research. In L. C. Moll (Ed.), *Vygotsky and education.* New York: Cambridge University Press.

Coleman, J. C. (1978). Current contradictions in adolescent theory. *Journal of Youth and Adolescence, 7,* 1–11

Commons, M. L., Richards, F. A., & Armon, C. (1984). *Beyond formal operations: Late adolescent and adult cognitive development.* New York: Praeger.

Cook, A. S., & Dworkin, D. S. (1992). *Helping the bereaved: Therapeutic interventions for children, adolescents and adults.* New York: Basic Books.

Cooley, C. H (1902). *Human nature and the social order.* New York, Charles Schribner's Sons.

Creasey, G., Jarvis, P., & Berk, L. (1998). Play and social competence. In O. Saracho & B. Spodek (Eds.), *Multiple perspectives on play in early childhood education* (pp. 116–143). Albany, NY: State University of New York Press.

Croghan, R., Griffin, C., Hunter, J., & Phoenix, A. (2006). Style failure: Consumption, identity and social exclusion. *Journal of Youth Studies, 9,* 463–478.

Cromer, R. F. (1987). Language growth with experience without feedback. *Journal of Psycholinguistic Research, 16,* 223–231.

Crystal, D. (1996). Language play and linguistic intervention. *Child Language Teaching and Therapy, 12,* 328–344.

Csikszentmihalyi, M., & Larson, R. (1984). *Being adolescent: Conflict and growth in the teenage years.* New York: Basic Books.

Cushman, F. (2008). Crime and punishment: Distinguishing the roles of causal and intentional analyses in moral judgement. *Cognition, 108*(2), 353–380.

Damon, W., & Hart, D. (1988). *Self-understanding in childhood and adolescence.* New York: Cambridge University Press.

Darwin C. (1859). *On the Origin of Species.* London: John Murray.

Davies, B. E., Moon, R. M., Sachs, M. C., & Ottolini, C. Y. (1998). Effects of sleep position on infant motor development. *Pediatrics, 102*(5), 1135–1140.

Davies, R. (2005). Mothers' stories of loss: Their need to be with their dying child and their child's body after death. *Journal of Child Health Care, 9*(4), 288–300.

DeCasper, A. J., & Fifer, W. P. (1980). Of human bonding: Newborns prefer their mothers' voices. *Science, 280*(6), 1174–1176.

References

DeCasper, A. J., & Spence, M. J. (1986). Prenatal maternal speech influences newborns' perception of speech sounds. *Infant Behavior and Development, 9*, 133–150.

DfES (2007). Raising expectations: Staying in education and training post-16. London: Her Majesty's Stationery Office. Available online at: www.education.gov.uk/search/results?q=Raising+expectations%3A+staying+2education+and+training+post-16

Demetriou, A., Christon, C., Spanoudis, G., & Platsdou, M. (2002). The development of mental processing: Efficiency, working memory, and thinking. *Monographs of the Society for Research in Child Development, 67*(1), Serial no.268, 1–154.

Department of Health (2008). End of life care strategy. London: Department of Health. Available online at: www.endoflifecareforadults.nhs.uk/assets/downloads/2pubs_EoLC_Strategy_1.pdf

Diamond, A. D. (1985). Development of the ability to use recall to guide action as indicated by infants' performance on AB. *Child Development, 56*(4), 868–883.

Diamond, L. M. (2000). Sexual identity, attractions, and behavior among young sexual-minority women over a two-year period. *Developmental Psychology, 36*(2), 241–250.

Donaldson, M. (1978). *Children's minds.* London: Croom Helm.

Dunn, J. (1988). *The beginnings of social understanding.* Oxford: Blackwell.

Dwyer, K. M., Booth-LaForce, C., Fredstrom, B. K., Rubin, K. H., Rose-krasnor, L., & Burgess, K. B. (2010). Attachment, social information processing, and friendship quality of early adolescent girls and boys. *Journal of Social and Personal Relationships, 27*(1), 91–116.

Earles, J. L., & Salthouse, T. A. (1995). Interrelations of age, health, and speed. *Journal of Gerontology: Psychological Sciences, 50B*(2), 33–41.

Eisenberg, N., & Fabes, R. A. (2006). Prosocial development. In W. Damon, R. M. Lemer, & N. Eisenberg (Eds.), *Handbook of child psychology:* Vol. 3: *Social, emotional, and personality development* (6th ed., pp. 701–778). New York: Wiley.

Eisenberg, N., Valiente, C., Fabes, R. A., Smith, C. L., Reiser, M., Shepard, S. A., Losoya, S. H., Guthrie, I. K., Murphy, B. C., & Cumberland, A. J. (2003). The relations of effortful control and ego control to children's resiliency and social functioning. *Developmental Psychology, 39*(4), 761–776.

Elias, C. L., & Berk, L. (2006). Self regulation in young children: Is there a role for sociodramatic play? *Early Childhood Research Quarterly, 17*(2), 216–238.

Ellaway, A., Kirk, A., Macintyre, S., & Mutrie, N. (2006). Nowhere to play? The relationship between the location of outdoor play areas and deprivation in Glasgow. *Health & Place, 13*(2), 557–561.

Enzinger, C., Fazekas, F., Matthews, P. M., Ropele, S., Schmidt, H., Smith, S., & Schmidt, R. (2005). Risk factors for progression of brain atrophy in aging: six-year follow-up of normal subjects. *Neurology. 64*(10), 1704–1711.

Epstein, J. L (1986). Friendship selection: Developmental and environmental influences. In E. C. Mueller & C. R. Cooper (Eds.), *Process and outcome in peer relationships.* New York: Academic Press.

Erikson, E. (1950). *Childhood and society.* New York: W. W. Norton.

Evans, J. L. (2006). The emergence of language: A dynamical systems account. In Erika Hoff & Marilyn Shatz (Eds.) *Blackwell handbook of language development.* Oxford: Blackwell

Fan, Y., Batmanghelich, N., Clark, C. M., Davatzikos, C., & Alzheimer's Disease Neuroimaging Initiative. (2008). Spatial patterns of brain atrophy in MCI patients, identified via high-dimensional pattern classification, predict subsequent cognitive decline. *Neuroimage, 39*, 1731–1743.

Fantz, R. L. (1963). Pattern vision in newborn infants. *Science, 140*, 296–297.

Faulkner, K. W. (1997). Talking about death with a dying child. *American Journal of Nursing, 97*, 65–69.

Fawcett, L. M., & Garton, A. F. (2005). The effect of peer collaboration on children's problem-solving ability. *British Journal of Educational Psychology, 75*(2), 157–169.

Fein, G. G. (1986). Pretend play. In D. Gorlitz & J. F. Wohlwill (Eds.), *Curiosity, imagination and play.* Hillsdale NJ: Erlbaum.

Fenson, L., Dale, P. S., Reznick. J. S., Bates, E., Thal, D. J., & Pethick, S. J. (1994). Variability in early communicative development. *Monographs of the Society for Research in Child Development, 59*(5), Serial No.542).

Fentress J. C., & Mcleaod, P. J. (1986). Motor patterns in development. In E. M. Blass (Ed.), *Handbook of behavioural neurobiology: Vol. 8: Developmental psychology and developmental neurobiology.* New York: Plenum.

Fernald, A. (1989). Intonation and communicative intent in mothers' speech to infants: Is the melody the message? *Child Development, 60*(6), 1497–1510.

Fernald, A. (1985). Four-month-old infants prefer to listen to motherese. *Infant Behaviour and Development, 8*, 181–195.

Field, D. (1981). Can preschool children really learn to conserve? *Child Development, 52*(1), 326–334.

Fischer, J. L., Sollie, D. L., Sorell, G. T., & Green, S. K. (1989). Marital status and career stage influences on social networks of young adults. *Journal of Marriage and the Family, 51*(2), 521–534.

Flavell, J. H., & Miller, P. H. (1998). Social cognition. In D. Kuhn & R. S. Siegler (Eds.), *Handbook of child psychology:* Vol. 2. (5th ed., pp. 851–898). New York: John Wiley.

Flavell, J. H., Miller, P. H., & Miller, S. A. (1993). *Cognitive development* (3rd ed.). Englewood Cliffs, NJ: Prentice Hall.

Flint, M. (1982). Male and female menopause: A cultural put on. In A. M. Voda, M. Dinnerstein, & S. R. O'Donnell (Eds.), *Changing perspectives on menopause* (pp. 363–378). Austin, TX: University of Texas Press.

Ford, J., Rugg, J., & Burrows, R. (2002). Conceptualising the contemporary role of housing in the transition to adult life in England. *Urban Studies, 39*, 2455–2467.

Fotenos, A. F., Mintun, M. A., Snyder, A. Z., Morris, J, C., & Buckner, R. L. (2008). Brain volume decline in aging: Evidence for a relation between socioeconomic status, preclinical alzheimer disease, and reverse. *Archives of Neurology, 65*(1), 113–120.

Fraley, R. C., Waller, N. G., & Brennan, K. A. (2000). An item-response theory analysis of self-report measures of adult attachment. *Journal of Personality and Social Psychology, 78*, 350–365.

Freud, A. (1958). Adolescence. In A. Freud, *The writings of Anna Freud: Volume 5: (1956-1965). Research at the Hampstead Child-Therapy Clinic and other papers.* Indiana, PA: Indiana University of Pennsylvania.

Freud, S. (1917). *A general introduction to psychoanalysis.* New York: Washington Square Press.

Freund, A. M., & Ritter, J. O. (2009). Midlife crisis: A debate. *Gerontology, 55*(5), 582–591.

Friedberg, L. (2003). The impact of technological change on older workers: evidence from data on computers. *Industrial and Labor Relations Review, 56*, 511–529.

Frisen, A., & Holmqvist, K. (2010). Physical, sociocultural, and behavioral factors associated with body-esteem in 16-year-old Swedish boys and girls. *Sex Roles, 63*, 373–385.

Furstenberg, F., Kefalas, M., & Napolitano, L. (2005). *Marriage is more than being together: The meaning of marriage among young adults in the United States.* Network on Transitions to Adulthood Research Network Working Paper. Available online at: www.transad.pop.upenn. edu/downloads/kefalasmarriagenorms.pdf

Furth, H. G. (1973). Further thoughts on thinking and language. *Psychological Bulletin, 79*(3), 215–216.

Galloway, J. C., & Thelen, E. (2004). Feet first: Object exploration in young infants. *Infant Behavior and Development, 27*, 107–112.

Garbarino, J. J. (1998). Comparisons of the constructs and psychometric properties of selected measures of adult attachment. *Measurement & Evaluation in Counseling & Development, 31*, 28–45.

Garvey, C. (1990). *Play.* Cambridge, MA: Harvard University Press.

Gershkoff-Stowe, L., & Thelen, E. (2004). U-shaped changes in behavior: A dynamic systems perspective. *Journal of Cognition and Development, 5*, 11–36.

Gibson, E. J., & Walk, R. D. (1960). The 'visual cliff'. *Scientific American, 202*, 64–71.

Gibson, E. J., & Spelke, E. S. (1983). The development of perception. In P. Mussen (Series Ed.) & J. H. Flavell & E. Markman (Eds.), *Handbook of child psychology: Vol 3: Cognitive development* (4th ed., 1–76) New York: Wiley.

Gilligan, C. (1982). *In a different voice: Psychological theory and women's development.* Cambridge, MA: Harvard University Press.

Gilligan, C. (1996). The centrality of relationships in psychological development: A puzzle, some evidence and a theory. In G. G. Noam & K. W.

Fischer (Eds.), *Development and vulnerability in close relationships.* Hillsdale NJ: Erlbaum.

Gold, E. B., Sternfield, B., Kelsey, J. L., Brown, C., et al. (2000). Relation of demographic and lifestyle factors to symptoms in a multi-racial/ethnic population of women 40–55 years of age. *American Journal of Epidemiology, 152*(5), 463–473.

Goldfarb, W. (1947). Variations in adolescent adjustment of institutionally-reared children. *American Journal of Orthopsychiatry, 17*, 449–457.

Gopnik, A. (1993). How we know our minds: The illusion of first-person knowledge of intentionality. *Behavioral and Brain Sciences, 16*, 1–14.

Gopnik, A., & Meltzoff, A. N. (1997). *Words, thoughts, and theories.* Cambridge, MA: Bradford, MIT Press.

Gordon-Salant, S., Yeni-Konshian, G., Fitzgibbons, P. J., & Barrett, J. (2006). Age-related differences in identification and discrimination of temporal cues in speech segments. *Journal of the Acoustical Society of America, 119*(4), 2455–2466.

Graber, J. A., & Brooks-Gunn, J. (2001). Body image. In R. M. Lerner & J. V. Learner (Eds.), *Adolescence in America.* Santa Barbara, CA: ABC-CLIO.

Grady, C. L., Springer, M. V., Hongwanishkul, D., McIntosh, A. R., & Winocur, G. (2006). Age-related changes in brain activity across the adult lifespan. *Journal of Cognitive Neuroscience, 18*, 227–241.

Graham, P., & Rutter, M. (1985). Adolescent disorders. In M. Rutter and L. Hersov (Eds.), *Child and adolescent psychiatry: Modern approaches* (4th ed). Oxford: Blackwell Scientific.

Greig, A., & Taylor, J. (1999). *Doing research with children.* London: Sage.

Groos, K. (1898). *The play of animals.* New York: Appleton.

Grossbart, T. A., & Sarwer, D. B. (2003). Psychosocial issues and their relevance to the cosmetic surgery patient. *Seminars in Cutaneous Medical Surgery, 22*(2), 136–147.

Guest, S. D., Davidson, A. J., Rulison, K. L., Moody, J., & Welsch (2007). Features of groups and status hierarchies in girls' and boys' early adolescent peer networks. *New Directions for Child and Adolescent Development, 118*, 43–60.

Guisinger, S. J., & Blatt, S. J. (1994). Individuality and relatedness: Evolution of a fundamental dialectic. *American Psychologist, 49*, 104–111.

Gunnar, M. R., & Quevedo, K. (2007). The neurobiology of stress and development. *Annual Review of Psychology, 58*, 145–173.

Haight, W. L., & Miller, P. J. (1993). *Pretending at home.* Albany, NY: SUNY Press.

Hale, S. (1990). A global developmental trend in cognitive processing speed. *Child Development, 61*, 653–663.

Hall, G. S. (1904). *Adolescence: Its psychology and its relations to physiology, anthropology, sociology, sex, crime, religion and education.* New York: Appleton.

Harkness, S., & Super, C. M. (1995). Culture and parenting. In M. H. Bornstein (Ed.), *Handbook of parenting,* Vol 3. Hillside, NJ: Erlbaum.

References

Harlow, H. F. (1958). The nature of love. *American Psychologist, 13*, 673–685.

Harlow, H. F., & Harlow, M. K. (1966). Social deprivation in monkeys. In M. L. Haimowitz and N. R. Haimowitz (Eds.), *Human development*. New York: Thomas Y. Crowell.

Harlow, H. F., & Zimmerman, R. R. (1959). Affectional responses in the infant monkey. *Science 130*(3373), 421–432.

Harris, M. (1992). *Language experience and early language development: From input to uptake*. Hove, East Sussex: Lawrence Erlbaum.

Harris, M., Barlow-Brown, F., & Chasin, J. (1995a). The emergence of referential understanding: Pointing and the comprehension of object names. *First Language, 15*, 19–34.

Harris, M., Yeeles, C., Chasin, J., & Oakley, Y. (1995b). Symmetries and asymmetries in early lexical comprehension and production. *Journal of Child Language, 22*, 1–18.

Harris, P. L. (2006). Social cognition. In W. Damon & W. R. Lerner (Eds.), *Handbook of child psychology*, Vol 2 (6th ed.) New York: Wiley.

Harris, P. L. (1989). Object permanence in infancy. In A. Slater & J. G. Bremner (Eds.), *Infant development: Recent advances*. Hove, East Sussex: Lawrence Erlbaum).

Hartup, W. W. (1996). The company they keep: Friendships and their developmental significance. *Child Development, 67*, 1–13.

Hayden, K. M., Zandi, P. P., Lyketsos, C. G., Khachaturian, A. S., Bastian, L. A., Charoonruk, G., Tschanz, J. T., Norton, M. C., Pieper, C. F., Munger, R. G., Breitner, J. C., Welsh-Bohmer, K. A., & Cache County Investigators (2006). Vascular risk factors for incident Alzheimer disease and vascular dementia: The Cache County study. *Alzheimer Disease and Associated Disorders, 20*(2), 93–100.

Hazan, C., & Shaver, P. (1987). Romantic love conceptualized as an attachment process. *Journal of Personality and Social Psychology, 52*, 511–524.

Hazan, C., & Shaver, P. (1990). Love and work: An attachment-theoretical perspective. *Journal of Personality and Social Psychology, 59*, 270–280.

Heath, S. (2008). Housing choices and issues for young people in the UK: A review of recent research on the housing choices and issues for young people in the UK. York: Joseph Rowntree Foundation. Available outline at: www.ecotec.com/pdfs/2325-young-people-housing.pdf

Hedlund, B., & Ebersole, P. (1983). A test of Levinson's midlife re-evaluation. *Journal of Genetic Psychology, 143*(2), 189–192.

Herkert, B. (2000). Communicating grief, *OMEGA – Journal of Death & Dying, 41*, 93–116

Hermans, H., & Oles, P. (1999). Midlife crisis in men: Affective organization of personal meanings. *Human relations, 52*, 1403–1426.

Hewes, J. (2010). Voices from the field – learning through play: A view from the field. In R. E. Tremblay, R. G. Barr, and R. De V. Peters, & M. Boivin (Eds.), *Encyclopedia on early childhood development* [online]. Montreal, Quebec: Centre of Excellence for Early Childhood Development. Available online at: www.enfant-encyclopedie.com/pages/PDF/HewesANGps.pdf

Hines, M. and Brooks, G. (2005) *Sheffield Babies Love Books: An Evaluation of the Sheffield Bookstart Project*. Sheffield: University Sheffield.

Hochschild, A., & Machong, A. (1989). The second shift: Working parents and the revolution at home. New York: Viking Penguin.

Hodges J., & Tizard B. (1989). IQ and behavioural adjustment of ex-institutional adolescents. *Journal of Child Psychology and Psychiatry, 30*(1), 53–75.

Hopkins, B. (1991). Facilitating early motor development: An intracultural study of West Indian mothers and their infants living in Britain. In J. K. Nugent, B. M. Lester & T. B. Brazelton (Eds.), *The Cultural Context of Infancy*, Vol 2. Norwood, NJ: Ablex.

Hoss, R. A., & Langlois, J. H. (2003). Infants prefer attractive faces. In O. Pascalis & A. Slater (Eds.), *The development of face processing in infancy and early childhood* (pp. 27–38). New York: NOVA Science.

Houston-Price, C., & Nakai, S. (2004). Distinguishing novelty and familiarity effects in infant preference procedures. *Infant and Child Development, 13*, 341–348.

Howe, N., Moller, L., & Chambers, B. (1994). Dramatic play in day care: What happens when doctors, cooks, bakers, pirates and pharmacists invade the classroom? In H. Goelman, E. Jacobs, H. Goelman, E. Jacobs (Eds.), *Children's play in child care settings* (pp. 102–118). Albany, NY: State University of New York Press.

Hughes, M. (1975). Egocentrism in preschool children. Unpublished PhD thesis, University of Edinburgh, UK.

Hutt, C. (1966). Exploration and play in children. *Symposia of the Zoological Society of London, 18*, 61–81.

Inoff-Germain, G., Chrousos, G., Arnold, G., Nottelmann, E., & Cutler, G. (1988). Relations between hormone levels and observational measures of aggressive behavior of young adolescents in family interactions. *Developmental Psychology, 24*, 129–139.

Iverson, P., Kuhl, P. K., Akahane-Yamada, R. Diesch, E., Tohkura, Y., Ketterman, A., & Siebert, C. (2003). A perceptual interference account of acquisition difficulties in non-native phonemes. *Cognition, 87*, B47–B57.

Jaffee, S., & Hyde, J. S. (2000). Gender differences in moral orientation: A meta-analysis. *Psychological Bulletin, 126*(5), 703–726.

James, W. (1890). *The principles of psychology*. New York: Dover.

Jenkins, S. R. (1989). Longitudinal prediction of women's careers: Psychological, behavioural, and social-structural influences. *Journal of Vocational Behavior, 34*, 204–235.

Jusczyk, P. W. (2002). Language development: From speech perception to first words. In A. Slater & M. Lewis (Eds.), *Introduction to infant development* (pp. 147–164). Oxford: Oxford University Press.

Kagan J. (2003). Biology, context and developmental inquiry. *Annual Review of Psychology, 54*, 1–23.

Kagan, J., Articus, D., Snidman, N., Feng, W. Y., & Hendler, J. (1994). Reactivity in infants: A cross-national comparison. *Developmental Psychology, 30*(3), 342–343.

Kaye, K., & Brazelton, T. B. (1971). Mother–infant interaction in the organization of sucking. Paper presented to the Society for Research in Child Development, Minneapolis, MN, March 1971.

Kaye, K., & Fogel, A. (1980). The temporal structure of face-to-face communication between mothers and infants. *Developmental Psychology, 16*, 454–464.

Kellehear, A. (2005). Compassionate Cities: Public health and end of life care. Abingdon: Routledge.

Kellehear, A., & O'Connor, D. (2008). Health promoting palliative care: A practice example. *Critical Public Health, 18*(1), 111–115.

Killen, M. (2007). Children's social and moral reasoning about exclusion. *Current Directions in Psychological Science, 16*, 32–36.

Killen, M., & Stangor, C. (2001). Children's social reasoning about inclusion and exclusion in gender and race peer group contexts. *Child Development, 72*(1), 174–186.

Kim, U., & Berry, J. W. (1993). *Indigenous psychologies: Research and experience in cultural context*. Newbury Park, CA: Sage.

Kirchmeyer, C. (2006). The different effects of family on objective career success across gender: A test of alternative explanations. *Journal of Vocational Behaviour, 68*, 323–346.

Kirkpatrick, L. A., & Davis, K.E. (1994). Attachment style, gender, and relationship stability: A longitudinal analysis. *Journal of Personality and Social Psychology, 66*, 502–512.

Kitchener, K. S., Lynch, C. L., Fischer, K. W., & Wood, P. K. (1993). Developmental range of reflective judgement: The effect of contextual support and practice on developmental stage. *Developmental Psychology, 29*(5), 893–906. Available online at: https://gseweb. harvard.edu/zddl/articlesCopy/Kitchener-etal1993DevRangeReflectJudgem.pdf

Kivipelto, M., Ngandu, T., Fratiglioni, L et al. (2005) Obesity and Vascular Risk Factors at Midlife and the Risk of Dementia and Alzheimer Disease Arch Neurol. 2005;62:1556-1560

Kohlberg, L. (1966). A cognitive-developmental analysis of children's sex-role concepts and attitudes. In E. E Maccoby (Ed.), *The development of sex differences*. Stanford, CA: Stanford University Press.

Kohlberg, L. (1958). The development of modes of moral thinking and choice in the years 10 to 16. Unpublished doctoral thesis, University of Chicago.

Kübler-Ross, E. (1969) *On death and dying*. New York: Macmillan.

Kuhl, P., Stevens, E., Hayashi, A., Deguchi, T., Kiritani, S., & Iverson, P. (2006). Infants show a facilitation effect for native language phonetic perception between 6 to 12 months. *Developmental Science, 9*, 13–21.

Ladd, G. W., & Price, J. M. (1993). Playstyles of peer-accepted and peer-rejected children on the playground. In C. H. Hart (Ed.), *Children on playgrounds: Research perspectives and applications*. New York: SUNY Press.

Lamb, M. E. (1977). Father–infant and mother–infant interaction in the first year of life. *Child Development, 48*, 167–181.

Lamb, T., & Yang, J. F. (2000). Could different directions of infant stepping be controlled by the same locomotor central pattern generator? *Journal of Neurophysiology, 83*, 2814–2824.

Leaper, C. (2002). Parenting girls and boys. In M. H. Bornstein (Ed.), *Handbook of parenting, Vol 1: Children and Parenting*. Mahwah, NJ: Lawrence Erlbaum.

Leslie, A., & Thaiss, L. (1992). Domain specificity in conceptual development: Neuropsychological evidence from autism. *Cognition, 43*, 225–251.

Lester, S., & Russell, W. (2008). *Play for a change: Play, policy and practice: A review of contemporary perspectives*. London: National Children's Bureau.

Levinson D. J. (1987) *The seasons of a man's life*, New York: Alfred Knopf.

Levinson, D. J., with Levinson, J. D. (1996). *The seasons of a woman's life*. New York: Alfred Knopf.

Levinson, D. J., with Darrow, C. N., Klein, E. B., Levinson, M. H., & McKee, B. (1978). *The seasons of a man's life*. New York: Ballantine Books.

Levinson, D. J. (1986). A conception of adult development. *American Psychologist, 41*, 3–13.

Levy, M. B., & Davis, K. E. (1988). Lovestyles and attachment styles compared: Their relations to each other and to various relationship characteristics. *Journal of Social and Personal Relationships, 5*, 439–471.

Lewis, K, & Brooks-Gunn, J. (1979). *Social cognition and the acquisition of the self*. New York: Plenum.

Lewis, M. (1990). Social knowledge and social development. *Merrill-Palmer Quarterly, 36*, 93–116.

Liebal, K., Behne, T., Carpenter, M., & Tomasello, M. (2009). Infants use shared experience to interpret pointing gestures. *Developmental Science, 12*, 264–271. Available online at: http://email.eva.mpg.de/~tomas/pdf/LiebalEtal_SharedExperience_2009.pdf

Lieven, E. (1994). Crosslinguistic and crosscultural aspects of language addressed to children. In C. Gallaway and B. Richards (Eds.), *Input and interaction in language acquisition*. Cambridge: Cambridge University Press.

Linn, M. C., & Peterson, A. C. (1985). Emergence and characterization of sex differences in spatial ability: A meta-analysis. *Child Development, 56*(6), 1479–1498.

Lynn, J. (2001). Serving patients who may die soon and their families: The role of hospice and other services. *Journal of the American Medical Association, 285*, 925–932.

Maccoby, E. E. (2002) Gender and group processes. *Current Directions in Psychological Science. 11*, 54–58.

References

Maccoby, E. E. (2003) Parenting effects. In J. G. Borkowski, S. L. Ramey, & M. Bristol-Power (Eds.), *Parenting and the child's world*. Mahwah, NJ: Erlbaum.

MacDonald, K. B., & Parke, R. D. (1986). Parent–child physical play: The effects of sex and age of children and parents. *Sex Roles, 15*, 367–378.

Maciejewski, P. K., Zhang, B., Block, S. D., & Prigerson, H. G. (2007). An empirical examination of the stage theory of grief. *Journal of the American Medical Association, 297*(7), 716–723.

Maclean, M., Bryant, P., & Bradley, L. (1987). Rhymes, nursery rhymes and reading in early childhood. *Merrill-Palmer Quarterly, 33*, 255–281.

Main, M., & Goldwyn, R. (1988). *Adult attachment classification system: Version 3.2*. Unpublished manuscript, Department of Psychology, University of California, Berkeley, CA.

Marcia, J. E. (1987). The identity status approach to the study of ego identity development. In T. Honess & K. Yardley (Eds.), *Self and Identity perspectives across the lifespan*. London: Routledge & Kegan Paul.

Marcia, J. (2002). Identity and psychosocial development in adulthood. *Identity, 2*, 7–28.

Marmot, M., Shipley, M., Brunner, E., & Hemingway, H. (2001). Relative contribution of early life and adult socioeconomic factors to adult morbidity in the Whitehall II Study. *Journal of Epidemiology and Community Health, 55*, 301–307.

Martin, C. L., & Fabes, R. A. (2001). The stability and consequences of young children's same sex peer interactions. *Developmental Psychology, 37*, 413–446.

Martin, M., & Willis, S. L. (2005). *Middle adulthood: A lifespan perspective*. Thousand Oaks, CA: Sage.

Martin, P., & Bateson, P. (1993). *Measuring behaviour: An introductory guide* (2nd ed.). Cambridge: Cambridge University Press.

Marvin, R. S., Cooper, G., Hoffman, K., & Powell, B. (2002). The circle of security project: Attachment-based intervention with caregiver-pre-school child dyads. *Attachment & Human Development, 4*, 107–124.

Mastropieri, D., & Turkewitz, G. (1999). Perinatal experience and neonatal responsiveness to vocal expression of emotion. *Developmental Psychobiology, 35*(3), 204–214.

Matsumoto, A. (1999). *Sexual differentiation of the brain*. Boca Raton, FL: CRC Press.

Mattson, S. N., Roesch, S. C., Fagerlund, A., Autti-Rämö, I., Lyons Jones, K., May, P. A., Adams, C. M., Kovovalova, V., Riley, E. P., & the CIFASD (2010). Toward a neurobehavioral profile of fetal alcohol spectrum disorders. *Alcoholism: Clinical & Experimental Research, 34*(9), 1640–1650.

Matychuk, P. (2005). The role of child-directed speech in language acquisition: A case study. *Language Sciences, 27*, 301–379.

Mayer, R. E. (2008). Applying the science of learning: Evidence-based principles for the design of multimedia instruction. *American Psychologist, 63*(8), 760–769.

McCabe, M. P., Ricciardelli, L. A., & Finemore, J. (2002). The role of puberty, media, and popularity with peers as strategies to increase weight, decrease weight and increase muscle tone among adolescent boys and girls. *Journal of Psychosomatic Research, 52*, 145–153.

McMaster, J., Pitts, M., & Poyah, G. (1997). The menopausal experiences of women in a developing country: There is a time for everything – To be a teenager, a mother and a granny. *Women and Health, 26*, 1–14.

Meltzoff, A. N., & Moore, M. K. (2000). Resolving the debate about early imitation. In A. Slater & D. Muir (Eds.), *The Blackwell reader in developmental psychology* (pp. 151–155). Oxford: Blackwell.

Menary, R. (2007). *Cognitive integration: Mind and cognition unbounded*. Basingstoke: Palgrave Macmillan.

Metcalf, P., & Huntington, R. (1991). *Celebrations of death: The anthropology of mortuary ritual*. Cambridge: Cambridge University Press.

Metz, D., & Underwood, M. (2005). *Older richer fitter: Identifying the customer needs of Britain's ageing population*. London: Age Concern Books.

Mead, G. H. (1934). *Mind, self and society from the standpoint of a social behaviourist*. Chicago, IL: University of Chicago Press.

Miles, S., Cliff, D., & Burr, V. (1998). 'Fitting in and sticking out': Consumption, consumer meanings and the consumption of young people's identities. *Journal of Youth Studies, 1*, 81–96.

Miles, S. (2000). *Youth lifestyles in a changing world*. Buckingham: Open University Press.

Miller, J. G., & Bersoff, D. M. (1992). Culture and moral judgment: How are conflicts between justice and interpersonal responsibilities resolved? *Journal of Personality and Social Psychology, 62*(4), 541–554.

Milner, M. (2004). *Freaks, geeks, and cool kids: American teenagers, schools, and the culture of consumption*. New York: Routledge.

Mitchell, G. (2008). Palliative care: A patient-centred approach. Oxford: Radcliffe Publishing

Munakata, Y. (1998). Infant perseveration and implications for object permanence theories: A PDP model of the AB task. *Developmental Science, 1*(2), 161–184.

Nazzi, T., & Bertoncini, J. (2003). Before and after the vocabulary spurt: Two modes of word acquisition? *Developmental Science, 6*, 136–142.

Nebot, M., Borrell, C., & Villalbi, J. R. (1997). Adolescent motherhood and socio-economic factors: An ecological approach. *European Journal of Public Health, 7*, 144–48.

Newcomb, A. F., Bukowski, W. M., & Pattee, L. (1993). Children's peer relations: A meta-analyic review of popular, rejected, neglected, controversial, and average sociometric status. *Psychological Bulletin, 113*, 99–128.

Newell, K. M., Vaillancourt, D. E., & Sosnoff, J. J. (2006). Aging complexity and motor performance. In J. E. Birren & K. W. Schaie (Eds.) *Handbook of the psychology of aging* (6th ed.) Burlington, MA: Academic Press.

Nicolson, R. I., Fawcett, A. J., & Dean, P. (2001). Developmental dyslexia: The cerebellar deficit hypothesis. *Trends in Neurosciences, 24*(9), 508–511.

Norgate, S. H. (1997). Research methods for studying the language of blind children. In N. H. Hornberger & D. Corson (Eds.), The encyclopedia of language and education: Vol. 8: Research methods in language and education. Dordrecht, The Netherlands: Kluwer Academic Publishers.

Norman, P., Gregory, I., Dorling, D., & Baker, A. (2008). Geographical trends in infant mortality: England and Wales, 1970–2006. *Health Statistics Quarterly, 40,* 18–29.

Nottlemann, E. D., Susman, E. J., Inoff-Germain, G., Cutler, G., Loriaux, D. L., & Chronsos, G. P. (1987). Gonadal and adrenal hormone correlates of adjustment in early adolescence. In R. M. Lerner & T. T. Foch (Ed.), *Biological-psychosocial interaction in early adolescence.* Hillsdale, NJ: Erlbaum.

Nunes, T., Schliemann, A. D., & Carraher, D. W. (1993). *Street mathematics and school mathematics.* New York: Cambridge University Press.

Oates, J. M., & Grayson, A. (2004). Cognitive and language development in children. Oxford/Buckingham: Blackwell/Open University Press.

O'Brien, M., & Huston, A. C. (1985). Development of sex-typed play behavior in toddlers. *Developmental Psychology, 21,* 866–871.

Obler, L. K. (2005). Language in adulthood. In J. B. Gleason (Ed.) *The development of language* (6th ed.). Boston, MA: Allyn & Bacon.

Ojeman, G. A. (1984). Common cortical and thalamic mechanisms for language and motor functions. *American Journal of Physiology, 246,* 901–903.

ONS, (2010). Population trends No. 142 Newport, South Wales: ONS. Available online at: **www.statistics.gov.uk/populationtrends/downloads/poptrends142web.pdf**

Ozer, D. J., & Benet-Martinez, V. (2006). Personality and the prediction of consequential outcome. *Psychology, 57,* 402–421.

Parker, J. G., & Seal, J. (1996). Forming, losing, renewing and replacing friendships: Applying temporal parameters to the assessment of children's friendship experiences. *Child Development, 67*(5), 2248–2268.

Parker J., & Gottman J. (1989). Social and emotional development in a relational context: Friendship interactions from early childhood to adolescence. In T. Berndt & G. Ladd (Eds.), *Peer relationships in child development.* New York: Wiley.

Parkes, C. M. (1986) *Bereavement: Studies of grief life* (2nd edition). London: Tavistock.

Parkes, C. M (1972). *Bereavement: Studies of grief in adult life.* Harmondsworth: Penguin.

Parten, M. B. (1932). Social participation among pre-school children. *Journal of Abnormal and Social Psychology, 27,* 243–269.

Patiniotis, J., & Holdsworth, C. (2005). 'Seize that chance!': Leaving home and transitions to higher education. *Journal of Youth Studies, 8*(1), 81–95.

Pellegrini, A. D. (1990). Elementary school children's playground behavior: Implications for social-cognitive development. *Children's Environment Quarterly, 7*(2), 8–16.

Pellegrini, A. D. & Perlmutter, J. (1989). Parental distancing strategies and children's fantasy play. In M. Bloch and A. Pellegrini (Eds.), *The ecological context of children's play.* Norwood, NJ: Ablex.

Pellegrini, A. D., & Perlmutter, J. (1987). Children's fantasy verbal play with parents and peers. *Educational Psychology, 7,* 269–281.

Pellegrini, A. D. & Smith P. K. (1998). Physical activity play: The nature and function of a neglected aspect of play. *Child Development, 69*(3), 577–598.

Perry, W. G. (1970). *Forms of intellectual and ethical development in the college years: A scheme.* New York: Holt, Rhinehart & Winston.

Philips, S. D. (1982). Career exploration in adulthood. *Journal of Vocational Behaviour, 20,* 129–140.

Phoenix, A. (2005). Young people and consumption: Commonalities and differences in the construction of identities. In B. Tufte, B., J. Rasmussen, & L.B. Christensen, (Eds.) *Frontrunners or Copycats?* (pp. 79–95). Copenhagen: Copenhagen Business School Press.

Piaget, J., & Inhelder, B. (1969). *The psychology of the child.* London: Routledge & Kegan Paul.

Piaget, J. (1962). *Play dreams and imitation.* New York: Norton.

Piaget, J. (1932). *The moral judgement of the child.* (Published in English, 1952). London: Kegan Paul.

Piaget, J. (1923). *Language and thought of the child.* London: Routledge.

Pinker, S. (2003). Language as an adaptation to the cognitive niche. In M. Christiansen & S. Kirby (Eds.), *Language evolution: States of the art.* New York: Oxford University Press.

Pinker, S. (1994). *The language instinct.* New York: William Morrow.

Pinquart, M., & Sörensen, S. (2000). Influences of socioeconomic status, social network, and competence on subjective well-being in later life: A meta-analysis. *Psychology and Aging, 15*(2), 187–224.

Pistole, M. C. (1989). Attachment in adult romantic relationships: Style of conflict resolution and relationship satisfaction. *Journal of Social and Personal Relationships, 6,* 505–510.

Proffitt, J. B., Coley, J. D., & Medun, D. L. (2000). Expertise and category-based induction. *Journal of Experimental Psychology Learning Memory and Cognition, 26,* 811–28.

QAA (2010) *Quality Assurance Agency benchmark for psychology.* London: Quality Assurance Agency.

Quinn, P. C. & Slater, A. (2003). Face perception at birth and beyond. In O. Pascalis & A. Slater, *The development of face processing in infancy and early childhood: Current perspectives* (pp. 3–11). Hauppauge, NY: NOVA Science.

Quinn, P., Yahr, J., Kuhn, A., Slater, A. M., & Pascalis (2002). Representation of the gender of human faces by infants: A preference for female. *Perception, 31*(9), 1109–1121.

Ragow-O'Brien, D., Hayslip, B., & Guarnaccia, C. A. (2000). The impact of hospices on attitudes toward funerals and subsequent bereavement adjustment. *Journal of Death and Dying, 41*(4), 291–305.

References

Ray, D., Bratton, S., Rhine, T., & Jones, L. (2001). The effectiveness of play therapy: Responding to the critics. *International Journal of Play Therapy, 10*(1), 85–108.

Reiner, W. G., & Gearhart, J. P. (2004). Discordant sexual identity in some genetic males with cloacal exstrophy assigned to female sex at birth. *New England Journal of Medicine, 350*(4), 333–341.

Reis, H. T., Lin, Y., Bennett, M. E., & Nezlek, J. B. (1993). Change and consistency in social participation during early adulthood. *Developmental Psychology, 29*, 633–645.

Reissland, N. (1988). Neonatal imitation in the first hour of life: Observations in rural Nepal. *Developmental Psychology, 24*, 464–469.

Rhodes, S. R. (1983). Age-related differences in work attitudes and behaviour: A review and conceptual analysis. *Psychological Bulletin, 93*, 328–367.

Richards, M., Hardy, R., & Wadsworth, M. E. (2003). Does active leisure protect cognition? Evidence from a national birth cohort. *Social Science and Medicine, 56*, 785–792.

Ridgers, N. D., Fairclough, S. J., & Stratton, G. (2010). Variables associated with children's physical activity levels during recess: The A-CLASS project. *International Journal of Behavioral Nutrition and Physical Activity, 7*, 4. www.ijbnpa.org/content/7/1/74

Robertson, J., & Robertson, J. (1989). *Separation and the very young.* London: Free Association Press.

Roggman, L. A., Langlois, J. H., & Huhhs-Tait, L. (1987). Mothers, infants, and toys: Social play correlates of attachment. *Infant Behavior and Development, 10*, 233–237.

Rohrich, R. J. (2000). The millennium cosmetic surgery: Who are we? Where are we going? *Plastic Reconstruction Surgery, 105*(1), 225.

Rosenberg, M. (1979). *Conceiving the self.* New York: Basic Books.

Rosenblatt, P. C. (1993). The social context of private feelings. In M. S. Stroebe, W. Stroebe, & R. O. Hansson (Eds.), *Handbook of bereavement: Theory, research and intervention.* New York: Cambridge University Press.

Rosenbloom, C., & Bahns, M. (2006). What can we learn about diet and physical activity from master athletes. *Holistic Nursing Practice, 20*(4), 161–166.

Rothbaum F., Weisz, J., Pott, M., Miyake, K., Morelli, G. (2000). Attachment and culture: Security in the United States and Japan. *American Psychologist, 55*, 1093–1104.

Rubia, K., Overmeyer, S., Taylor, E., Brammer, M., Williams, S. C., Simmons, A., Andrew, C., & Bullmore, E. T. (2000). Functional frontalisation with age: Mapping neurodevelopmental trajectories with fMRI. *Neuroscience & Biobehavioural Reviews, 24*(1), 13–19.

Rubin, K. H., Bukowski, W. M., & Parker, J. G. (2006). Peer interactions, relationships, and groups. In W. Damon, R. M. Lerner & N. Eisenberg (Eds.), *Handbook of child psychology: Vol. 3: Social, emotional, and personality development* (6th ed., pp. 571–645). New York: Wiley.

Rubin, K. H., Fein, G. G., & Vandenberg, B. (1983). Play. In E. M. Hetherington (Ed.) *Handbook of child psychology* Vol. 4: Socialization, personality, and social development (4th ed., pp. 693–744). New York: Wiley

Ruble, D. N., & Martin, C. L (2006). Gender development. In W. Damon, R. M. Lerner, & N. Eisberg (Eds.), *Handbook of child psychology: Vol. 3: Social, emotional and personality development,* (6th ed. pp. 858–932). New York: John Wiley.

Rutter, M. (1991). *Maternal deprivation reassessed* (2nd ed.). Harmondsworth: Penguin.

Rymer, R. (1993). *Genie: A scientific tragedy.*

Sallis, J. F., Conway, T. L., Prochaska, J. J., McKenzie, T. L., Marshall, S. J., & Brown, M. (2001). The association of school environments with youth physical activity. *American Journal of Public Health, 91*, 618–620.

Salthouse, T. A. (2009). When does age-related cognitive decline begin? *Neurobiology of Aging, 30*, 507–514.

Sameroff, A. J. (1991). The social context of development. In M. Woodhead, R. Carr, & P. Light (Eds.), *Becoming a person.* London: Taylor & Francis.

Sameroff, A. J. & Chandler, M. J. (1975). Reproductive risk and the continuum of caretaker casualty. In F. D. Horowitz (Ed.), *Review of child development research* (Vol. 4). Chicago, IL: University of Chicago Press.

Samson, M. M., Meeuwsen, I. B., Crowe, A., Dessens, J. A., Duursma, S. A., & Verhaar, H. J. (2000). Relationships between physical performance measures, age, height and body weight in healthy adults. *Age and Ageing, 29*(3), 235–242.

Sassler, S., Ciambrone, D., & Benway, G. (2008). Adulthood upon returning to the parental home. *Sociological Forum, 23*, 670–698.

Schulenberg, J. E., & Zarrett, N. R. (2006). Mental health during emerging adulthood: Continuity and discontinuity in courses, causes, and functions. In J. J. Arnett & J. L. Tanner (Eds.), *Emerging adults in America: Coming of age in the 21st century* (pp. 135–172). Washington, DC: American Psychological Association.

Seale, C. (1991). Caring for people who die. Paper presented at British Sociological Association Conference on Health and Society, University of Manchester.

Selman, R. L. (1980). *The growth of interpersonal understanding.* New York: Academic Press.

Sen, M. G., Yonas, A., & Knill, D. C. (2001). Development of infants' sensitivity to surface contour information for spatial layout. *Perception, 30*, 167–176.

Shahidi J., Bernier, N., & Cohen, S. R. (2010). Quality of life in terminally ill cancer patients: Contributors and content validity of instruments. *Journal of Palliative Care, 26*(2), 88–93.

Shan, Z., Liu, J. Z., Sahgal, V., Wang, B., & Yue, G. H. (2005). Selective atrophy of left hemisphere and frontal lobe of the brain in old men. *Journal of Gerontology, 60*(2), 165–174.

Shatz, M., & Gelman, R. (1973). The development of communication skills: Modifications in the speech of young children as a function of listener. *Monographs of the Society for Research in Child Development*, Serial number 152, *38*(5).

Shirley, M. M. (1933). The first two years: A study of 25 babies. *Post natal and locomotor development: Vol. 1*. Minnneapolis, MN: University of Minnesota Press.

Shulman, S., & Ben-Artzi, E. (2003). Age-related differences in the transition from adolescence to adulthood and links with family relationships. *Journal of Adult Development, 10*, 217–226.

Shweder, R. A. (1994). Are moral intuitions self-evident truths? *Criminal Justice Ethics, 13*(2), 24–31.

Siegal, M., & Beattie, K. (1991). Where to look first for children's knowledge of false beliefs. *Cognition, 38*, 1–12.

Siegal, M., & Peterson, C. C. (1994). Children's theory of mind and the conversational territory of cognitive development. In C. Lewis & P. Mitchell (Eds.), *Origins of an understanding of mind*. Hove, East Sussex: Erlbaum.

Siegler, R. S. (1998). *Children's Thinking* (3rd ed.) Upper Saddle River, NJ: Prentice Hall.

Signorella, M. L., Jamison, W., & Krupa, M. H. (1989). Predicting spatial performance from gender stereotyping in activity preferences and in self-concept. *Developmental Psychology, 25*, 89–95.

Simmons, R. G., & Blyth, D. A. (1987). *Moving into adolescence: The impact of pubertal change and school context*. New York: Aldine De Gruyter.

Simonton, D. K. (1990). Creativity in the later years: Optimistic prospects for achievement. *Gerontologist, 30*, 626–631.

Singh L., Morgan J., & Best, C. (2002). Infants' listening preferences: Baby talk or happy talk? *Infancy, 3*(3), 365–394.

Sinnott, J. D. (1996). The developmental approach: Postformal thought as adaptive intelligence. In F. Blanchard-Fields & T. M. Hess (Eds.), *Perspectives on cognitive change in adulthood and aging* (pp. 358–383). New York: McGraw-Hill.

Sinnott, J. D. (1994). *Interdisciplinary handbook of life span learning*. Westport, CT: Greenwood.

Slater, A. (2004). Novelty, familiarity and infant reasoning. *Infant and Child Development, 13*, 353–355.

Slater, A., & Johnson, S. P. (1998). Visual sensory and perceptual abilities of the newborn: Beyond the blooming, buzzing confusion. In F. Simion, G. Butterworth (Eds.), *The development of sensory, motor and cognitive capacities in early infancy: From perception to cognition*. Hove, East Sussex: Psychology Press/Erlbaum (UK) Taylor & Francis.

Slater, A., Quinn, P. C., Brown, E., Hayes, R. (1999). Intermodal perception at birth: Intersensory redundancy guides newborn infants' learning of arbitrary auditory–visual pairings. *Developmental Science, 2*, 333–338.

Slobin, D. I. (1972). Children and language: They learn the same way all around the world. *Psychology Today, 6*(2), 74–82.

Smetana, J. G., & Letourneau, K. J. (1984). Development of gender constancy and children's sex-typed free play behaviour. *Developmental Psychology, 20*, 691–696.

Smilansky, S. (1968). *The effects of sociodramatic play on disadvantaged preschool children*. New York: Wiley.

Smith, L. B., Thelen, E., Titzer, R., & McLin, D. (1999). Knowing in the context of acting: The task dynamics of the A-not-B error. *Psychological Review, 106*(2), 235–260. Available online at: www.indiana.edu/cogdev/labwork/SmithThelen1999.pdf

Smith, P., & Pellegrini, A. (2008) Learning through play. *Encyclopedia on early childhood development*. Available online at: www.pre-kventura.org/Portals/48/Learning%20Through%20Play.pdf

Snarey, J. R. Reimer, J., & Kohlberg, L. (1985). The development of social-moral reasoning among kibbutz adolescents: A longitudinal cross-cultural study. *Developmental Psychology, 21*(1), 3–17.

Snow, C. (1972). Mothers' speech to children learning language. *Child Development, 43*, 549–565.

Snowdon, D. (2002). *Aging with grace: What the nun study teaches us about leading longer, healthier and more meaningful lives*. New York: Bantum.

Sokol, B. W., Chandler, M. J., & Jones, C. (2004). From mechanical to autonomous agency: The relationship between children's moral judgements and their developing theories of mind. *New directions for child and adolescent development. Special Issue: Connections between theories of mind and sociomoral development, 103*, 19–36.

Spelke, E. S. (1998). Nativism, empiricism and the origins of knowledge. *Infant Behaviour and Development, 21*(2), 181–200.

Spencer, H. (1873). *The principles of psychology*. New York: D. Appleton & Co.

Stevens, M. M., & Dunsmore, J. C. (1996). Adolescents who are living with a life-threatening illness. In C. A. Corr & D. E. Balk (Eds.), *Handbook of adolescent death and bereavement* (pp. 107–135), New York: Springer.

Stroebe, M.S. (1998). New directions in bereavement research: Exploration of gender differences. *Palliative Medicine, 12*(1), 5–12.

Super, D. E., Savickas, M. L., & Super, C. M. (1996). The life-span, life-space approach to careers. In D. Brown, L. Brooks, & associates (Eds.), *Career choice and development* (3rd ed.). San Francisco, CA: Jossey-Bass.

Tamis-LeMonda, C. S., Bornstein, M. H., & Baumwell, L. (2001). Maternal responsiveness and children's achievement of language milestones. *Child Development, 72*(3), 748–767.

The Royal College of Obstetrics and Gynaecology (2004) Clinical green top guidelines: Management of HIV in pregnancy. Available online at: www.rcog.org.uk/womens-health/clinical-guidance/management-hiv-pregnancy-green-top-39

Thelen, E. (1995). Motor development: A new synthesis. *American psychologist, 50*, 79–95.

References

Thiessen, E. D., Hill, E. A., & Saffron, J. R. (2005). Infant-directed speech facilitates word segmentation. *Infancy, 1,* 53–71.

Thornton, R., & Light L. L. (2006). Language comprehension and production in normal aging. In J. E. Birren & K. W. Schaie (Eds.), *Handbook of the psychology of aging.* Boston, MA: Elsevier Academic Press.

Thorpe, G. (1993). Enabling more dying people to remain at home. *British Medical Journal, 307*(6909), 915–918.

Timperio, A., Crawford, D., Telford, A., & Salmon, J. (2004). Perceptions about the local neighborhood and walking and cycling among children. *Preventative Medicine, 38,* 39–47.

Tizard, B., & Hodges, J. (1978). The effect of early institutional rearing on the development of eight-year-old children. *Journal of Child Psychology and Psychiatry, 19,* 99–118.

Tomasello, M. (2006). Acquiring linguistic constructions. In D. Kuhn & R. Siegler (Eds.), *Handbook of child psychology: Vol 2: Cognition, perception and Language* (pp. 255–298). New York: Wiley.

Turiel, E. (1983). *The development of social knowledge: Morality and convention.* Cambridge: Cambridge University Press.

Uchino, B. N., Cacioppo, J. T., & Keicolt-Glaser, J. K. (1996). The relationship between social support and physiological processes: A review with emphasis on underlying mechanisms and implications for health. *Psychological Bulletin, 119,* 488–531.

Upton, P., & Eiser, C. (2006). School experiences after treatment for a brain tumour. *Child: Care, Health and Development, 32*(1), 9–17.

Urberg, K. A., & Kaplan, M. G. (1989). An observational study of race-, age-, and sex-heterogeneous interaction in preschoolers. *Journal of Applied Developmental Psychology, 10,* 299–311.

Valenzuela, M., Breakspear, M., & Sachdev, P. (2007). Complex mental activity and the aging brain: Molecular, cellular and cortical network mechanisms. *Brain Research Reviews, 56,* 198–213.

Van IJzendoorn, M. H. (1992). Intergenerational transmission of parenting: A review of studies in nonclinical populations. *Developmental Review, 12,* 76–99.

Van IJzendoorn, M. H., Kroonenberg, P. M. (1990). Cross-cultural consistency of coding the strange situation. *Infant Behavior and Development. 13*(4), 469–485.

Van IJzendoorn, M., & Kroonenberg, P. (1988). Cross-cultural patterns of attachment: A meta-analysis of the strange situation. *Child Development, 59,* 147–156.

Viholainen, H., Ahonen, T., Cantell, M., Lyytinen, P., & Lyytinen, H. (2002). Development of early motor skills and language in children at risk for familial dyslexia. *Developmental Medicine & Child Neurology, 44,* 761–769.

Von Hofsten, C. (2007). Action in development. *Developmental Science, 10,* 54–60.

Vygotsky, L. S. (1986). The genetic roots of thought and speech. In A. Kozulin (Trans. & Ed.), *Thought and language.* Cambridge, MA: MIT Press.

Vygotsky, L. S. (1978). *Mind in society: The development of higher psychological processes.* Cambridge, MA: Harvard University Press.

Vygotsky, L. S. (1962). *Thought and language,* New York: Wiley.

Wade, B., & Moore, M. (1998). An early start with books: Literacy and mathematical evidence from a longitudinal study. *Educational Review, 50,* 135–145.

Walker, L. J. (1989). A longitudinal study of moral reasoning. *Child Development, 60,* 157–166.

Ward, B. J., & Tate, P. A. (1994). Attitudes among NHS doctors to requests for euthanasia. *British Medical Journal, 308,* 1332.

Waro Aikins, J., Bierman, K. L., & Parker, J. G. (2005). Navigating the transition to junior high school: The influence of pre-transition friendship and self-system characteristics. *Social Development, 14,* 42–60.

Wartner, U. G., Grossmann, K., Fremmer-Bombik, E., & Suess, G. (1994). Attachment patterns at age six in south Germany: Predictability from infancy and implications for preschool behavior. *Child Development, 65,* 1014–1027.

Waterman, A. S. (1992). Identity as an aspect of optimal psychological functioning. In G. R. Adams, T. P. Gullotta, & R. Montemayor (Eds.), *Adolescent identity formation* (pp. 50–72). Newbury Park, CA: Sage.

Waters, G., & Caplan, D. (2005). The relationship between age, processing speed, working memory capacity, and language comprehension. *Memory, 13*(3–4), 403–413.

Wellman, H. M., & Gelman, S. A. (1998). Knowledge acquisition in foundational domains. In D. Kuhn, R. S. Siegler (Eds.), *Handbook of child psychology: Vol. 2: Cognition, perception, and language* (5th ed., pp. 523–573). New York: Wiley.

Wendell, C., Zonderman, A., Metter, J., Najjar, S. S., & Waldstein, S. R. (2009). Carotid intimal medial thickness predicts cognitive decline among adults without clinical vascular disease. *Stroke, 40,* 3–180.

Werker, J. F. (1989). Becoming a native listener: A developmental perspective on human speech perception. *American Scientist, 77*(1), 54–59.

Whitbourne, S. K. (2005). *Adult development and aging: Biopsychological perspectives* (2nd ed.). Hoboken, NJ: Wiley.

White, L., & Edwards, J. N. (1990). Emptying the nest and parental well-being: An analysis of national panel data. *American Sociological Review, 55,* 235–242.

WHO (1990). Technical report series 804: Cancer pain and palliative care. Geneva: WHO.

Wiesner, M., & Ittel, A. (2002). Relations of pubertal timing and depressive symptoms to substance use in early adolescence. *Journal of Early Adolescence, 22,* 5–23.

Willis, S. L., & Schaie, K. W. (2005). Cognitive functioning in the baby boomers: Longitudinal and cohort effects. In S. K. Whitbourne & S. L.

Willis (Eds.), *The baby boomers grow up* (pp. 205–234). Hillsdale, NJ: Lawrence Erlbaum.

Wimmer, H., & Perner, J. (1983). Beliefs about beliefs: Representation and constraining function of wrong beliefs in young children's understanding of deception. *Cognition, 13,* 103–128.

Wold, G. (2004). *Basic geriatric nursing.* St Louis, MO: Mosby.

Wood, D., Wood, H., & Middleton, D. (1978). An experimental evaluation of four face-to-face teaching strategies. *International Journal of Behavioral Development, 2,* 131–147.

Woodward, A. L., & Markman, E. M. (1998). Early word learning. In D. Kuhn & R. S. Siegler (Eds.), *Handbook of child psychology: Vol. 2: Cognition, perception, and language* (5th ed., pp. 371–420). New York: Wiley.

Woollett, A., & Pheonix, A. (1991). Psychological views of mothering. In A. Phoenix, A. Woollett, & E. Lloyd (Eds.), *Motherhood: Meanings, practices and ideologies.* London: Sage.

Woolley, J. D. (1997). Thinking about fantasy: Are children fundamentally different thinkers and believers than adults? *Child Development, 68,* 991–1011.

Yan, B., & Arlin, P. K. (1995). Nonabsolute/relativistic thinking: A common factor underlying models of postformal reasoning? *Journal of Adult Development, 2,* 223–240.

Yung, L. M., Laher, I., Yao, X., Chen, Z. Y., Huang, Y., & Leung, F. P. (2009). Exercise, vascular wall and cardiovascular diseases: An update (Part 2). *Sports Science, 39*(1), 45–63.

Zarbatany, L., McDougall, P., & Hymel, S. (2000). Gender-differentiated experience in the peer culture: Links to intimacy in preadolescence. *Social Development, 9,* 62–79.

Zhang, L. F. (2002). Thinking styles and cognitive development. *The Journal of Genetic Psychology, 163,* 179–195.

Index